# THE LAW OF
# HARBOURS AND
# PILOTAGE

*By*

## R. P. A. DOUGLAS, o.b.e.
*Legal Adviser to the British Ports Federation*

AND

## G. K. GEEN, m.sc.
*Extra Master*

**THIRD EDITION**

**|L|L|P|**

LONDON   NEW YORK   HAMBURG   HONG KONG
LLOYD'S OF LONDON PRESS LTD.
1989

Lloyd's of London Press Ltd.
Legal Publishing and Conferences Division
One Singer Street, London EC2A 4LQ

USA AND CANADA
Lloyd's of London Press Inc.
Suite 523, 611 Broadway
New York, NY 10012 USA

GERMANY
Lloyd's of London Press GmbH
59 Ehrenbergstrasse
2000 Hamburg 50, West Germany

SOUTH EAST ASIA
Lloyd's of London Press (Far East) Ltd.
Room 1101, Hollywood Centre
233 Hollywood Road
Hong Kong

© R. P. A. Douglas,
G. K. Geen 1989

This book is the third edition of both *Harbour Law* (2nd ed. 1983)
and *The Law of Pilotage* (2nd ed. 1983)

*British Library Cataloguing in Publication Data*
Douglas, R.P.A.
The law of harbours and pilotage.—3rd ed
1. Great Britain. Shipping. Pilotage. Law
2. Great Britain. Harbours & ports. Law
I. Title   II. Geen, G.K.   III. Douglas, R.P.A.
Harbour law   IV. Geen, G.K. Law of pilotage
344.103'966

ISBN 1–85044–168–5

Text set 10 on 12 pt Ehrhardt by
Promenade Graphics Ltd.
Cheltenham, Glos.
Printed in Great Britain by
Bookcraft Ltd.
Midsomer Norton

# PREFACE TO THE THIRD EDITION

This book is the third edition of both *Harbour Law* and *The Law of Pilotage*.

Since the Second Edition of *Harbour Law* was published in September 1983 there have been a number of important changes in the law relating to harbours. In particular, the Dangerous Vessels Act 1985 and the Ports (Finance) Act 1985 have come into force and the Dangerous Substances in Harbour Areas Regulations 1987 have introduced a uniform and modernised (although not in many respects substantially new) code of powers as respects dangerous substances in harbours. There has also been new harbour legislation for the prevention of pollution including the Prevention of Oil Pollution Act 1986, the Prevention of Pollution (Reception Facilities) Order 1984 and the Merchant Shipping (Reception Facilities for Garbage) Regulations 1988.

However, probably the most important change in harbour law has been in relation to marine pilotage. The Pilotage Act 1987 has swept away the complex statutory structure, stemming originally, for the most part, from the Pilotage Act 1913, described in the Second Edition of *Pilotage Law*, and made the provision of pilotage services a function of harbour authorities.

A new edition of *Harbour Law* therefore seemed to be called for and it also seemed clear that this should include the new pilotage functions of harbour authorities.

It seemed appropriate to include in this edition chapters on the division of control between Master and Pilot, Ship and Tugs and Ship and Harbour Master (corresponding to chapters in *Pilotage Law*). These chapters, and the history of pilotage law before the Pilotage Act 1913 contained in Appendix 1, are the work of Captain G. K. Geen.

The Appendix setting out the Harbours Act 1964 included in the two previous editions of *Harbour Law* has been omitted from this one. With the repeal of sections 9 and 10 of the 1964 Act by the Ports (Finance) Act 1985 this no longer seemed to be justified.

We are grateful to Mr M. Compton, Health and Safety Adviser to the British Ports Federation, for his help in relation to the passage in this edition dealing with the Docks Regulations 1988.

*November 1988*

R. P. A. DOUGLAS
G. K. GEEN

# CONTENTS

# BIBLIOGRAPHY

*All references are to paragraph numbers*

|  | Para. |
|---|---|
| Abbott, Charles, *A Treatise of the Law Relative to Merchant Ships and Seamen*, 2nd edn., London, 1804 | 398 |
| Board of Trade, *Report of Departmental Committee on Pilotage* (Cd. 5571), London, 1911 | 713 |
| *Coulson & Forbes on Waters and Land Drainage*, 6th edn. | 2, 7 |
| Hene, Derek H., *The Law of Sea and Air Traffic*, London 1955 | 604 |
| Kent, James, *Commentaries on American Law*, vol. 3, 3rd edn., New York, 1836 | 552 |
| *MacLachlan's Treatise on the Law of Merchant Shipping*, 7th edn., London, 1932 | 549 |
| Marsden, *The Law of Collisions at Sea, British Shipping Laws*, vol. 4, 11th edn., London, 1961 | 551, 604 |
| Royal Commission, *Report from the Commissioners appointed to inquire into the Laws and Regulations relating to Pilotage in the United Kingdom* (1836), xxviii | 713 |
| Royal Commission, Canada, *Report of Royal Commission on Pilotage*, Ottawa, 1968 | 399, 554, 562, 602, 604 |
| Temperley, *Merchant Shipping Acts, British Shipping Laws*, vol. 2, 7th edn. | 467 |

# TABLE OF CASES

*All references are to paragraph numbers*

# TABLE OF LEGISLATION

*All references are to paragraph numbers*

# CHAPTER 1

# HARBOURS AND HARBOUR
# AUTHORITIES GENERALLY

**1.** This book deals with the law relating to harbours in Great Britain which are managed by harbour authorities under statutory powers (other than "fishery harbours" and "marine works" which are described below) for the purpose of providing a service to other persons. Some passages, for example those dealing with the construction of works below high water mark, inevitably go somewhat wider. Much of the law relating to the harbours mentioned above also applies in relation to harbours of the kinds briefly referred to in paragraph 23 at the end of this chapter but this book does not discuss the law as it applies in particular to each of those kinds of harbour.

**2.** In the case of *R. v. Hannam*[1] Lord Esher, M.R., said that a harbour in its ordinary sense was a place to shelter ships from the violence of the sea and where ships were brought to load and unload goods. He added that the quays were a necessary part of the harbour. In *Hunter v. Northern Marine Insurance Company*[2] where the meaning of the word "port" was in issue, Lord Herschell said that: "A port is a place where a vessel can lie in a position of more or less shelter from the elements, with a view to the loading or discharge of cargo." At common law, therefore, "harbour" and "port" seem to be synonymous for most purposes although it appears on the authority of a treatise, *de Portibus Maris*, ascribed to Sir Matthew Hale, that a place which is a mere haven, natural or artificial, for the safe riding of ships (and has no facilities for loading or unloading goods) is also a "harbour".[3] Most questions which now arise on whether something is, or is within, a harbour involve consideration of one of the statutory definitions of "harbour" referred to below, all of which are in very wide terms, or the definition of the limits of a particular harbour contained in a local Act of Parliament or statutory order. A question which occasionally arises in relation to the definitions of "harbour" in public general statutes is whether a particular area of water is sufficiently enclosed or sheltered by land to be regarded as a harbour. This, of course, is a question of fact.

**3.** For the purposes of the Merchant Shipping Act 1894 "harbour" is defined in section 742 of that Act as including "harbours, properly so called, whether

---

1. *R. v. Hannam* (1886) 2 T.L.R. 234.
2. *Hunter v. Northern Marine Ins. Co.* (1888) 13 App. Cas. 717.
3. See *Coulson & Forbes on Waters and Land Drainage*, 6th edn., p.83.

1

natural or artificial, estuaries, navigable rivers, piers, jetties, and other works in or at which ships can obtain shelter, or ship and unship goods or passengers".

4. For the purposes of the Harbours Act 1964 "harbour" is defined in section 57(1) of that Act as "any harbour, whether natural or artificial, and any port, haven, estuary, tidal or other river or inland waterway navigated by sea-going ships, and includes a dock, wharf, and in Scotland a ferry or boat slip being a marine work, . . . ". "Dock" is defined in the Harbours Act 1964 as "a dock used by sea–going ships" and "wharf" as "any wharf, quay, pier, jetty or other place at which sea-going ships can ship or unship goods or embark or disembark passengers". It was held in the *Salt Union* v. *Wood*[4] that a "sea-going ship" is a ship that in fact goes to sea and not merely one that could go to sea.

5. The Harbours Act 1964 defines a harbour authority for the purposes of that Act as "any person in whom are vested under this Act, by another Act or by an order or other instrument (except a provisional order) made under another Act or by a provisional order powers or duties of improving, maintaining or managing a harbour". The definition of "harbour authority" for the purposes of the Merchant Shipping Act 1894 includes, but is not limited to, persons managing harbours under statutory powers.

6. Other important definitions of "harbour" or "harbour area" and "harbour authority" are contained in the Prevention of Oil Pollution Act 1971 (paragraph 211 *post*), the Prevention of Pollution (Reception Facilities) Order 1984 (paragraph 221 *post*) and the Dangerous Substances in Harbour Areas Regulations 1987 (paragraphs 165 to 168 *post*).

7. Nearly all harbours with a significant degree of commercial or recreational use are managed under statutory powers. One reason for this is that, to quote from the Sixth Edition of *Coulson & Forbes on Waters and Land Drainage*, which refers to the authority of Hale: "The privilege of erecting ports at which customable goods may be landed and of taking dues and tolls as incident thereto is part of the royal prerogative and can only belong to a subject as a franchise by grant or prescription from the Crown or by Act of Parliament." Harbour authorities which rely on grant or prescription from the Crown are now very rare and do not include any major harbour authorities.

8. Another reason why statutory powers are necessary to manage a harbour is that the construction and maintenance of harbour works below high water mark may be open to challenge in the courts, unless such construction and maintenance is authorized by statute, on the grounds that the works interfere with the public right of navigation. Furthermore, harbour authorities for significant harbours need to have powers to regulate the activities of other persons using the harbour and in particular the movement and berthing of ships within the harbour. Adequate powers for these purposes can only be obtained by or under statute.

9. The local circumstances of the numerous harbours in Great Britain are extremely varied. This is perhaps one reason why harbour authorities still operate

4. *Salt Union* v. *Wood* [1893] 1 Q.B. 370.

to a large extent under *local* statutory powers. The nature and functions of harbour authorities vary too. This aspect is dealt with in the next chapter. In the case of each harbour authority the limits of the harbour for which they are responsible are specified in their statutes. Different limits may sometimes be specified for different purposes.

10. Local statutory provisions under which a harbour authority manage their harbour may be contained in a local Act of Parliament or in subordinate legislation made under the Harbours Act 1964—the relevant enabling powers.are described later. By virtue of the Private Legislation Procedure (Scotland) Act 1936 a private Bill cannot normally be promoted in relation to a harbour in Scotland. Instead application may be made to the Secretary of State for Scotland for a provisional order which, if made by him, is subject to confirmation by Parliament by means of a Confirmation Bill submitted to Parliament by the Secretary of State. Subsequent references in this book to local Acts of Parliament include references to Scottish provisional orders confirmed by Parliament. Some smaller harbours are still managed under powers conferred by provisional orders made and confirmed under the General Pier and Harbour Act 1861 but this Act is now virtually obsolete. Under section 17(3) of the Harbours Act 1964 an application for an order under the General Pier and Harbour Act 1861 cannot be entertained by the Secretary of State for Transport where he is satisfied that the objects to be achieved can be achieved by a harbour revision or empowerment order (or by a combination of such orders) under the Act of 1964.

11. Although the functions of harbour authorities vary the form of local statutory harbour provisions generally follow broadly similar patterns. The Harbours, Docks and Piers Clauses Act 1847, which embodied the provisions normally included at that time in local harbour Acts so as to enable these to be incorporated by reference in future Acts without unnecessary repetition, contains a fairly comprehensive code of operational powers which includes powers for the harbour authority's harbour master to regulate a number of matters, including the movement and mooring of vessels, and confers quite wide powers for the harbour authority to make by-laws. Until recently the local Acts and orders of most harbour authorities incorporated the greater part of this operational code, often with some modifications, and new local harbour Acts and orders still frequently incorporate substantial parts of it. However, over the past 20 years or so new local measures, particularly in the case of major harbours, have often replaced old-fashioned provisions of the Clauses Act with modern powers, including, in particular, new powers to regulate vessels in the harbour and to make by-laws. These modern powers have tended to follow a common pattern. The more important of them, as well as some still common and effective provisions of the Clauses Act, are described later.

12. The statement that harbour authorities still operate mainly under powers contained in local Acts and orders needs to be qualified in the case of the few remaining nationalized harbours and the formerly nationalized harbours for which Associated British Ports are the harbour authority. The only harbour authority for

3

nationalized harbours is now the British Waterways Board who manage their few small harbours to a large extent under powers contained in the Transport Acts of 1962 and 1968, most of which apply to all the nationalized transport authorities. Associated British Ports have a code of powers relating to all their harbours which is set out in Schedule 3 to the Transport Act 1981. These powers are similar to, but in some respects wider than, those of a nationalized harbour authority under the Transport Acts. A few provisions of those Acts continue to apply to Associated British Ports. However, in addition to the general powers referred to in this paragraph, local Acts and orders are also of considerable importance at the nationalized harbours and those of Associated British Ports.

13. Prior to the Harbours Act 1964 there was little general legislation relating particularly to harbours. This was no doubt because, for reasons mentioned earlier, they were regarded as essentially local undertakings. A few old Acts still unrepealed, such as the Harbours Act 1814, the General Pier and Harbour Act 1861 and the Act amending it of 1862, the Harbours and Passing Tolls etc. Act 1861, the Harbours Transfer Act 1862, the Harbours Transfer Act 1865 and the Harbours Loans Act 1866, are now either obsolete or of very minor importance. The Merchant Shipping Act 1894, however, contained important provisions relating to harbours, the Explosives Act 1875 and the Petroleum (Consolidation) Act 1928 each imposed on harbour authorities a duty to make by-laws (now repealed by the Dangerous Substances in Harbour Areas Regulations 1987) and the statutes now consolidated in the Prevention of Oil Pollution Act 1971 also imposed important duties on harbour authorities. Legislation relating to pilotage and the regulation of dock workers' employment was, and is, also of great importance to harbour authorities.

14. The Harbours Act 1964 stemmed from the recommendations contained in the Report of the Committee of Inquiry into the major ports of Great Britain published in 1962 usually known as the "Rochdale Report" from the name of the Chairman of the Committee, Viscount Rochdale. This Act was concerned mainly with the central organization of harbours. The status of harbour authorities as independent bodies was not greatly diminished and, as indicated above, they continue to operate mainly under local powers (subject to some qualification in the case of the nationalized and formerly nationalized harbours) but in this connection the Harbours Act included provisions for subordinate legislation which were intended to provide a cheaper and more expeditious alternative to private Bills. These provisions are described later. The one really important general power for harbour authorities contained in the Harbours Act was the power, also discussed later, to levy ship, passenger and goods dues.

15. The Harbours Act 1964 established the National Ports Council with mainly advisory powers although also with powers to promote training and research, initiate measures for the amalgamation or reconstitution of harbour authorities and the duty to determine objections to dues levied by harbour authorities. The Act also provided for major harbour development to be subject to control by the Secretary of State for Transport in the national interest and authorized the Secretary

of State to make capital loans (and, originally, also grants) to harbour authorities. As indicated below, both the National Ports Council and the system for the control of major harbour development contained in the 1964 Act have now been abolished.

16. The main purpose of the Docks and Harbours Act 1966 was to provide for the licensing of port employers. The object of this was to secure a major reduction in the number of such employers and, together with the Dock Labour Scheme of 1967, it was an integral part of the operation to introduce a new system of permanent employment for dock workers. The licensing authorities are harbour authorities for ports which are included in the Dock Workers Employment Scheme and there are rights of appeal to the Secretary of State against their decisions. As mentioned above, these licensing provisions are closely linked to the provisions of the Dock Workers Employment Scheme and apply only to ports to which that Scheme applies. The 1966 Act also conferred some further important powers on harbour authorities including powers to carry out "harbour operations" as defined in the Harbours Act 1964 (except "the marking or lighting of a harbour or any part thereof" the reason for this exception being that any harbour authority which needed to carry out this operation already had power to do so), to purchase land by agreement and to acquire port businesses (businesses engaged wholly or mainly in carrying out "harbour operations") or shares in port businesses by agreement.

17. "Harbour operations" are defined in section 57(1) of the Harbours Act 1964 as—

   (a) the marking or lighting of a harbour or any part thereof;
   (b) the berthing or drydocking of a ship;
   (c) the warehousing, sorting, weighing or handling of goods on harbour land or at a wharf;
   (d) the movement of goods or passengers within the limits within which the person engaged in improving, maintaining or managing a harbour has jurisdiction or on harbour land;
   (e) in relation to a harbour (which expression for the purposes of this paragraph does not include a wharf)—
      (i) the towing, or moving of a ship which is in or is about to enter or has recently left the harbour;
      (ii) the loading or unloading of goods; or embarking or disembarking of passengers, in or from a ship which is in the harbour or the approaches thereto;
      (iii) the lighterage or handling of goods in the harbour; and
   (f) in relation to a wharf,—
      (i) the towing or moving of a ship to or from the wharf;
      (ii) the loading or unloading of goods, or the embarking or disembarking of passengers, at the wharf in or from a ship;

"harbour land" is defined in section 57(1) as land adjacent to a harbour and occupied wholly or mainly for the purposes of activities there carried on and "wharf" is defined in that section as any wharf, quay, pier, jetty or other place at which sea-going ships can ship or unship goods or embark or disembark passengers.

18. The Ports (Financial Assistance) Act 1981 as amended by section 5 of the

Transport (Finance) Act 1982 and section 2 of the Ports (Finance) Act 1985 authorized the Secretary of State, with the consent of the Treasury, to give financial assistance (not exceeding, in aggregate, £500 million) to the Port of London Authority (PLA) and the Mersey Docks and Harbour Company (MDHC) for measures taken by them to reduce the number of persons employed in, or in ports adjacent to, their respective ports, being measures taken with a view to restoring the profitability of their undertakings, and for the carrying on of their undertakings while such measures are being taken. The Ports (Reduction of Debt) Act 1983 enabled the Secretary of State with the consent of the Treasury to reduce the debts to the Government of the PLA by up to £48 million and those of the MDHC by up to £36 million. The amounts of debt thus written off are to count against the limit of £500 million referred to above on financial assistance to these two bodies.

19. Parts I and II of the Transport Act 1981 provided, respectively, for the introduction of private capital into the harbour undertakings of the British Railways Board (then managed by their subsidiary Sealink) and the British Transport Docks Board. These undertakings are discussed in the next chapter. Part III of the Transport Act 1981 abolished the National Ports Council and made a number of consequential and other amendments to the Harbours Act 1964.

20. Section 66 of the Transport Act 1982 empowered the Secretary of State to authorize or direct a harbour authority to do in connection with their harbour anything which it appears to the Secretary of State the authority ought to do in the interests of national defence. A harbour authority or any other person who suffers injury, loss or damage in consequence of anything done in pursuance of an authorization or direction given under this section is entitled to receive compensation from the Secretary of State. Section 27(6) of the Transport Act 1962 contains a similar power for the Secretary of State to give directions in the interests of national defence to the harbour authorities for the nationalized harbours (and other bodies managing nationalized transport undertakings) but contains no provision for compensation. It ceased to apply to the harbours managed by the British Transport Docks Board when that body was reconstituted under Part II of the Transport Act 1981 and no longer applies to the harbours managed by Sealink Harbours Limited.

21. The Ports (Finance) Act 1985 repealed sections 9 and 10 of the Harbours Act 1964 which contained provisions for the control of major harbour development by the Secretary of State. It also, as described later, included important provisions relating to the borrowing powers of harbour authorities and the audit of their accounts.

22. The Dangerous Vessels Act 1985 contained powers for a harbour master to give directions prohibiting the entry into, or requiring the removal from, a harbour, of certain highly dangerous vessels. This Act is discussed in detail later.

23. The Pilotage Act 1987, discussed in Chapter 12 *post*, abolished the former statutory pilotage system and made pilotage a function of harbour authorities.

24. Before concluding this chapter it is proposed to refer briefly to the kinds of harbours with which this book is not primarily concerned. These are—

(a) Harbours managed otherwise than under statutory powers. This category includes (*inter alia*) wharves and jetties constructed and maintained by virtue of licences granted by harbour authorities under powers (referred to later) to license the construction of works below high water mark. Although no major harbours fall within this category it does include two or three not insignificant commercial ports, particularly the Port of Par.

(b) "Own-account" harbours. These are harbours (usually wharves or jetties) operated under statutory powers wholly or mainly for the export of goods manufactured by the operators (or their associated companies) or for the import of goods to be used by the operators for the purposes of their own business or those of associated companies. A typical example of such a harbour is a jetty managed by an oil company for their own purposes under powers conferred by a local Act of Parliament or a harbour empowerment order made under the Harbours Act 1964. A person managing such a harbour is, technically, a harbour authority for all statutory purposes and, if the harbour is a jetty or wharf, usually has a measure of control over a limited area of adjacent water.

(c) Fishery harbours. These do not comprise all those harbours which are concerned mainly with the fishing industry. Indeed the main fishing harbours are not within this category. A "fishery harbour" is defined in section 21(7) of the Sea Fish Industry Act 1951 for the purposes of that section as a small harbour ("harbour" being defined in that subsection as including any haven, cove or other landing place) which in the opinion of the Secretary of State for Transport and the Minister of Agriculture, Fisheries and Food is principally used by the fishing industry. Section 21 does not apply to Scotland and the harbours in question are therefore all in England and Wales. The harbours which at the beginning of 1951 were fishery harbours are named in Schedule 4 to the Sea Fish Industry Act 1951 and section 21(8) of that Act provides that a harbour shall not be deemed to have become, or ceased to be, a fishery harbour since the beginning of that year unless and until it is declared to have done so by an order made by the Minister of Agriculture, Fisheries and Food and the Secretary of State for Transport acting jointly. For the purposes of the Harbours Act 1964 and Part III of the Docks and Harbours Act 1966 "fishery harbour" has the same meaning as in section 21 of the Sea Fish Industry Act 1951. Most general enactments relating to harbours and harbour authorities apply to fishery harbours and the harbour authorities which manage them. But the responsible Minister for most purposes is the Minister of Agriculture, Fisheries and Food instead of the Secretary of State for Transport.

(d) Marine works. "Marine work" is defined for the purposes of the Harbours Act 1964 in section 57(1) of that Act as amended by the Transport Act 1968. This definition also applies for the purposes of Part III of the Docks and Harbours Act 1966 and, by virtue of section 5 of the Harbours Act 1964, for the purposes of the Harbours, Piers and Ferries (Scotland) Act 1937. Briefly, a marine work as so defined is a harbour, ferry or boatslip in Scotland—

    (i) which, in the opinion of the Secretary of State for Scotland and the Secretary of State for Transport (strictly, now, "in the opinion of the

7

Secretary of State", since, technically, that office is indivisible) is principally used or required for the fishing industry; or

(ii) which, being situated in certain specified areas in the north of Scotland
is, in the opinion of the Secretary of State for Scotland and the Secretary
of State for Transport principally used or required for the fishing or
agricultural industries or the maintenance of communications between
any place in those areas and any other place in Scotland. Harbours, ferries or boatslips vested in certain specified bodies are excluded from the
definition.

Again, most general enactments relating to harbours and harbour authorities
apply to marine works and the harbour authorities responsible for them but the
responsible Minister for most purposes is the Secretary of State for Scotland.

The Harbours, Piers and Ferries (Scotland) Act 1937 contains provisions for
the acquisition, construction and maintenance of marine works by local authorities
in Scotland.

(e) Dockyard ports. These are naval harbours. Their respective limits are
defined by Orders in Council under the Dockyard Ports Regulation Act 1865. At
each dockyard port the navigation both of Her Majesty's ships and others are subject to rules and regulations made by Order in Council under the Act of 1865. In
respect of each such port there is a Queen's Harbour Master to superintend the
execution of the Dockyard Ports Regulation Act and Orders in Council made
thereunder. It is not uncommon for a dockyard port to be within, or overlap, the
limits of a commercial harbour. In such cases the powers of the Queen's Harbour
Master have precedence over those of the harbour authority. In practice, however,
the Queen's Harbour Master and the harbour authority's harbour master generally liaise closely and it appears that such overlapping jurisdictions seldom give rise
to serious difficulty.

# CHAPTER 2

# TYPES OF HARBOUR AUTHORITY

25. Although the variety of harbour authorities (that is to say, harbour authorities for harbours of the kind referred to in paragraph 1 above) is such that no precise classification is possible there are two main grounds on which distinctions can be made, namely—
   (a) the functions performed by the harbour authority, and
   (b) the nature of the body, e.g., nationalized undertaking, local authority, company or "port trust".

26. The main functions of harbour authorities, which are discussed later in some detail, may perhaps be classified, in general terms, as follows:
   (a) the provision and maintenance of harbour facilities, i.e, quays, wharves, etc.;
   (b) conservancy functions, including lighting and bouying the harbour, the removal of wrecks and other obstructions and maintenance dredging— clearing up pollution might also be regarded as falling under this head;
   (c) regulating the activities of other persons at the harbour including, in particular, regulating the movement and berthing of ships in the harbour by means of directions and by-laws and licensing dredging and the construction of works in the harbour by other persons;
   (d) carrying out harbour operations including, in particular, cargo-handling activities; and
   (e) the provision of a pilotage service.

27. Some harbour authorities, including nearly all the major ones, undertake all these classes of function. They include those harbour authorities, such as the Port of London Authority (PLA), the Tees and the Hartlepool Port Authority, the Forth Ports Authority, the Clyde Port Authority and the Port of Tyne Authority, and Associated British Ports at the Humber and Southampton, which are responsible for all kinds of harbour authority functions throughout a major estuary.

28. Following the recommendations of the Rochdale Report (see paragraph 14 *ante*), steps were taken in the 1960s and early 1970s towards the amalgamation of dock and conservancy functions in major estuaries but there are still some harbour authorities, of which the Harwich Harbour Conservancy Board are a major example, which do not themselves provide harbour facilities but are engaged

9

solely in conservancy functions and the regulation of shipping. Conversely, there are a few important harbour authorities, such as the Felixstowe Dock and Railway Company, which are mainly concerned with the management of docks and whose conservancy jurisdiction is limited to a relatively small area in the vicinity of their docks.

**29.** Turning to the various kinds of bodies which manage harbours under statutory powers, about a third of the harbours in Great Britain, including the great port of Southampton and the Humber ports were, by virtue of the Transport Act 1962, vested in the British Transport Docks Board (BTDB) which were constituted by that Act. The harbours in question were formerly vested in the British Transport Commission to whom they were transferred from the former Railway Companies by the Transport Act 1947, except that the undertakings of the former Humber and Southampton Conservancy Boards were transferred to the BTDB by harbour reorganization schemes under the Harbours Act 1964 (certain harbours were also transferred by such schemes or by local Act of Parliament from the BTDB to other harbour authorities).

**30.** On 31 December 1982, pursuant to section 5(1) of the Transport Act 1981, the BTDB were reconstituted under the name of "Associated British Ports". Under the provisions of Part II of the Transport Act 1981 Associated British Ports continue, as a statutory corporation, to manage their harbours under substantially the same powers as the BTDB. With a few exceptions, the provisions of the Transport Acts 1962 and 1968 no longer apply but a similar, and in some respects rather wider, code of powers for Associated British Ports is set out in Schedule 3 to the 1981 Act. The controls which, under the Transport Acts, the Secretary of State exercises over nationalized transport undertakings no longer apply to Associated British Ports and the financial provisions of those Acts, including borrowing and charging powers, have also ceased to apply. Schedule 3 to the 1981 Act includes new borrowing powers for Associated British Ports and a new power to charge for services and facilities. Associated British Ports now charge ship, passenger and goods dues under section 26 of the Harbours Act 1964 (and combined charges under section 27A of the Act inserted by the Transport Act 1981) as do other harbour authorities.

**31.** Under Part II of the Transport Act 1981, Associated British Ports are controlled by a company, formed by the Secretary of State and registered under the Companies Act 1985, known as Associated British Ports Holdings plc in substantially the same way as if they were a wholly owned subsidiary of that company. In particular, under section 7(4) of the 1981 Act, the directors of Associated British Ports (of which there must be not less than five nor more than 13) are appointed by Associated British Ports Holdings plc for such period as that company may determine. Under Section 11(1) of the 1981 Act the directors of Associated British Ports must pay to Associated British Ports Holdings plc such sums as appear to the directors to be justified by the profits of Associated British Ports (this corresponding to the dividends which a subsidiary pays its holding company). But Associated British Ports Holdings plc has no power to give directions to the directors of

Associated British Ports as respects the exercise of their powers and duties as a harbour authority.

**32.** The provisions of Part II of the Transport Act 1981, under which a statutory board with no share capital is to some extent controlled by a company formed and registered under the Companies Act 1985 but the directors of the board are, nevertheless, not subject to direction by the company, are thought to be unique. This, it is submitted, is an ingenious and subtle concept which enables the introduction of private capital and the commercial flexibility of a company formed under the Companies Act (Associated British Ports Holdings plc's memorandum of association enables it to carry out a wide variety of activities) to be reconciled with the principles usually associated with the carrying out of important powers and duties conferred and imposed by Parliament for public purposes.

**33.** Not all the British Transport Commission's harbours were vested by the Transport Act 1962 in the BTDB. Several, broadly speaking the "packet ports" which at that time were mainly concerned with the transport of passengers to and from the Continent or Ireland, were vested in the British Railways Board (BRB) and a few small harbours at the seaward ends of canals were vested in the British Waterways Board (BWB).

**34.** The BRB's ports were managed, together with the Board's shipping services, by a subsidiary known as "Sealink". Section 2 of the Transport Act 1981 required that Sealink should form a company under the Companies Act 1948 and transfer to that company (which would be a subsidiary of Sealink) Sealink's harbour undertaking. This has been done and BRB's harbours are now managed by Sealink Harbours Limited.

**35.** The BRB, having disposed of their securities in Sealink, the harbours managed by Sealink Harbours Limited have ceased to be nationalized and the relevant provisions of the Transport Acts 1962 and 1968 no longer apply. In addition to local Acts and orders the provisions of Schedule 1 to the Transport Act 1981 apply to these harbours.

**36.** A number of harbours are managed by local authorities. These include the major harbour of Bristol and the new harbours developed at Scapa Flow in Orkney and Sullom Voe in the Shetlands for the exploitation of North Sea oil. The management of a harbour by a local authority has implications from the financial point of view in that the relevant local harbour legislation generally provides for payments and receipts in respect of the harbour undertaking to be carried to, and form part of, the general rate fund. Where the harbour undertaking have made a profit in any year the local authority are often enabled to set aside all or part of it as a reserve to meet future contingencies in connection with the undertaking but where the port loses money the deficit may be met from the rates. Harbour authorities which are local authorities are, as such, exempt from corporation tax to which other harbour authorities are liable if they make a profit.

**37.** The harbour authorities for several harbours are companies but in nearly all cases, and for all three of the important harbours concerned—Mersey, Manchester Ship Canal and Felixstowe—the companies in question were constituted by local Acts of Parliament and not under the Companies Acts. The Mersey Docks and Harbour Company were established by the Mersey Docks and Harbour Act 1971 (which dissolved the former Mersey Docks and Harbour Board). The directors of that company include up to three persons appointed by the Government and one or two persons appointed by the directors in consultation with the trade unions recognized by the company in negotiations with their employees, together with six or seven directors elected by shareholders.

**38.** Most harbour authorities in Great Britain, including those for the majority of the great commercial ports, are bodies of the kind commonly known (the expression does not seem to have appeared in any statute or to have any judicial authority) as "port trusts". A port trust may perhaps be described as an *ad hoc* body created by, or under, statute for the purpose of managing a harbour and not having a share capital. Examples of port trusts are the PLA, the Tees and Hartlepool Port Authority, the Clyde Port Authority and the Medway Ports Authority. The Milford Haven Conservancy Board and the Harwich Harbour Conservancy Board, although their functions, as their names imply, are mainly in the conservancy field, are also port trusts, and many small and medium harbours throughout Great Britain are managed by port trusts.

**39.** The constitutions of port trusts have been a subject of controversy for many years. Originally, most members of port trusts were elected or appointed by particular interests concerned with the harbour or by a Minister of the Crown on the recommendation of, or after consultation with, such interests which generally included shipowners, importers and exporters of goods through the port, local authorities in the area and dock labour.

**40.** In recent years a different pattern has been adopted for all the port trusts which are harbour authorities for major harbours and in several other cases. A typical example is the constitution of the Port of Tyne Authority as reconstituted by the Port of Tyne Authority (Constitution) Revision Order 1974 which is set out in Appendix A. The concept is a relatively small Board consisting of a majority of members appointed by the Secretary of State not representative of particular interests but drawn from a specified range of relevant knowledge and experience, together with the chief executive officer and several other executives appointed by the Board. In a few cases this concept has been modified to give a measure of special treatment to local authorities or take account of special circumstances.

**41.** The "representative" basis of appointment mentioned in paragraph 39 *ante* has been retained for most small and medium port trusts. A question which is sometimes raised is whether a member appointed in this way, although not a delegate, has a duty to protect the interests by, or by reference to, whom he was appointed as well as to the harbour authority. In the author's view the only duty of such a member, in his capacity as a member of the port trust, is, at meetings of the Board, or committees of the Board, to seek to promote the best interests of the harbour authority. In short, such a member does not sit on the Board of the port trust as a representative. This is emphasized in cases where provisions of the Commissioners Clauses Act 1847 are incorporated with the local Acts of the port trust (although they seldom are in recent Acts and orders) by the Declaration which a member is required to make by section 12 of the Commissioners Clauses Act to faithfully and impartially, according to the best of his skill and judgment, execute all the powers and authorities reposed in him as a Commissioner by virtue of the harbour authority's statutes.

# CHAPTER 3

# BASIC DUTIES, POWERS AND LIBILITIES OF HARBOUR AUTHORITIES

**42.** In order to ascertain the law relating to any particular harbour authority reference must be made to their local Acts and orders (as well as the general law). However, in addition to the fact that local enactments often follow a common pattern, there are certain basic principles which apply generally.

**43.** The powers granted to a harbour authority by Parliament are in virtually all cases conferred for the purpose of providing a public service. Until recent years powers to construct and/or manage and maintain harbours were generally in permissive terms, but it is clear that even although the terms of a special Act of Parliament establishing a body for the purpose of carrying on an undertaking are permissive the statute may by implication impose a duty on the body concerned to establish and maintain the service in question. *Gardner* v. *London, Chatham and Dover Railway Co.*[1] and *Re Salisbury Railway and Market House Co.*[2] are cases in point.

**44.** The intention of Parliament to impose a duty to operate the harbour even where the harbour authority's statutory powers are generally in permissive terms can be inferred if the relevant Acts and orders incorporate section 33 of the Harbours, Docks and Piers Clauses Act 1847, or include a provision to the same effect, which is nearly always the case. That section provides that: "Upon payment of the rates made payable by this and the special Act (i.e., the Act which incorporates section 33), and subject to the other provisions thereof, the harbour, dock and pier shall be open to all persons for the shipping and unshipping of goods and the embarking and landing of passengers." (As indicated later section 26 of the Harbours Act 1964, which authorizes harbour authorities to levy dues, translates the reference to rates in section 33 of the Clauses Act as incorporated in a harbour authority's statutes so as to apply to charges under section 26.) In the case of *Thoresen Car Ferries Ltd.* v. *Weymouth and Portland Borough Council*,[3] Donaldson, J., said that a harbour authority's duty under section 33 was to keep their harbour open (to any person wishing to use it) subject to the right of others to use it. No doubt this duty is subject to the physical limitations of the harbour.

---

1. *Gardner* v. *London, Chatham and Dover Railway Co.* (1867) L.R. 2 Ch. App. 201.
2. *Re Salisbury Railway and Market House Co.* [1967] 3 W.L.R. 651; 111 S.J. 495; [1967] 1 All E.R. 813.
3. *Thoresen Car Ferries Ltd.* v. *Weymouth and Portland Borough Council* [1977] 2 Lloyd's Rep. 614.

**45.** It appears however that (even in the absence of a power to appropriate particular facilities as mentioned below) a harbour authority may by contract grant a regular user of the harbour, such as a ferry operator, a right to use a berth at certain times and will not be in breach of section 33 because other users are not able to use the berth at those times. But a harbour authority are not obliged to enter into a commitment that a berth will be available to a particular user at particular times even although, in the case of a user who wishes to provide a regular service at specified times, the use of the berth on any other basis may not be commercially practicable—*Thoresen Car Ferries* v. *Weymouth and Portland Borough Council.* The special legislation of most harbour authorities for significant commercial harbours now includes a provision authorizing the harbour authority, notwithstanding the provisions of section 33, to appropriate particular harbour facilities for the exclusive or preferential use of a particular user or for a particular kind of traffic.

**46.** Other important cases on the interpretation of section 33 of the 1847 Act emphasize that it must be given a wide construction. In *LNER* v. *British Trawlers Federation*[4] it was held that the marketing of fish when landed must be regarded as part of the process of shipping and unshipping within the meaning of section 33 and that access to the docks must include access with such a vehicle as the party seeking access deems necessary. Lord Macmillan said: "The harbour is to be open to all for the purpose of unshipping goods. It is manifest that this must include the consequential purpose of removing the goods unshipped, and such removal necessitates the employment of the appropriate vehicles." He pointed out that, by virtue of the definition in section 2 of the 1847 Act, "the harbour, dock or pier" included, for the purposes of section 33, works connected therewith. In *J. H. Piggot and Son* v. *Docks and Inland Waterways Executive*[5] it was held that tugowners are entitled by section 33 in the ordinary course of their business to employ their tugs in providing towage services to vessels entering or leaving a harbour for the shipping or unshipping of goods and/or embarking or landing of passengers. In *Garland and Flexman* v. *Wisbech Corporation*[6], a case which did not turn primarily on the construction of section 33, it was stated, *per curiam*, that section 33 is really dealing with the question of access to the installations in the geographical area of the harbour or pier. "It means that the public can go on to those premises for the purpose of doing, and there do, the things specified in the section, that is to say, shipping or unshipping of goods and embarking and landing of passengers." It should perhaps be pointed out that, at many ports, the rights of persons themselves to undertake the shipping or unshipping of goods are now subject to the provisions as respects the licensing and registration of port employers referred to in Chapter 11 *post*.

**47.** In recent local harbour legislation the duties of the harbour authority concerned are usually expressly stated and this is now the case with nearly all major harbour authorities. The general duties and powers of Associated British Ports are stated in section 9 of the Transport Act 1981. This section is set out in Part I of

---

4. *LNER* v. *British Trawlers Federation* [1934] A.C. 279.
5. *J. H. Pigott and Son* v. *Docks and Inland Waterways Executive* [1953] 1 Q.B. 338.
6. *Garland and Flexman* v. *Wisbech Corporation* [1962] 1 Q.B. 151.

Appendix B. Part II of Appendix B sets out section 5 of the Port of London Act 1968 which states the general powers and duties of the PLA. The special legislation of the harbour authorities for nearly all major commercial harbours now contain general statements of powers and duties in substantially similar terms.

**48.** Although the terms of these provisions—to take such action for the specified purposes as the harbour authority consider necessary or desirable or expedient—confer a discretion, this must be exercised reasonably and in good faith for the purpose which the relevant legislation was designed to achieve which is in virtually all cases the provision of port services and facilities to meet the needs of the public.

**49.** Where a harbour authority have a statutory duty to maintain their harbour, which it is submitted is nearly always the case, it would seem that the harbour cannot be closed and the undertaking discontinued except by means of an Act of Parliament. There may be some doubt about this in the case of a harbour authority which is a company. However, in the *Salisbury Railway and Market House* case referred to above[7] it was held that the company concerned, which, although created by statute, had registered under Part VIII of the Companies Act 1948 and had then gone into a members' voluntary winding up, could not, without statutory sanction, abandon its functions relating to the market house.

**50.** Under section 666 of the Companies Act 1985 an unregistered company may be wound up by the court in certain specified circumstances. There is no recent authority on whether an unregistered company with subsisting statutory duties can be wound up under this provision but having regard to the *Salisbury Railway and Market House* case it seems that the better view is that such a company cannot be completely wound up and dissolved except by Act of Parliament. This view seems to be supported by the judgments of the Court of Appeal in *Re Woking Urban Council (Basingstoke Canal) Act 1911*.[8]

**51.** It has been suggested that a port trust is an unregistered company for the purposes of the Companies Act 1985 and that it is therefore arguably possible for a port trust to be wound up under section 666 of that Act. However, it does not appear that a port trust is in any sense a company. The contrary view would appear to involve the proposition that every body corporate is such. Thus, for example, local authorities and bodies such as the BBC would be liable to be would up by the court. It seems unlikely that Parliament intended to achieve such a result.

**52.** It may indeed often be doubtful whether a harbour authority can close even a significant part of their harbour without statutory authority. In particular, where section 33 of the Harbours, Docks and Piers Clauses Act 1847 is not only incorporated by a harbour authority's special legislation in relation to their harbour as a whole but also by an Act or order which authorizes the construction of a specific dock or jetty it would seem that, unless the authority's special legislation provides to the contrary, that facility cannot be closed without further legislation. In order to

7. *Ante*, fn.2.
8. *Re Woking Urban Council (Basingstoke Canal) Act 1911* [1914] 1 Ch. 300.

overcome this difficulty some harbour authorities have recently included in their special legislation a declaration that section 33 as incorporated with that legislation shall not be construed as derogating from the power of the harbour authority to discontinue any part of their undertaking.

53. Harbour authorities are nearly all bodies created by statute and as such subject to the doctrine of *ultra vires*, that is to say, they can only do what is expressly authorized by or under statute or such things as are reasonably incidental to what is expressly authorized. The case of the *Dundee Harbour Trustees* v. *Nicol*[9] arose from the Trustees seeking to diversify their activities by letting out boats for excursions. This was challenged by a commercial firm in that line of business who brought an action against them on the grounds that the Trustees had no power to undertake this activity. In giving judgment against the Trustees Lord Haldane said: "It is now well settled that the answer to the question whether a corporation created by statute has a particular power depends exclusively on whether that power has been expressly given to it or can be implied from the language used."

54. With regard to harbour authorities' powers for the acquisition and disposal of land, section 38(1) of the Docks and Harbours Act 1966 provides that a harbour authority may for the purpose of any of their statutory powers or statutory duties acquire by agreement any land wherever situated. Some harbour authorities already possessed such a power under their special legislation. Section 23 of the Harbours, Docks and Piers Clauses Act 1847 authorizes a harbour authority with whose special legislation the section is incorporated to "lease or grant the use or occupation of any warehouses, buildings, wharves, yards, cranes, machines, or other conveniences provided by them for the purpose of this or the special Act, at such rents, and upon such terms and conditions as shall be agreed upon between the undertakers and the persons taking the same, providing that no such lease be granted for a longer term than three years". This section, which it will be noted authorizes the grant of leases for operational harbour purposes and not the disposal of surplus land, is sometimes incorporated with a modification omitting the limitation to a three years' term.

55. The special legislation of most harbour authorities for major harbours now contains a general power to dispose of land belonging to them in such manner, whether by way of sale, exchange, lease, the creation of any easement, right or privilege or otherwise, for such periods, upon such conditions and for such consideration as they think fit. Sometimes this power is limited, in terms, to land no longer required for the purposes of the harbour undertaking and would not therefore authorize the grant of a lease for operational harbour purposes, e.g., the lease of a berth to the intent that the lessees will operate it. If section 23 of the Harbours, Docks and Piers Clauses Act 1847 is incorporated with a harbour authority's special legislation such leases can be granted under that provision and in at least one case—Article 31 of the Port of Tyne Reorganization Scheme 1967—the special legislation includes, in addition to a power to dispose of surplus land, a

9. *Dundee Harbour Trustees* v. *Nicol* [1915] A.C. 550.

modern provision authorizing the harbour authority to grant operational leases. However, it would seem that, even in the absence of an express power for the purpose, a harbour authority with express general powers and duties to manage their harbour probably have implied power to grant leases, licences, etc, where they consider that this would be in the interests of the efficient and economical management of the harbour.

**56.** Some harbour authorities for major harbours have power under their special legislation to make, and submit to the Secretary of State, orders for the compulsory acquisition of land which they require for the purposes of their harbour undertakings. For this purpose the Acquisition of Land Act 1981, which contains the standard procedural code for the compulsory purchase of land, is generally applied. The Transport Act 1962 confers powers for the compulsory acquisition of land on the harbour authorities for nationalized harbours. In the case of Associated British Ports such powers are now contained in paragraph 19 of Schedule 3 to the Transport Act 1981.

**57.** The property in the bed of a harbour is *prima facie* vested in the Crown. In some cases however it is vested in the harbour authority by grant or charter from the Crown or by prescription and occasionally it is so vested in another person. Most harbour authorities do not own the bed of their harbour and, although such ownership has advantages, particularly in relation to the construction of works below high water mark, it is certainly not essential for the management of a harbour.

**58.** Although there appears to be no direct authority, there seems no reason to doubt that the principle established in *Hammersmith and City Railway Co. Ltd.* v. *Brand*[10] and discussed in *Allen* v. *Gulf Oil Refining Ltd.*[11] that where a body are authorized by statute to construct (and therefore by implication to use) works in a specific position they will not be liable for nuisance in respect of the use of those works reasonably and without negligence for the purpose envisaged by the statute, applies to harbour authorities. (However, in such cases a harbour authority may be liable to pay compensation under Part I of the Land Compensation Act 1973 where the value of an interest in land is depreciated by certain kinds of nuisance—the "physical factors" described in section 1(2) of the Land Compensation Act 1973—caused by the use of a work, e.g., a dock, the construction of which was specifically authorized by statute.)

**59.** It is well established that a harbour authority will be liable if they, or their servants, fail to exercise reasonable care and skill in carrying out the harbour authority's functions. In the Privy Council case of *East London Harbour Board* v. *Caledonian Shipping Co.*[12] the harbour authority were held to be liable for the negligence of their harbour master in directing the movement and mooring of vessels. In *Edwards* v. *Falmouth Harbour Commissioners*[13] the Falmouth Harbour Commissioners

10. *Hammersmith and City Railway Co. Ltd* v. *Brand* (1869) L.R. 4 H.L. 171.
11. *Allen* v. *Gulf Oil Refining Ltd.* [1981] A.C. 1001.
12. *East London Harbour Board* v. *Caledonian Shipping Co.* [1908] A.C. 271.
13. *Edwards* v. *Falmouth Harbour Commissioners* (1884) 54 L.J. Adm. 42.

were held to be liable for the action of their harbour master who gave orders for a ship to be beached in such a manner that she was damaged. In *The Ratata*[14] Preston Corporation, as harbour authority for the Ribble, were held liable for damage caused by the failure of their servants to exercise reasonable care and skill in carrying out a towage operation. In *The Framlington Court*,[15] it was held that the PLA were responsible for the negligence of their dock-master in ordering the *Framlington Court*, under powers conferred on the dock-master by the Port of London Act 1920, to get under way when he was aware of an obstruction at the dock entrance (although in the event the plaintiffs failed because of contributory negligence on the part of the master of the *Framlington Court*—if the case had been heard after the passing of the Law Reform (Contributory Negligence) Act 1945 the result would have been different). It seems clear that the fact that the negligence of a harbour master relates to the exercise of statutory powers vested, in terms, directly in him (see para 122 *post*) makes no difference to the vicarious liability of the harbour authority who employ him. See also in this connection *A. F. Henry and MacGregor* v. *Aberdeen Harbour Commissioners*.[16]

**60.** The duties of a harbour authority in carrying out conservancy functions are discussed in more detail in Chapter 5. It was held in *Mersey Docks and Harbour Board Trustees* v. *Gibbs*[17] that a harbour authority are liable for damage occasioned by their failure to take reasonable care that their dock (so far as they keep it open for public use) may be used by those who choose to navigate it without danger to their lives or property. But it appears from *Queen of the River Steamship Co.* v. *River Thames Conservators*[18] that a harbour authority are not liable for damage caused by an obstruction in their harbour which they are not aware of and could not reasonably be expected to be aware of.

**61.** Under sections 2 and 3 of the Merchant Shipping (Liability of Shipowners and Others) Act 1900 as amended by section 19 of, and Schedule 5 to, the Merchant Shipping Act 1979, a harbour authority may limit their liability (whether arising under common law or under statute) for loss or damage occurring on any distinct occasion to any vessel or vessels or to any goods, merchandise or other things whatsoever on board any vessel or vessels, unless the loss or damage resulted from their personal act or omission committed with the intent to cause such loss or damage or recklessly and with knowledge that such loss would probably result. It seems therefore that a harbour authority will always be entitled to limit their liability for such loss or damage as is mentioned above which results from an act or omission on the part of a servant or agent of the harbour authority.

**62.** Where a harbour authority are entitled to limit their liability as mentioned in the preceding paragraph the extent of that limitation turns on the tonnage of the largest registered British ship which, at the time when the loss or damage in

14. *The Ratata* [1898] A.C. 513.
15. *The Framlington Court* (1936) 56 Ll.L.Rep. 200.
16. *A. F. Henry and MacGregor* v. *Aberdeen Harbour Commissioners* (1943) 76 Ll.L.Rep. 107.
17. *Mersey Docks and Harbour Board Trustees* v. *Gibbs* (1866) L.R. 1 H.L. 93.
18. *Queen of the River Steamship Co.* v. *River Thames Conservators* (1907) 96 L.T.

question occurs, is, or within the previous five years has been, within the harbour authority's limits of jurisdiction (excluding any ship which is, or was, within that area by reason only that she was built or fitted out there, or that she took shelter within or passed through that area on a voyage between two places outside that area, or that she has loaded or unloaded mails or passengers within that area). The amount of that limitation is to be calculated by applying to this tonnage the formula for calculating limits of liability specified in paragraph 1(*b*) of Article 6 of the Convention on Limitation of Liability for Maritime Claims 1976 (which Convention, by virtue of section 17 of the Merchant Shipping Act 1979, has the force of law in the United Kingdom and is set out in Part I of Schedule 4 to that Act, related and incidental provisions being specified in Part II of that Schedule) read with the related provisions of that Convention and with those of Part II of Schedule 4 to the Merchant Shipping Act 1979. (In relation to pilotage, special provisions as to the limitations of a harbour authority's liability apply. These are specified in paragraphs 486 to 495 *post*.)

63. Under section 74 of the Harbours, Docks and Piers Clauses Act 1847, which, or an equivalent provision, is nearly always incorporated in the special legislation of harbour authorities, a shipowner is absolutely liable for damage caused by his ship to harbour works except, it appears from the decision of the House of Lords in *River Wear Commissioners* v. *Adamson*,[19] where this is due to an Act of God.

64. Under the Convention on Limitation of Liability for Maritime Claims 1976, as in force in the United Kingdom by virtue of the Merchant Shipping Act 1979, a shipowner whose ship damages harbour works may, unless it is proved that the damage resulted from his personal act or omission committed with the intent to cause the damage, or recklessly and with knowledge that the damage would probably result, limit his liability in accordance with the formula specified in paragraph 1(*b*) of Article 6 of the Convention which is related to the tonnage of the ship concerned.

65. The Convention also provides that shipowners and salvors may, on a similar basis, limit their liability in respect of the costs of wreck removal. However, by virtue of paragraph 3 of Part II of Schedule 4 to the Merchant Shipping Act 1979, this provision will not apply unless the Secretary of State for Trade, by order, provides for the establishment of a fund to compensate harbour authorities for consequential reductions in the amounts recoverable by them in claims for such costs. No such order has yet been made.

---

19. *River Wear Commissioners* v. *Adamson* (1877) 2 App. Cas. 743.

# CHAPTER 4

# PROVISION OF HARBOUR FACILITIES BY HARBOUR AUTHORITIES AND OTHERS

**66.** In any harbour the basic works, the quays, wharves and jetties, will be constructed to a large extent below high water mark in navigable waters and it is often necessary to dredge a channel of sufficient depth for ships to reach these works in safety. The law in relation to the construction of works, and dredging, below high water mark is in a number of respects the same for harbour authorities as for other persons but, as indicated below, there are certain differences.

**67.** At common law the construction of works below high water mark in navigable waters so as to interfere with the public right of navigation is an actionable nuisance. In the case of the *Attorney-General* v. *Terry*[1] the owner of a wharf at the port of Sandwich who sought to extend his wharf about three feet into the River Stour was restrained from doing so in an action for nuisance brought by the Attorney-General on the relation of Sandwich Corporation who at that time were the harbour authority for the port. It was held both in the court of first instance and in the Court of Appeal that the wharf as extended would in fact obstruct navigation. It appeared from the judgment of Jessell, M.R., in the court of first instance, that even if obstruction to navigation had not been proved the extension of the wharf would still be restrained because it might become an obstruction in the future. However, having regard to the judgments of the House of Lords in *Orr-Ewing* v. *Colquhoun*,[2] it seems doubtful whether that is good law. It appears that even if an erection below high water mark obstructs navigation it may not be a nuisance if it results in a direct public benefit, to the same public as use the navigation, which outweighs the inconvenience caused to them by the obstruction—e.g., works to straighten the sides of a harbour of irregular shape might not be a nuisance even if they are to some extent an obstruction to navigation—*per* Jessell, M.R., in *Attorney-General* v. *Terry*. In *Iveagh* v. *Martin*[3] Paull, J., said, in relation to the position where the owner of the foreshore erects thereon a permanent building such as a quay, that in a proper case the public "may have the right in an action properly constituted to obtain a mandatory injunction ordering the owner of the quay to remove the quay on the

1. *Attorney-General* v. *Terry* (1874) L.R. 9 Ch. 423.
2. *Orr-Ewing* v. *Colquhoun* (1877) 2 App. Cas. 839.
3. *Iveagh* v. *Martin* [1960] 1 Q.B., at p. 273.

grounds that it seriously interferes with their rights of navigation" (he added that he could see no evidence that such a cause of action existed in the particular case he was dealing with).

**68.** Any significant quay, wharf or jetty at a harbour is likely to obstruct navigation to some extent. In general, therefore, such works should be authorized by an Act of Parliament or by a harbour revision order under section 14 of the Harbours Act 1964 (in the case of an existing harbour authority), or a harbour empowerment order under section 16 of that Act (in the case of a prospective harbour authority).

**69.** The special legislation of a harbour authority sometimes contains a general power for them to construct works in their harbour. For example, under section 62 of the Port of London Act 1968 the Port of London Authority have power to lay down, maintain and operate in and over the River Thames such works and equipment as are required for or in connection with the exercise by them of any of their functions.

**70.** As indicated below, at some harbours (according to the terms of the relevant special legislation) the licence from the harbour authority which is required by any person other than that authority before constructing works below high water mark, or dredging, in the harbour, may remove any need to obtain statutory powers for the purpose.

**71.** In addition to statutory authority, a variety of statutory licences and consents, each related to different considerations, have to be obtained before the construction of works, or dredging, below high water mark can be undertaken. Perhaps the most important of these is the consent required from the Secretary of State under section 34 of the Coast Protection Act 1949 for the purpose of securing safety of navigation.

**72.** Under section 34(1) of the Coast Protection Act 1949, as amended by the Merchant Shipping Act 1988, the consent of the Secretary of State is required before any person may

    (a) construct, alter or improve any works on, under or over any part of the seashore lying below the level of mean high water springs;

    (b) deposit any object or any materials on any such part of the seashore as aforesaid; or

    (c) remove any object or any materials from any part of the seashore lying below the level of mean low water springs, if the operation (whether while being carried out or subsequently) causes or is likely to result in obstruction or danger to navigation.

**73.** Section 35(1) of the Coast Protection Act excepts certain operations from the restriction imposed by section 34(1). These exceptions include "the carrying out of any dredging operations (including the deposit of dredged materials) authorized by any local Act in accordance with the provisions thereof" but the construction of works authorized by a local Act is not excepted. The exceptions also include any work carried out by, or in accordance with a licence or permission granted by, (a harbour authority or navigation authority) in pursuance of any Act, where

(i) the Act requires that if the approval of the Secretary of State is not previously obtained to the work other conditions must be complied with; and

(ii) the said approval has been so obtained or the said conditions are complied with.

So far as works licensed by a harbour authority are concerned, it is believed that this exception applies only to works licensed by the PLA under section 66 of the Port of London Act 1968. Under section 76(1) of that Act a work on the bed of the River Thames licensed by the PLA is not to be carried out unless it has been previously approved in writing by the Secretary of State or, if such approval has not been obtained, the licence imposes a condition that the work will be immediately removed if the Secretary of State requires it.

74. Section 34(3) of the Coast Protection Act requires the Secretary of State, if he is of opinion that any operation for which an application is made to him under section 34 will cause or is likely to result in obstruction or danger to navigation, either to refuse consent or give his consent subject to such conditions as he may think fit having regard to the nature and extent of the obstruction or danger which it appears to him would otherwise be caused or be likely to result. The new subsection (4A) inserted by the Merchant Shipping Act 1988 provides that conditions imposed by the Secretary of State under section 34—

(a) shall (subject to the Secretary of State's power to revoke them) either remain in force for a specified period or remain in force without limit of time;

(b) shall, in addition to binding the person to whom consent is given, bind, so far as is appropriate, any person who for the time being owns, occupies, or enjoys any use of the works in question;

(c) may, if the condition relates to the provision of any lights, signals or other aids to navigation or to the stationing of guard ships in the vicinity of the works in question or to the taking of any other measures for the purpose of controlling the movements of ships in the vicinity of those works, be varied by the Secretary of State in the interests of the safety of navigation; and

(d) may be revoked by the Secretary of State if he thinks fit to do so.

75. The scope of section 34 of the Coast Protection Act 1949 was considered in the case of *Harwich Harbour Conservancy Board* v. *The Secretary of State for the Environment, East Suffolk County Council and Stour River Estate*.[4] The question at issue was whether the Secretary of State, in considering whether to give his consent to the construction of a marina, was entitled to take into account not only whether the proposed works would, in themselves, constitute an obstruction or danger to navigation (either directly or by causing siltation) but also whether the

---

4. *Harwich Harbour Conservancy Board* v. *The Secretary of State for the Environment, East Suffolk County Council and Stour River Estate* [1975] 1 A.C. 334.

additional vessels which would be likely to be attracted to the area by the works would obstruct or endanger navigation. It was held that section 34(1) did not enable the Secretary of State to refuse his consent to the construction of a work on the ground that the work might be used by vessels which he desired to exclude from the area (and accordingly, in the case under consideration, that the Secretary of State for the Environment had been wrong in refusing to deal with that issue under the Town and Country Planning Acts on the ground that it was a matter to be considered by the Secretary of State (for Trade at that time) under the Coast Protection Act). (It was, however, indicated that possible obstruction by boats actively using the work— e.g., by a boat tied up at a jetty, could be taken into account.)

**76.** This limitation of the scope of the Secretary of State's jurisdiction under section 34 has now been removed by the new subsection (3A) inserted in the section by the Merchant Shipping Act 1988. This provides that in the case of a proposal to construct, alter or improve any works on, under or over any part of the seashore lying below the level of mean high water springs references in subsection (1) or (3) of section 34 to an operation being likely to result in obstruction or danger to navigation shall be construed as including a reference to its being likely to have such a result by reason of any use intended to be made of the works in question when constructed, altered or improved. This clearly enables the Secretary of State to take into account the sort of consideration which was held in the *Harwich* case to be outside his jurisdiction under section 34.

**77.** At many harbours (including nearly all important commercial harbours) the harbour authority's special legislation prohibits persons other than the harbour authority from constructing works below high water mark or dredging without first obtaining a licence from the harbour authority. In recent years most harbour authorities for major harbours have adopted provisions for this purpose which follow a common pattern, although with some variations.

**78.** Sections 37 to 41 of the Medway Ports Authority Act 1973, which are set out in Appendix C, are a typical example of the current powers of a major harbour authority to license works and dredging. It will be noted that under section 37(1) a person may be granted a licence to construct, etc., works below high water mark "notwithstanding interference with public rights of navigation and other public rights by such works . . . ". Although it may be arguable that a provision in this form merely enables the harbour authority to grant a licence for works which, when constructed, may interfere with public rights, it seems that the better view is that a licence granted under this provision authorizes the licensee to construct and maintain the works in question without being liable for nuisance on the grounds that the works interfere with the public rights of navigation or fishing (provided no doubt that the licensee is not guilty of negligence and that his use of the works is reasonable). If this view is correct a licence granted under a provision of this kind removes the need there might otherwise be to obtain statutory powers to authorize the construction and maintenance of the works. This view appears to be endorsed by the judgment of Lord Templeman in the House of Lords in *Tate and Lyle*

*Industries Ltd. and Another* v. *Greater London Council and Another.*[5] His Lordship referred to the cases of *Kearns* v. *The Cordwainers' Co.*[6] and *Attorney-General* v. *Thames Conservators*[7] as showing that no action would lie for an interference with the public right of navigation caused by works licensed by the PLA under section 243 of the Port of London (Consolidation) Act 1920 (that section, which has been replaced by section 66 of the Port of London Act 1968—a modern licensing power of the kind referred to above—did not refer expressly to the public right of navigation).

79. Section 38(4) of the Medway Ports Authority Act 1973 states that the issue of a licence to dredge under section 38 shall not confer statutory authority for the carrying out of the work covered by the licence. This is a standard provision. It removes any doubt that where dredging is authorized by the harbour authority the Secretary of State's consent under the Coast Protection Act is still required (because the exception under section 35(1) of that Act for dredging authorized by statute does not apply).

80. What considerations can a harbour authority take into account in exercising their discretionary powers to license works and dredging by other persons? In some cases the form of the licensing powers in a harbour authority's special legislation indicate that safety of navigation is the only consideration (and there is thus an almost complete overlap with the control exercised by the Secretary of State under section 34 of the Coast Protection Act) but where these powers are on the lines of those set out in Appendix C or otherwise do not provide expressly or by implication that the licensing power is geared exclusively to navigational considerations it seems that the scope may be wider. In the case of *Rex* v. *Port of London Authority ex parte Kynoch*[8] it was held that in considering whether to grant a licence for another person to construct works in the River Thames the PLA were entitled to take into account that the proposed works would be used for purposes competitive with works which they had statutory powers to provide. It seems that the range of considerations which a harbour authority may take into account under licensing provisions of the kind set out in Appendix C depends on the range of the harbour authority's general powers and duties. A harbour authority whose functions are virtually limited to conservancy are probably only entitled to take navigational considerations into account. But it appears that a harbour authority responsible for the full range of harbour authority functions are entitled also to take into account whether the proposed works are necessary or desirable for the trade of the port, having regard to the works which both they and other persons have provided or may provide and the good planning and efficient management of the port generally.

81. It will be noted that the licensing powers set out in Appendix C provide for

5. *Tate and Lyle Industries Ltd. and Another* v. *Greater London Council and Another* [1983] 2 Lloyd's Rep. 117.
6. *Kearns* v. *The Cordwainers' Co.* (1859) 6 C.B. (N.S.) 388.
7. *Attorney-General* v. *Thames Conservators* (1862) 1 H. & M.1.
8. *Rex.* v. *Port of London Authority ex parte Kynoch* [1919] 1 K.B. 176.

appeals to Ministers against decisions of the harbour authority—to the Secretary of State for Trade in relation to works and to the Secretary of State for Transport in relation to dredging. Following a transfer of functions from the Secretary of State for Trade to the Secretary of State for Transport this appellate function is now vested exclusively in the latter.

82. As indicated above there is a considerable overlap between the Secretary of State's jurisdiction under section 34 of the Coast Protection Act 1949 and the powers of harbour authorities to regulate the construction of works and dredging by other persons below high water mark in their harbours. With a view to reducing this overlap section 37 of the Merchant Shipping Act 1988 contains an enabling power for the Secretary of State by regulations to disapply section 34 as respects any operations of a kind falling within the Secretary of State's jurisdiction under that section which a harbour authority have power to license or otherwise regulate under their local Acts and orders. This regulation-making power may be exercised either on the application of the harbour authority concerned or on the Secretary of State's own motion after consulting the harbour authority. Regulations to disapply section 34 at a harbour may supplement and adapt the harbour authority's existing works licensing powers. Section 37 of the 1988 Act provides that where section 34 of the 1949 Act has been disapplied as mentioned above the Secretary of State may redetermine an application already determined by the harbour authority even in the absence of an appeal if he considers that it would be appropriate for him to do so in the interest of safe navigation. He must, however, initiate the procedure for this purpose within 30 days after the harbour authority's determination.

83. Section 37 of the Merchant Shipping Act 1988 also requires all harbour authorities with works licensing powers before an operation which they have licensed has been begun to furnish the Hydrographer of the Navy with written particulars of the operation with a plan showing where it is to be carried out and, once the operation has been carried out, to furnish the Hydrographer with a notification of that fact and with such plans and additional information relating to the completed operation as he may require for the purpose of determing whether, and if so what, changes should be made to any chart or other publication produced under his superintendence.

84. Part II of the Food and Environmental Protection Act 1985 which provides for deposits in the sea to be licensed, and replaced the Dumping at Sea Act 1974, sets up another hurdle to be surmounted before works may be constructed below high water mark. The purpose of this licensing system is to protect the marine environment and the living resources which it supports. It seems that the prohibition imposed by section 5 of the Food and Environmental Protection Act on the deposit of substances or articles in the sea except in pursuance of a licence applies to the construction of harbour works subject to the exceptions mentioned below. This might seem incongruous but when the point was taken at the Committee stage in the House of Lords of the Bill which became the Dumping at Sea Act 1974 it was stated that "it is important for those charged with the responsibility of

safeguarding the marine environment to be in a position to maintain an effective oversight of operations which could conceivably introduce or release heavy metals or other persistent substances into the food chain via marine life". The Deposits in the Sea (Exemptions) Order 1985 provides that a licence under Part II of the Food and Environmental Protection Act is not required for the operations specified in the Schedule to that Order. These include the deposit of any article in connection with the provision of moorings or aids to navigation by a harbour authority or lighthouse authority or by any other person if the consent of a harbour authority or lighthouse authority is required.

85. The licensing authority for the purposes of Part II of the Food and Environmental Protection Act 1985 is the Minister of Agriculture, Fisheries and Food in England and Wales and the Secretary of State for Scotland in Scotland. The Act confers a right on the applicant for, or the holder of, a licence to make written representation relating to a decision of the licensing authority and requires such representations to be considered. Part II of the Food and Environmental Protection Act is also important to harbour authorities in relation to dredging since the deposit at sea of dredged spoil needs to be licensed under Part II.

86. As mentioned earlier, most land below high water mark is vested in the Crown and where it is proposed to construct harbour works below high water mark it is therefore usually necessary to purchase or lease the site from the Crown Estate Commissioners. Under section 3 of the Crown Estate Act 1961, the Crown Estate Commissioners are required (subject to section 4 of that Act), on the sale, lease or other disposal of any land of the Crown Estate, to obtain the best consideration in money or money's worth which in their opinion can reasonably be obtained, having regard to all the circumstances of the case but excluding any element of monopoly value attributable to the extent of the Crown's ownership of comparable land. Section 4(1) of the Act of 1961 provides as follows:

for the development, improvement or general benefit of any land of the Crown Estate, the Commissioners with the consent of Her Majesty signified under the Royal Sign Manual may dispose of land or of a right or privilege over or in relation to land, without consideration or for such consideration as they think fit where the land is to be used and occupied, or the right or privilege is to be enjoyed—

   (a) for the purposes of any public or local authority, or for the purposes of any authority or person exercising powers conferred by or under any enactment for the supply of water; or

   (b) for the construction, enlargement, improvement or maintenance of any road, dock, sea-wall, embankment, drain, water-course or reservoir; or

   (c) for providing, enlarging or improving a place of religious worship, residence for a minister of religion, school, library or scientific institution, or any communal facilities for recreation, or the amenities of, or means of access to any land or building falling within this paragraph; or

   (d) for any other public or charitable purpose in connection with any land of the Crown Estate, or tending to the welfare of persons residing or employed on any such land.

87. It has been argued that the Crown Estate Commissioners have a discretion to sell or lease land for the construction of docks (and the other public purposes

mentioned in section 4(1) of the Crown Estate Act 1961) at less than the full commercial price (excluding monopoly value which incidentally has not proved easy to assess in the case of land under the sea). This argument turns on whether the words "for the development, improvement or general benefit of any land of the Crown Estate" at the beginning of section 4(1) include land which the Commissioners are disposing of as mentioned in the subsection. The legal advisers to the Crown Estate Commissioners take the view that the words at the beginning of section 4(1) refer only to land retained by the Commissioners. This construction (which may be supported by a comparison with section 55 of the Settled Land Act 1925 as read with section 107 of that Act) gives section 4(1) a very limited application—and results in the Commissioners charging high purchase prices or (more usually) rents, for the sites of harbour works below high water mark.

88. It is perhaps worth mentioning at this point that a harbour authority's works below high water mark are usually subject to provisions on the lines of sections 42 to 45 of the Medway Ports Authority Act 1973 set out in Appendix D. These are designed to prevent danger to navigation.

89. In addition to works below high water mark harbour authorities commonly provide storage sheds and other facilities for harbour purposes on land adjoining the harbour (in which, of course, they must first have or acquire the necessary rights or interests). Section 21 of the Harbours, Docks and Piers Clauses Act 1847 contains express powers for this purpose but is seldom now incorporated in special harbour legislation. The special legislation of most harbour authorities for major harbours now contains general powers to provide, maintain and operate warehousing services and facilities and services and facilities for the consignment of goods on routes which include the port premises, e.g., section 5 of the Port of London Act 1968 set out in Part II of Appendix B. Indeed, if a harbour authority have the capacity as a statutory corporation to manage a harbour (not solely from the conservancy angle) the power to provide warehouses, etc., on land in which they have a sufficient interest appears to be implicit.

90. Subject to what is said in the next paragraph about development below low water mark, permission is required under the Town and Country Planning Act 1971, or, as the case may be, the Town and Country Planning (Scotland) Act 1972, for the construction of harbour works but, as mentioned below, development by harbour authorities is in some cases permitted by virtue of the Town and Country Planning General Development Order 1977 or its Scottish equivalent.

91. It appears that the jurisdiction of a local planning authority does not extend beyond low water mark except possibly where the land in question is within the general administrative area of the local authority concerned, e.g., in a tidal estuary falling *intra fauces terrae*. In the Scottish case of *Argyll and Bute District Council* v. *Secretary of State for Scotland*,[9] which seems to be the only authority directly in point, the Lord Justice-Clerk, Lord Wheatley, held that the jurisdiction of a planning authority in Scotland did not apply below low water mark even where the site

9. *Argyll and Bute District Council* v. *Secretary of State for Scotland* 1977 S.L.T. 33.

concerned was within the general jurisdiction of the local authority. In England and Wales, however, the authorities, although not directly in point, appear to indicate that planning control probably does apply to land below low water mark which is within the general jurisdiction of the authority in question.

92. Under the Town and Country Planning General Development Order 1988 and the equivalent order in force in Scotland certain development by harbour authorities and their lessees is permitted without the permission of the local planning authority or the Secretary of State for the Environment.

93. This authorized development is specified in Class B of Part 17 of Schedule 2 to the 1988 Order and consists, subject to certain exceptions and qualifications, of development by a harbour authority or their lessees of a harbour authority's operational land for the purpose of shipping or in connection with the embarking, disembarking, loading, discharging or transport of passengers, livestock or goods at a harbour. Section 222 of the Town and Country Planning Act 1971 defines "operational land" in relation to statutory undertakers (which include harbour authorities) as—"(a) land which is used for the purpose of carrying on their undertaking; and (b) land in which an interest is held for that purpose, not being land which, in respect of its nature and situation is comparable rather with land in general than with land which is used, or in which interests are held, for the purpose of the carrying on of statutory undertakings". Section 223 of the Town and Country Planning Act 1971 specifies certain circumstances in which land of statutory undertakers is to be treated as not being operational land. Except for some differences in relevant dates the corresponding Scottish provisions are in substantially similar terms.

94. Another class of development authorized by the General Development Order which is relevant in relation to harbour authorities is that specified in Class A of Part 11 of Schedule 2 to that Order. This consists, subject to certain qualifications, of development authorized (i) by any local or private Act of Parliament or (ii) by any order approved by both Houses of Parliament or (iii) by any order made under section 14 or section 16 of the Harbours Act 1964 (i.e., harbour revision and empowerment orders), which designates specifically both the nature of the authorized development and the land upon which it may be carried out. Again, the corresponding Scottish provisions are in similar terms.

95. Under Article 4 of the General Development Order the Secretary of State or a local planning authority (subject in most cases to the Secretary of State's approval) may give directions restricting development permitted under the General Development Order.

96. The European Community's Directive on Environmental Assessment (EEC/85/337) provides that for certain projects which may have an important impact on the environment information about environmental effects must be provided by the developer and taken into account by the competent authority before deciding whether to give development consent to the project. Annex I to the Directive specifies classes of projects for which an environmental assessment is always required. These include "trading ports and also inland waterways and ports

29

for inland waterway traffic which permit the passage of vessels of over 1350 tonnes" (it appears that the creation of a new navigable water area is envisaged). Annex II to the Directive specifies class of projects which are to be made subject to an environmental assessment where the Member State considers that their characteristics so require. These include harbours, including fishing harbours and yacht marinas. They also include the modification of a project included in Annex I. The Directive does not apply to "projects the details of which are adopted by a specific act of national legislation". In the United Kingdom therefore it does not apply to a project which is specifically authorized by an Act of Parliament.

**97.** In the United Kingdom, harbour development of the kind which the Directive envisages as requiring environmental assessment would usually be specifically authorized by a Local Act of Parliament. Where such development is not so authorized it will nearly always be either:

(a) works authorized by a harbour revision or empowerment order (see paragraph 68 *ante*) which (as indicated in paragraph 94 *ante*) have the benefit of deemed planning permission under Class XII of the Town and Country Planning General Development Order; or

(b) works below low water mark constructed by a harbour authority under a general works power in their special legislation or by another person pursuant to a licence granted by the harbour authority (see paragraph 77 *ante*) where the relevant power enables the licensed works to be constructed and maintained notwithstanding interference with the public right of navigation and statutory authorization for the works is not therefore required.

In both these cases the normal planning consent procedures, by reference to which the Directive on Environmental Assessment is implemented in most cases, do not apply except possibly where the site of proposed works below low mark (in England and Wales) to be constructed under a general works power or pursuant to a licence is situated in an estuary *intra fauces terrae* (see paragraph 91 *ante*).

**98.** Regulations have been made under section 2 of the European Communities Act 1972 to implement the Directive in these two cases. The procedure for making harbour revision and empowerment orders specified in Schedule 3 to the Harbours Act 1964 has been amended by the Harbour Works (Assessment of Environmental Effects) Regulations 1988 so as to provide for environmental assessments in appropriate cases (see paragraph 334 *post*). As respects harbour works constructed below low water mark under a general works power or pursuant to a licence, the Harbour Works (Assessment of Environmental Effects) Regulations 1989 apply to works below the low water mark of medium tides involved in the construction of a harbour (as widely defined in section 57 of the Harbours Act 1964—see paragraph 4 *ante*) or in the making of modifications to an existing harbour, being works which are—

(a) not subject to planning control pursuant to the Town and Country Planning Act 1971 or the Town and Country Planning (Scotland) Act 1972 or pursuant to orders made under either of those Acts; and

(b) not specifically described in or authorized to be carried out by a harbour revision or empowerment order or by a provisional order (as defined in section 57 of the Harbours Act 1964); and

(c) not specifically described in or authorized to be carried out by any enactment conferring powers to carry out works at a harbour.

These regulations provide for an application to the Secretary of State for consent to the carrying out of operations under the Coast Protection Act 1949 (see paragraphs 72–76 *ante*), or notice to the Secretary of State from a harbour authority pursuant to regulations under section 37(2) of the Merchant Shipping Act 1988 that application has been made for a licence to carry out operations (see paragraph 82 *ante)* or an application to the Secretary of State for the approval of operations pursuant to any other Act (see paragraph 73 *ante*) to trigger the consideration by the Secretary of State (in relation to harbour works other than works affecting fishery harbours or marine works—see paragraphs 24(c) and (d) *ante*) of whether the works in question are harbour works to which the regulations apply and, if so, whether they constitute a project within Annex I to the Directive or a project within Annex II whose characteristics require that it should be made subject to an environmental assessment. If the Secretary of State determines that an environmental assessment is required in order to comply with the Directive the proposed works must not be carried out without his consent under the regulations and he must direct the person wishing to carry out the works ("the developer") to furnish him with the information necessary to enable him to carry out such an assessment. In that event, the developer is required by the regulations to publish notice of his proposals and to provide the public with an opportunity to inspect the information and other documentation supplied to the Secretary of State and to make representations to the Secretary of State. The Secretary of State must consult suitable bodies with environmental responsibilities about the proposals and may, if he thinks fit, hold an inquiry. Where an environmental assessment has been held in accordance with the regulations the Secretary of State may consent to the carrying out of the proposed works either unconditionally, or subject to such conditions as he thinks fit, or may refuse consent, after considering all the relevant information, any representations received and the report of any inquiry held.

# CHAPTER 5

# THE CONSERVANCY FUNCTIONS OF HARBOUR AUTHORITIES

**99.** The conservancy functions of harbour authorities comprise dredging to maintain the navigational channels, the provision of lights, buoys and beacons to mark the channels and give warning of dangers, and the removal of wrecks and other obstructions to navigation. The purpose of these functions is to secure safe and convenient navigation in the harbour and their performance often involves surveying the bed of the harbour and the preparation of maps and charts.

**100.** The special legislation of most harbour authorities for major harbours authorizes the authority to deepen, dredge, scour and improve the bed and foreshore of the harbour and blast any rock in the harbour. Generally, any dredged material becomes the property of the harbour authority and may be used or disposed of as the authority think fit but such material must not be deposited below the level of high water except in such position as the Secretary of State may approve and subject to such conditions or restrictions as he may impose. As indicated in paragraph 73 *ante* a provision of this kind (at any rate if included in an Act of Parliament as distinct from subordinate legislation) removes the need to obtain consent under section 34 of the Coast Protection Act 1949 for the authorized dredging. Where the bed and foreshore of the harbour belong to the Crown, as is generally the case, the powers of the harbour authority are subject to the rights of the Crown and the Crown Estate Commissioners normally require some payment by the harbour authority in respect of dredged material.

**101.** Under section 634 of the Merchant Shipping Act 1894 the management of all lighthouses, buoys and beacons throughout England and Wales and the Channel Islands was vested in the Trinity House ("the master wardens and assistants of the guild, fraternity, or brotherhood of the most glorious and undivided Trinity and of St. Clement in the parish of Deptford Strond in the county of Kent, commonly called the corporation of the Trinity House of Deptford Strond") and the management of all lighthouses, buoys and beacons throughout Scotland and the adjacent seas and islands and the Isle of Man was vested in the Commissioners of Northern Lighthouses. The Trinity House and the Commissioners of Northern Lighthouses (and also the Commissioners of Irish Lights) are referred to in the Act of 1894 as the general lighthouse authorities. "Buoys and beacons" are defined in the Merchant Shipping Act 1894 as including all other marks and signs of the sea. It was however considered that this definition might not be wide enough

32

to include certain electronic aids to navigation and under section 34(3) of the Merchant Shipping Act 1979 the Secretary of State may by order provide that references or a particular reference to a buoy or beacon in the relevant Part of the Merchant Shipping Act shall be construed as including, in such circumstances as are specified in the order, equipment of a kind so specified which is intended as an aid to the navigation of ships.

102. The vesting of lighthouses, buoys and beacons in the general lighthouse authorities under section 634 of the Merchant Shipping Act 1894 was however expressed to be subject to any powers or rights then lawfully enjoyed or exercised by any person or body of persons having by law or usage authority over local lighthouses, buoys or beacons. Such persons or bodies of persons are referred to in the Act of 1894 as local lighthouse authorities.

103. Most harbour authorities with conservancy functions are local lighthouse authorities for the purposes of the Merchant Shipping Act 1894. Harbour authorities existing on 25 August 1894, when that Act came into force, who had power to provide lighthouses, buoys and beacons, as most of them had, became local lighthouse authorities under the terms of section 634. Where a harbour authority have been established subsequently their special legislation generally declares them to be a local lighthouse authority for the purpose of the Merchant Shipping Act 1894. It may be doubtful whether such a declaration included in subordinate legislation is effective. It seems however that where the undertaking of a harbour authority which is a local lighthouse authority is transferred, even by virtue of subordinate legislation, to another harbour authority the latter will assume the status of local lighthouse authority in relation to the undertaking in question.

104. The PLA are not a local lighthouse authority although they have power to place lights, buoys and beacons in or near the River Thames with the approval of Trinity House. Under section 196 of the Port of London Act 1968, sections 652 to 654 of the Merchant Shipping Act 1894 (which are referred to in paragraphs 105 and 106 *post*) apply in relation to lights, buoys and beacons erected or placed or proposed to be erected or placed by the PLA as if that authority were a local lighthouse authority.

105. Section 652 of the Merchant Shipping Act 1894 requires each general lighthouse authority to inspect all lighthouses, buoys and beacons provided by local lighthouse authorities within their area. Section 653 of the Act gives general lighthouse authorities firm control over the activities of local lighthouse authorities. Under this section a general lighthouse authority may, with the santion of the Secretary of State, and after giving due notice, direct a local lighthouse authority to lay down buoys, or to remove or discontinue any lighthouse, buoy or beacon, or to make any variation in the character of any lighthouse, buoy or beacon, or the mode of exhibiting lights in any lighthouse, buoy or beacon. Under the same section a local lighthouse authority are prohibited from taking any action in this field without the sanction of the general lighthouse authority. Section 653(3) provides that if a local lighthouse authority having power to erect, place or maintain any lighthouse, buoy or beacon, fail to do so, or fail to comply with the direction of a general light-

house authority with respect to any local lighthouse, buoy or beacon, Her majesty may, on the application of the general lighthouse authority, by Order in Council, transfer any powers of the local lighthouse authority with respect to the lighthouse, buoy or beacon in question, to the general lighthouse authority. The case where a local lighthouse authority do something, for example lay down a buoy, without the sanction of the general lighthouse authority is not expressly provided for but of course the general lighthouse authority could, with the sanction of the Secretary of State, direct the removal of a lighthouse, buoy or beacon which had been erected or laid down without their consent.

106.  Section 654 of the Merchant Shipping Act 1894 contains provisions for the voluntary surrender of any lighthouse, buoy or beacon by a local lighthouse authority to the general lighthouse authority.

107.  Sections 77 and 78 of the Harbours, Docks and Piers Clauses Act 1847, which are still incorporated with the special legislation of some harbour authorities (although the latter is never incorporated with modern legislation), contain provisions which overlap those of section 653 of the Merchant Shipping Act 1894. Section 77 requires the harbour authority to lay down such buoys for the guidance of vessels as they are directed to do by Trinity House (in England and Wales) or by the Commissioners of Northern Lighthouses (in Scotland). It differs from the corresponding provision of section 653 of the Merchant Shipping Act 1894 in that Trinity House or the Commissioners of Northern Lighthouses, as the case may be, do not have to obtain the sanction of the Secretary of State before giving a direction. Section 78, which, as mentioned above, is not in practice incorporated in modern legislation, prohibits the harbour authority from erecting any lighthouse or beacons, or exhibiting or permitting the exhibition of, any light, beacon or sea mark without the sanction in writing of Trinity House (in England and Wales) or the Commissioners of Northern Lighthouses (in Scotland). It appears to overlap the corresponding provisions of section 653 of the Merchant Shipping Act 1894 almost completely.

108.  Nearly all harbour authorities have dual, and to some extent overlapping, powers to remove wrecks. Sections 530 and 532 of the Merchant Shipping Act 1894 confer powers for this purpose on all harbour authorities. These sections are set out in Part I of Appendix E but the special legislation of most harbour authorities extends and supplements their application. An example of this is section 46 of the Medway Ports Authority Act 1973 which is set out in Part II of Appendix E. Furthermore, the special legislation of nearly all harbour authorities contains a provision for the protection of Crown interests in wrecks on the lines of section 47 of the Medway Ports Authority Act 1973 which is set out in Part III of Appendix E (under section 741 of the Merchant Shipping Act 1894 that Act does not, except where specially provided, apply to Her Majesty's ships).

109.  In addition to these wreck raising powers under the Merchant Shipping Act 1894 the special legislation of nearly all harbour authorities either incorporates section 56 of the Harbours, Docks and Piers Clauses Act 1847, which empowers the harbour authority's harbour master to remove wrecks or other obstructions

which impede navigation, or includes powers to the same effect. Section 56 of the Harbours, Docks and Piers Clauses Act 1847 is set out in Part IV of Appendix E. The special legislation of a few harbour authorities contains provisions in a rather different form from those referred to above. In particular, the special legislation of the PLA does not build on sections 530 and 532 of the Merchant Shipping Act 1894 but contains wreck removal powers—sections 121 and 122 of the Port of London Act 1968 which are set out in Part V of Appendix E—which combine most of the features of section 56 of the Harbours, Docks and Piers Clauses Act 1847 and section 530 of the Merchant Shipping Act 1894 as commonly modified.

110. The logic of the dual wreck raising powers of most harbour authorities appears to be that where the removal of a wreck is urgently necessary the harbour master can take action on his own initiative under section 56 of the Harbours, Docks and Piers Clauses Act 1847 (which extends to other obstructions and "any floating timber which impedes the navigation" as well as wrecks) but that where action is not urgently necessary, and particularly where there may be some doubt whether a wreck does impede navigation, it is more appropriate for the harbour authority to proceed under section 530 of the Merchant Shipping Act 1894. It seems that before taking action under that section, the harbour authority must themselves form an opinion that a vessel sunk, stranded or abandoned in their harbour or in or near any approach thereto, is, or is likely to become, an obstruction or danger to navigation.

111. Section 530 of the Merchant Shipping Act 1894, although, unlike section 56 of the Harbours, Docks and Piers Clauses Act, it is limited to wrecks, is wider in that it authorizes the harbour authority, in terms, not merely to remove, but to destroy, the vessel (in *The Crystal*,[1] Lord Macnaughton expressed doubt whether the power to "remove" contained in section 56 included power to destroy) and also to light or buoy a wreck pending its raising, removal or destruction.

112. There were also important differences between the two sections in that section 56 of the Harbours, Docks and Piers Clauses Act 1847 imposes a liability on the owner of the wreck or other obstruction to repay the cost of removal whereas section 530 of the Act of 1894 only contains a power for sale. However, the standard supplement to the latter section exemplified by section 46 of the Medway Ports Authority Act 1973 enables the harbour authority to recover from the owner of the wreck any expenses reasonably incurred by the harbour authority under sections 530 and 530 of the Merchant Shipping Act 1894 which are not reimbursed out of the proceeds of the sale (if any).

113. In the case of *The Crystal* referred to above it was held that, although section 56 of the Harbours, Docks and Piers Clauses Act 1847 makes the owners of the wreck personally liable for the expenses of removal (even in the absence of negligence), the owners of the ship at the time when she becomes an obstruction will not be so liable if they abandon her before the harbour authority incur expense because "owner" in section 56 means the person who was the owner at the time

1. *The Crystal* [1894] A.C. 508.

when expenses were incurred by the harbour authority. The standard provision supplementing sections 530 and 532 of the Merchant Shipping Act 1894, in relation to particular harbour authorities, removes this possible difficulty so far as those sections are concerned by defining "owner" as the person who was the owner of the vessel at the time of her sinking, stranding or abandonment.

**114.** In the case of *Dee Conservancy Board* v. *McConnell*[2] it was held that where a ship becomes a wreck through the negligence of her owners or their servants the owners are liable at common law for the reasonable cost of removing the obstruction (the common law liability not being displaced by the harbour authority's statutory remedies) and cannot therefore escape liability by abandoning the wreck before the harbour authority incur expenditure.

**115.** The duties of a harbour authority in the conservancy field have been considered in several cases. In *St. Just Steam Ship Co. Ltd.* v. *Hartlepool Port and Harbour Commissioners*,[3] the issue was whether the Commissioners were liable for damage caused to a ship by a submerged wreck which the Commissioners thought had been dispersed but the continued existence, and position, of which (the judge found) they should have been aware of. In that case Mr Justice Wright (as he then was) said:

In those circumstances the law is now well established. The liability of the Commissioners in such a case does not directly depend upon the terms of the private Act. It depends on the special relations arising *de novo* as each ship enters the jurisdiction of the port, and it is a duty which had been very clearly expressed in a number of cases which is said to be analogous to the ordinary common law duty existing as between invitor and invitee; and it has been clearly expressed in the well known case of the *Mersey Docks and Harbour Board Trustees* v. *Gibbs*.[4]

**116.** In *Mersey Docks and Harbour Board Trustees* v. *Gibbs*,[5] which arose out of damage caused to a vessel entering one of the Mersey Board's docks by a bank of mud which had been allowed to accumulate there, Lord Westbury said:

Where such a body is constituted by statute, having the right to levy tolls for its own profit, in consideration of making and maintaining a dock or canal, there is no doubt of the liability to make good to the persons using it any damage occasioned by neglect in not keeping the works in proper repair:

and later:

The common law in such a case imposes a duty upon the proprietors to take reasonable care, so long as they keep it open for the public use of all who may choose to navigate it, that they may do so without danger to their lives or property.

**117.** In *The Neptun (Owners)* v. *Humber Conservancy Board*,[6] which arose from a ship stranding in the River Humber and subsequently becoming a total loss, Langton, J., endorsed the statements of the law in *Mersey Docks and Harbour Board*

2. *Dee Conservancy Board* v. *McConnell* [1928] 2 K.B. 159.
3. *St. Just Steam Ship Co. Ltd* v. *Hartlepool Port and Harbour Commissioners* (1929) 34 Ll.L. Rep. 344.
4. *Mersey Docks and Harbour Board Trustees* v. *Gibbs* (1866) L.R. 1 H.L. 93.
5. (1866) L.R. 1 H.L. 93.
6 *The Neptun (Owners)* v. *Humber Conservancy Board* (1937) 59 Ll.L. Rep. 158; 54 T.L.R. 195.

*Trustees* v. *Gibbs*[7] and *St. Just Steam Ship Co. Ltd.* v. *Hartlepool Port and Harbour Commissioners.*[8] He held that the duty of a buoyage and beaconage authority was analogous to that existing between invitor and invitee, and was to take reasonable care, so long as the authority kept the navigable highway open for the public use of all who chose to navigate it, that they might do so without danger to their lives or property. He observed in the course of his judgment that this duty

cannot be stated exactly as being a relation of invitor or invitee, since it is difficult to imagine the Board extending to the public an invitation to use the highway which *ex concessis* is already their legal right. Nevertheless, . . . the common law duty is the same as that owed by an invitor to an invitee, and it is not necessary to invent any particular single term to indicate the relationship between a public custodian and an individual who pays for the use and the work performed by such a custodian.

**118.** In the course of his judgment in *The Neptun case*,[9] Mr Justice Langton (with whom two Elder Brethren of Trinity House had sat as nautical assessors) made some interesting comments on the more detailed conservancy obligations of a harbour authority (it appears from his judgment that, having regard to the nature of the bed of the River Humber, the question of dredging did not arise). He said:

It remains, perhaps, to outline briefly the scope of the obligations of a buoyage and beaconage authority. For this purpose I have relied upon the services of the Elder Brethren. Neither they nor myself would wish this short schedule of duties to be considered as necessarily exhaustive, but in the complete absence of any assistance in this matter such as I should have expected to have received from the Humber Conservancy Board it has become necessary to lay down what I conceive to be a minimum of their obligations. A fair and useful method of approach to this subject seemed to me to be to ask my advisers what they, as experienced shipmasters entering the Humber without knowledge of its channels, would expect at the hands of the buoyage and beaconage authority appointed to lay down the marks for the navigation of the river. Speaking as shipmasters, and incidentally also as persons with no small knowledge of the special work connected with buoyage and beaconage, they tell me that they would expect as follows:—

(1) That the authority should have sounded and found the best navigable channel in the river.

(2) That having found it the authority should have placed sea marks of the nature of light-vessels, floats or buoys in the positions where they would be of the best advantage to navigation.

(3) That by night such sea marks should be provided with adequate lights to enable the channel to be easily found and properly kept by a vessel using it.

(4) That the authority had re-sounded the channel as and when opportunity presented itself.

(5) In view of the quickly shifting character of the river bed, that the authority had kept a vigilant watch upon the changes in the river bed and had altered, moved or renewed the sea marks in accordance with the changes ascertained.

(6) That records of the changes both in sounding and in movement of the marks should have been preserved for future reference and for the guidance of subsequent officials.

(7) That the authority should publish as conspicuously as possible such further information as would supplement the guidance given by sea marks.

7. (1866) L.R. 1 H.L. 93.
8. (1929) 34 Ll.L. Rep. 344.
9. *Ante,* fn.6.

For my part I accept unhesitatingly this comparatively short list of expectations as a fair statement of the minimum duties of a buoyage and beaconage authority upon a great and busy highway such as the Humber, and if one adds, upon the authority which I have quoted, that the Board should exercise reasonable care in the performance of all these duties I am of opinion that the legal position of the Humber Conservancy Board *vis-à-vis* the plaintiffs is defined with sufficient accuracy for present purposes.

**119.** In *The Tramontana II*[10] it was held that the defendants (the Ministry of Defence in respect of a Dockyard Port) having, in the exercise of their statutory powers, assumed responsibility for marking a wreck, owed a duty to all persons lawfully using the port to carry out that marking with reasonable skill and care.

**120.** The cases referred to in paragraphs 115 to 119 *ante* were decided before it became the practice to include in the special legislation of harbour authorities a statement of their general powers and duties. As indicated in paragraphs 46 and 47 such a provision, in relation to a harbour authority's conservancy functions, usually takes the form of an express duty to take such action as the harbour authority consider necessary or desirable for an incidental to the maintenance, operation, improvement and conservancy of their harbour.

**121.** Such a provision has not yet been judicially considered but it seems unlikely that the courts will hold that it abrogates, or overrides, a harbour authority's duty at common law to take reasonable care that those who lawfully use their harbour may do so in safety. The discretion conferred by such a statutory duty must be exercised reasonably and in good faith for the purpose for which it was conferred. On this basis a harbour authority would be bound to consider necesary any action which was required to satisfy their duty at common law.

10. *The Tramontana II* [1969] 2 Lloyd's Rep. 94.

## CHAPTER 6

# HARBOUR AUTHORITIES' POWERS TO REGULATE ACTIVITIES OF OTHER PERSONS AT HARBOURS

**122.** An essential characteristic of the harbour authority for a significant harbour is their powers to regulate the activities of other persons there. The powers of a harbour authority to control shipping in the harbour are of particular importance. Certain powers for this purpose are vested directly in the harbour master since it is often necessary for him to take action at short notice and on his own initiative.

**123.** Section 52 of the Harbours, Docks and Piers Clauses Act 1847 although (as indicated below) to some extent superseded, is still incorporated with the special legislation of most harbour authorities. It authorizes the harbour master to give directions—

For regulating the time at which and the manner in which any vessel shall enter into, go out of, or lie in or at the harbour, dock, or pier, and within the prescribed limits, if any, and its position, mooring or unmooring, placing and removing, whilst therein;

For regulating the position in which any vessel shall take in or discharge its cargo or any part thereof, or shall take in or land its passengers, or shall take in or deliver ballast within or on the harbour, dock or pier;

For regulating the manner in which any vessel entering the harbour or dock or coming to the pier shall be dismantled, as well for the safety of such vessel as for preventing injury to other vessels, and to the harbour, dock or pier, and the moorings thereof;

For removing unserviceable vessels and other obstructions from the harbour, dock or pier, and keeping the same clear;

For regulating the quantity of ballast or dead weight in the hold which each vessel in or at the harbour, dock or pier shall have during the delivery of her cargo, or after having discharged the same.

**124.** "The Harbour Master" is defined in section 2 of the Harbours, Docks and Piers Clauses Act 1847 so as to include, in addition to the harbour master himself, his assistants. The special legislation of most harbour authorities commonly defines the expression as including also any person authorized by the harbour authority to act in the capacity of harbour master.

**125.** Section 53 of the Harbours, Docks and Piers Clauses Act 1847 provides that—

The master of every vessel within the harbour or dock, or at or near the pier, or within the prescribed limits, if any, shall regulate such vessel according to the directions of the harbour master, made in conformity with this and the special Act: and any master of a vessel who, after notice of any such direction by the harbour master served upon him, shall not forthwith regulate such vessel according to such direction shall be liable to a penalty not exceeding twenty pounds.

This maximum penalty was increased to £50 by the Criminal Law Act 1977 and, by virtue of the Criminal Justice Act 1982, is now level 2 on the standard scale of fines introduced by that Act (which as increased by the Criminal Penalties etc. (Increase) Order 1984, is currently £100). The maximum penalty at a particular harbour may however depend on the terms of the local Act or order which incorporates section 53.

**126.** It was held in *The Excelsior*[1] that the master of a ship moored in a harbour, when directed by the harbour master to move her to a different berth, was required to comply with that direction even although, if that ship alone were to be considered, it would be injudicious to move the ship, it being the duty of the harbour master to consider the interests of all the shipping in the harbour.

**127.** The scope of section 52 of the Harbours, Docks and Piers Clauses Act 1847 was considered in the case of *The Guelder Rose*.[2] That case related to a direction at the harbour of Fowey that between the hours of sunrise and sunset certain vessels should proceed up the harbour at a pace not exceeding three miles an hour; that between sunset and sunrise they should anchor in a particular place specified by reference to a chart; that they should not at any time proceed above a specified point without the sanction of the harbour master; and that they should not at any time be moved within the limits of the harbour without notifying the harbour master, unless in either case they had a qualified pilot on board.

**128.** This direction was held to be *ultra vires* section 52. In relation to it Lord Justice Atkin said:

That does not appear to me to be in the least a matter for which jurisdiction was given to the harbour master. Speaking generally, it appears to me that the object of section 52 is fairly obvious. The harbour master is the person who controls the movements of the particular vessels when they are within the port on the occasion when they are within the port; and generally speaking, I have not the least doubt at all that his powers are given to him for the purpose of giving specific directions to specific ships for specific movements. Those are powers that must be exercised in the circumstances sometimes at once, or on an emergency in respect of which the procedure as to by-laws would be quite unreasonable and useless. The harbour master and his assistants are given equal powers. I am far from saying that there might not be good occasions on which the harbour master might give a direction which is to operate for more than the event of the particular voyage. For instance, Mr Nesbitt made the suggestion of a case where there was an obstruction in the harbour, which it was not contemplated would remain permanently within the harbour, and in respect of which I think it is very probable that the harbour master might give a general direction that as long as the obstruction remained vessels were to leave it either on the starboard or on the port side, or were to approach it in a particular way and at a particular tide. That seems to me to be something quite different from the general directions which were given in this case.

**129.** The decision in *The Guelder Rose* case was applied in the case of *Pearn* v.

1. *The Excelsior* (1868) L.R. 2 A. & E. 268.
2. *The Guelder Rose* [1927] 136 L.T. 226.

*Sargent*[3] where it was held that a direction at Looe Harbour that during specified hours (when a regatta would be in progress not in the whole harbour but in the 800 yards nearest the sea) no vessel should move within the harbour except with the express permission of the harbour master was *ultra vires* section 52. In the course of his judgment Lord Widgery, C.J., said:

The function of the harbour master under section 52 is to regulate the traffic; after all it is a public harbour where the public have a right to be there, and it is not the harbour master's function, as such, to keep them out. His function is to control and regulate them rather like a traffic policeman regulating traffic. Of course there will be cases when he has to go beyond these simple functions; of course there may be cases where necessity arises and he has to impose wider prohibitions for a particular time, but when that happens it is for consideration whether the directions he has given are reasonable for the emergency or circumstances which prompted them.

**130.** Following the case of *The Guelder Rose*,[4] section 52 of the Harbours, Docks and Piers Clauses Act 1847 as incorporated with the special legislation of particular harbour authorities is frequently modified by a declaration that the section, as incorporated—

(a) shall extend to empower the harbour master to give directions prohibiting the mooring of vessels in any particular part or parts of the harbour; and

(a) shall not be construed to require the harbour master in emergency to give particular directions in the case of every vessel in respect of which it is desired to exercise any of the powers of that section, but in pursuance of that section for all or any of the purposes thereof the harbour master shall be entitled in emergency to give general directions applicable to all vessels or to particular classes of vessels.

**131.** Although the harbour master's powers under section 52 of the Harbours, Docks and Piers Clauses Act 1847 have proved effective there seemed to be a case for harbour authorities for major harbours to have somewhat wider powers— powers which would, in particular, enable the harbour authority to lay down general and long term rules to regulate the movement etc. of ships by a simpler and more flexible method than the by-law procedure.

**132.** Most harbour authorities for major harbours and several others have now obtained, by means of private Act of Parliament or harbour revision order, wider and up-to-date powers to regulate the movement and berthing of ships. An example of such powers are those contained in sections 20 and 21 of the Medway Ports Authority Act 1973 which are set out in Appendix F. These sections are in the form which has been adopted, with slight variations, by all the harbour authorities which have obtained such powers. Section 20 enables the harbour authority to lay down general rules for the regulation of vessels navigating in the harbour. Rules for this purpose could also be included in by-laws but in modern conditions the by-law procedure may take too long in relation to such matters as the designation of routes and channels. Section 21 empowers the harbour master to enforce these rules and generally to direct the movement, etc., of individual ships (his

3. *Pearn* v. *Sargent* [1973] 2 A.C. 141.
4. [1927] 136 L.T. 226.

powers in this respect being similar to those under section 52 of the Harbours, Docks and Piers Clauses Act but in rather more flexible terms). Sections 23 to 27, also set out in Appendix F, contain the related procedural and enforcement provisions.

133. Some harbour authorities have also obtained general powers to regulate vessels at docks and section 22 of the Medway Ports Authority Act 1973, also included in Appendix F, is an example in the usual form. This again is a more flexible and convenient alternative to by-laws.

134. Under powers of the kind referred to in paragraph 132 the harbour authority are normally required to consult the General Council of British Shipping before giving, or before revoking or amending, a general direction relating to the navigation of vessels in the harbour. The Port of London Authority are required to obtain the actual agreement of this body before giving, revoking or amending such a direction.

135. It appears from the case of *Pearn* v. *Sargent* referred to in paragraph 129 *ante* that the harbour master's power to regulate the movement, etc., of vessels under section 52 of the Harbours, Docks and Piers Clauses Act 1847 does not include power to prohibit a ship from entering harbour although the power to regulate the time of entry no doubt enables a harbour master, where appropriate, to postpone entry for a considerable period. The principle appears to be that a power to regulate does not include power to prohibit. With regard to provisions of the kind referred to in paragraph 132 *ante*, in some cases these include power for the harbour authority to give a direction for prohibiting entry into the harbour of a vessel which for any reason would be, or be likely to become, a danger to other vessels in the harbour. Section 20(1)(*c*)(ii) of the Medway Ports Authority Act 1973 is an example of this. In most cases, however, the wider powers to regulate the movement, etc., of ships referred to in paragraph 132 do not include power to prohibit a ship from entering harbour.

136. It was considered that given the highly dangerous nature of some modern cargoes, and the catastrophe which could result if, say, a ship with defective steering collided with a gas carrier, there ought to be a clear power for a harbour master to prohibit a ship from entering, or to require a ship to leave, a harbour where, in his opinion, this was necessary to avoid the danger of a serious accident. This was the genesis of the Dangerous Vessels Act 1985.

137. Section 1 of the Dangerous Vessels Act enables a harbour master to give directions prohibiting the entry into, or requiring the removal from, the harbour of any vessel if, in his opinion, the condition of that vessel, or the nature or condition of anything it contains, is such that its presence in the harbour might involve:

    (a) grave and imminent danger to the safety of any person or property; or

    (b) grave and imminent risk that the vessel may, by sinking or foundering in the harbour, prevent or seriously prejudice the use of the harbour by other vessels.

138. The purpose of the Act is to enable the harbour master to take action to avoid a catastrophic accident. It does not give him *carte blanche* to exclude ships

from harbour. It does not entitle a harbour master to exclude a ship simply because, in his view, oil from the ship may pollute the harbour—although, if he has reason to believe that a ship which proposes to enter the harbour does not comply with the requirements of the Merchant Shipping (Prevention of Oil Pollution) Regulations 1983, he may, and indeed must, under regulation 33 of those regulations, report the matter to the Secretary of State, who may deny the ship entry to port if he is satisfied that it presents an unreasonable threat of harm to the marine environment (see paragraph 213 *post*).

**139.** Directions by a harbour master under section 1 of the Dangerous Vessels Act may be given:

(a) to the owner of the vessel or to any person in possession of the vessel;

(b) to the master of the vessel (no doubt the usual case); or

(c) to any salvor in possession of the vessel, or to any person who is the servant or agent of any salvor in possession of the vessel and who is in charge of the salvage operation.

Such directions may be given in any reasonable manner as the harbour master thinks fit and, at the time when he gives directions to any person, the harbour master must inform that person of the grounds for giving them.

**140.** In deciding whether to give directions under section 1 in any particular case, a harbour master must have regard to all the circumstances of that case and, in particular, to the safety of any person or vessel, whether in or outside the harbour, and including the vessel which would be the subject of his directions.

**141.** Section 2 of the Dangerous Vessels Act makes clear that the right of a harbour authority under section 2 and 3 of the Merchant Shipping (Liability of Shipowners and Others) Act 1900 to limit their liability for loss or damage to vessels and goods, etc., on board a vessel (see paragraph 61 *ante*) extends to liability for any loss or damage occurring outside the harbour in consequence of directions given by a harbour master in purported exercise of his powers under section 1 of the Act.

**142.** Section 3 of the Dangerous Vessels Act contains a power for the Secretary of State to override action taken by a harbour master under section 1. Where a harbour master has given directions under section 1 as respects any vessel, the Secretary of State may, for the purpose of securing the safety of any person or vessel (including the vessel to which the harbour master's directions relate), give directions to the harbour master requiring him to permit the vessel in question to enter and remain, or (as the case may be) to remain, in the harbour, and to take any action which he may specify in the directions for the purpose of enabling the vessel to do so or for any connected purpose.

**143.** If the Secretary of State gives directions under section 3 to a harbour master, the latter's directions under section 1 cease to have effect. A harbour master to whom directions are given under section 3 must give notice of those directions to the person to whom his directions under section 1 were given or, failing that, to any of the other persons to whom those directions might have been given, in such reasonable manner as he may think fit. It is the duty of the harbour master to take any action in relation to the vessel in question specified in the Secretary of State's directions, and of the harbour master and the harbour authority to take all such further action as may be reasonably necessary to enable the vessel to enter and remain, or to remain, in the harbour.

**144.** Section 4 of the Dangerous Vessels Act provides that the powers of a harbour master under section 1 are without prejudice to the Secretary of State's powers under section 12 of the Prevention of Oil Pollution Act 1971 which, as extended by the Merchant Shipping (Prevention of Pollution) (Intervention) Order 1980, confers on the Secretary of State wide powers to deal with shipping casualties which, in his opinion, will, or may, cause pollution (whether by oil or other substances) on a large scale. Section 4 also contains a saving for the functions of a receiver of wreck, or any officer or person who acts for a receiver of wreck, under sections 511, 512 and 516 of the Merchant Shipping Act 1894.

**145.** Section 5 of the Dangerous Vessels Act provides that a person who, without reasonable excuse, contravenes or fails to comply with any directions under section 1 shall be guilty of an offence and shall be liable on summary conviction to a fine not exceeding £25,000 and, on conviction on indictment, to a fine.

**146.** These penalties are very much higher than those which may be incurred for failing to comply with directions by a harbour master under section 52 of the Harbours, Docks and Piers Clauses Act 1847 or under any provision of a local harbour Act or order. It is a defence for a person charged under section 5 to show that he took all reasonable precautions and exercised all due diligence to avoid the commission of the offence.

**147.** By virtue of section 6 of the Dangerous Vessels Act, directions under section 1 cannot be given in relation to:

    (a)  any vessel belonging to Her Majesty or employed in the service of the Crown for any purpose, including any such vessel in the possession of a salvor; or

    (b)  any vessel which is a pleasure boat of 24 metres or less in length.

**148.** Powers for a harbour master (*inter alia*) to prohibit the entry into a harbour in certain circumstances, and to regulate the movements, of a vessel carrying a dangerous substance are contained in the Dangerous Substances in Harbour Areas Regulations 1987 which are discussed in the next chapter.

**149.** Under section 57 of the Harbours, Docks and Piers Clauses Act 1847 a harbour master may cause a vessel which has been "laid by or neglected as unfit for sea service" to be removed from the harbour at the expense of the owner of the vessel and "laid on any part of the strand or sea shore, or other place where the same may, without injury to any person, be placed". It was held in a Scottish case, the *Trustees of the Harbours of Peterhead* v. *Thomas Chalmers (The Clupea*[5]) that in disposing of a vessel after removing her from the harbour under the terms of section 57 the harbour master was not entitled to destroy her (which seems consistent with *The Crystal* referred to in paragraph 111 *ante* although that case was not cited) and that after the harbour master had removed the vessel from the harbour and

---

5. *Trustees of the Harbours of Peterhead* v. *Thomas Chalmers (The Clupea)*, Ct. of Sess., 20 January 1982.

laid her on the shore the control and possession of the vessel reverted to the owner.

**150.** The Merchant Shipping (Tankers) (EEC Requirements) Regulations 1981, made by the Secretary of State following a designation for the purpose under section 2(2) of the European Economic Communities Act 1972 to implement a Directive by the Council of the European Economic Community, apply to all tankers of 1,600 gross register tonnage or more carrying oil, gas or chemicals or to such tankers which are empty but whose tanks are not yet free of vapours given off by residues of oil, gas or chemical cargoes and have an atmosphere which has not been rendered non-flammable.

**151.** These regulations, whose requirements have been extended by the Merchant Shipping (Tankers) (EEC Requirements) (Amendment) Regulations 1982, provide that the master of a tanker to which they apply, before the tanker enters any harbour, must notify to the harbour master of that harbour certain specified information. This includes, in particular, the estimated time of the tanker's arrival at the pilot station or harbour limits of the harbour where the master intends first to berth her (unless the master does not intend to berth the tanker at the harbour which is being entered), the nature and quantity of any chemicals, gas or oil carried by the tanker, whether she is fitted with an inert gas system and information about any defect in the hull, machinery or equipment of the tanker which may:
  (i) affect materially the safe manoeuvrability of the tanker; or
  (ii) affect materially the safety of other vessels in or in the vicinity of or in the approaches to the harbour; or
  (iii) constitute a hazard to the marine environment; or
  (iv) constitute a hazard to persons or property on land or in the vicinity of the harbour.

**152.** The master of the tanker must notify the harbour master of any change in the information about defects in her which occur after it was originally notified but before she enters harbour or while she is in harbour.

**153.** These regulations also require the master of a tanker to which they apply to make available to any pilot who boards her to pilot her into harbour and, if he so requests, to the harbour master of any harbour at which the tanker calls, a check list in a form set out in the Schedule to the regulations. A pilot who boards a tanker to pilot her into harbour must notify the harbour master if the master fails to make a check list available to him in accordance with the regulations. A pilot who boards a tanker to pilot her into or out of harbour must, if he knows or believes that there are defects which may prejudice the safe navigation of the tanker which have not been notified to the harbour master by the master of the tanker in accordance with the regulations, notify the master of those defects. If subsequently, the pilot knows or believes that the master of the tanker has failed to notify the harbour master of the defects in question, the pilot must notify the harbour master himself.

**154.** Harbour authorities have wide powers to make by-laws to (among other things) regulate the movement of, or other activities in relation to, ships in harbours. Before discussing by-laws in more detail reference should be made to the

Collision Regulations. Under sections 21 and 22 of the Merchant Shipping Act 1979 the Secretary of State has powers to make regulations with regard (*inter alia*) to the prevention of collisions at sea.

**155.** Under the Merchant Shipping (Distress Signals and Prevention of Collisions) Regulations 1983 made under the enabling powers referred to above the regulations currently in force for these purposes are the International Regulations for Preventing Collisions at Sea 1972. These regulations apply to all vessels upon the high seas and in all waters connected therewith navigable by sea-going vessels. They therefore generally apply in harbours but not to land-locked artificial channels such as the Manchester Ship Canal; *The Hare.*[6] Rule 1(*b*) of the International Regulations states that "nothing in these Rules shall interfere with the operation of special rules made by an appropriate authority for roadsteads, harbours, rivers, lakes or inland waterways connected with the high seas and navigable by sea-going ships. Such special rules shall conform as closely as possible to these Rules". It therefore appears that a by-law made by a harbour authority, if inconsistent with the Collision Regulations, will prevail but that strong reasons are necessary to justify the making of such a by-law. It was held in the case of *The Carlotta*[7] that a harbour by-law which deals with the same subject-matter as a provision of the Collision Regulations will exclude the application of that provision.

**156.** The Collision Regulations comprise steering and sailing rules, rules prescribing the lights and shapes which vessels are to exhibit in various circumstances and rules for sound and light signals, including distress signals. Regulation 5(1) of the Merchant Shipping (Distress Signals and Prevention of Collisions) Regulations 1983 provides that where any of the Collision Regulations is contravened, the owner of the vessel, the master and any person for the time being responsible for the conduct of the vessel is guilty of an offence punishable as provided in the regulation. Under regulation 5(2) it is, however, a defence for any person charged under the regulations to show that he took all reasonable precautions to avoid the commission of the offence.

**157.** Returning to harbour by-laws, section 83 of the Harbours, Docks and Piers Clauses Act 1847, which is still incorporated with the special legislation of many harbour authorities, contains powers to make harbour by-laws for a number of specified purposes. This section is set out in Part I of Appendix G. A number of harbour authorities have now adopted more modern by-law making powers. The form of these powers varies but section 78 of the Medway Ports Authority Act 1973 set out in Part II of Appendix G is a typical example of a modern power to make general harbour by-laws.

**158.** In addition to these powers to make general by-laws many harbour authorities have a separate power to make by-laws for prescribing lights, signals and steering and sailing rules. The Dangerous Substances in Harbour Areas Regula-

---

6. *The Hare* [1904] P. 331.
7. *The Carlotta* [1899] P. 223.

tions 1987 include a power for harbour authorities to make by-laws as respects dangerous substances and this is discussed in the next chapter.

**159.** A set of model general harbour by-laws recommended (subject to consideration of local circumstances) by the Department of Transport and the British Ports Federation is set out in Part III of Appendix G.

**160.** The appropriate procedure for the making and confirmation of harbour by-laws (apart from the case of by-laws under the Dangerous Substances in Harbour Areas Regulations which is discussed in the next chapter) depends on the special legislation of the harbour authority in question. Section 85 of the Harbours, Docks and Piers Clauses Act 1847 specifies the procedure for the confirmation of by-laws made under section 83 of that Act but where section 83 is still incorporated in harbour authorities' special legislation the special Act always, or nearly always, prescribes that by-laws shall be subject to confirmation by the Secretary of State for Transport. The provisions of section 85 for confirmation by a judicial authority now therefore seldom, if ever, apply. The special legislation of most major harbour authorities now apply the provisions for the making and confirmation of by-laws contained in section 236 of the Local Government Act 1972 (in Scotland section 202 of the Local Government (Scotland) Act 1973) with appropriate modifications. These modifications always provide for by-laws to be confirmed by the Secretary of State for Transport. In the case of harbour authorities in England and Wales these modifications usually enable the Secretary of State to modify a harbour by-law submitted to him for confirmation (in Scotland the local government procedure includes power to modify).

**161.** By virtue of section 57 of the Criminal Justice Act 1988 by-laws made by a harbour authority (other than by-laws under the Dangerous Substances in Harbour Areas Regulations 1987) may provide for a maximum fine for contravention of the by-laws of up to level 4 on the standard scale (currently £1,000).

# CHAPTER 7

# DANGEROUS SUBSTANCES

162. Since 1 June 1987 the carriage, loading, unloading and storage of dangerous substances at harbours has been governed, mainly but not exclusively, by the Dangerous Substances in Harbour Areas Regulations 1987. These regulations, made by the Secretary of State for Transport under enabling powers contained in the Health and Safety at Work, etc. Act 1974, replaced former provisions for the regulation of dangerous substances in harbours contained in by-laws made under the Explosives Act 1875 and the Petroleum (Consolidation) Act 1928. They also replaced the Conveyance in Harbours of Military Explosives Regulations 1977, and certain sections of the Explosives Act 1875, the Explosives Act 1923, the Petroleum (Consolidation) Act 1928 and a number of provisions contained in local Acts and orders and by-laws made thereunder. As indicated below, however, some local Act provisions have been retained.

163. To a large extent the regulations cover substantially the same ground as the controls which they replaced. The most important of the substantive changes are—

    (a) the express powers for harbour authorities, through powers vested in their harbour masters, to control the entry into their dock estates of dangerous substances brought from inland;

    (b) the establishment of a licensing system to control the handling, etc., of explosives; and

    (c) the requirement for harbour authorities to prepare emergency plans and for emergency arrangements to be made at berths.

164. Regulation 3 describes what is a dangerous substance for the purpose of the regulations. Any substance (including any preparation or other mixture) which by reason of its "characteristic properties" creates a risk to the health and safety of any person when the substance is in a "harbour or harbour area" is a dangerous substance for this purpose. The "characteristic properties" are specified in column 1 of Part I of Schedule 1 to the regulations and include explosive, flammable and toxic properties. In addition, any substance or article which is within the definition of "dangerous goods" in regulation 1(2) of the Merchant Shipping (Dangerous Goods) Regulations 1981 is a dangerous substance for the purpose of the Dangerous Substances in Harbour Areas Regulations. Regulation 3 contains a number of detailed exceptions and qualifications. Perhaps the most important of

these is that under paragraph (2) of the regulations a substance or article which is brought into a harbour area from inland and which is not to be loaded onto a vessel as cargo is not to be treated as a dangerous substance for the purpose of the regulations except in the circumstances specified in regulation 3(2).

**165.** Under regulation 5(1) the Dangerous Substances in Harbour Areas Regulations apply in every "harbour" and "harbour area" (and also, as indicated below, under regulation 33 the explosives licensing provisions of the regulations may apply outside a "harbour" or "harbour area"). "Harbour", as defined in regulation 2, is a harbour which is *not* managed under statutory powers. In practice, it is rare for dangerous substances to be loaded or unloaded at a harbour managed otherwise than under statutory powers.

**166.** Most areas to which the regulations apply are within the definition of "harbour area" contained in regulation 2. That is to say, they are areas of water within the statutory jurisdiction of a "statutory harbour authority" defined in regulation 2 as a harbour authority within the meaning of section 57 of the Harbours Act 1964. Such a harbour authority is a person (in practice, a port trust, a company, a local authority, or Associated British Ports) in whom powers or duties of improving, maintaining or managing a harbour are vested by or under statute. "Harbour area" also includes any berth abutting on such a water area where the loading or unloading of any dangerous substances takes place whether or not that berth is for other purposes under the statutory jurisdiction of the harbour authority. Berth is defined in regulation 2 as any dock, pier, jetty, quay, wharf or similar structure at which a vessel may tie up and includes any plant or premises used for purposes ancillary or incidental to the loading or unloading of a dangerous substance *within the curtilage of that berth.*

**167.** "Harbour area" also includes any land within the statutory jurisdiction of the statutory harbour authority which is used in connection with the loading or unloading of vessels. It also includes a monobuoy connected to storage facilities in the harbour area and its monobuoy area.

**168.** Paragraph (*b*) of the definition of "harbour area" deals with the case where the limits of jurisdiction of statutory harbour authorities overlap, as happens in several cases. For the purpose of the regulations, the area where the limits of the two authorities concerned overlap falls within the harbour area comprising the harbour limits, berths or land within which are used by vessels navigating in the area of overlap to a greater extent that they use berths or land within the other overlapping limits. For example, the limits of the Harwich Conservancy Board overlap with those of the Felixstowe Dock and Railway Company. Most of the ships which navigate in the overlapping area use berths at Felixstowe and therefore that area is included in the harbour area comprising Felixstowe's limits.

**169.** Another qualification relates to wharves and jetties managed under statutory powers by oil or other companies for the purposes of their own traffic. These are usually called "own account" undertakings and are described in the latter part of the definition of "statutory harbour authority" in regulation 2. Where such an own-account undertaking, which usually includes a relatively small water area around the wharf or jetty, is within the limits of jurisdiction of another statutory harbour authority, as is usually the case, then the company concerned is not a statutory harbour authority for the purposes of the regulations and it follows, of course, that the wharf or jetty and the surrounding area within the jurisdiction of the company are included as part of the harbour area which comprises the statutory limits of jurisdiction within which the own account undertaking is situated. An example of this are the oil jetties at Milford Haven which were constructed by oil companies under statutory powers. For the purpose of these regulations they are within the harbour area which comprises the limits of jurisdiction of the Milford Haven Port Authority.

170. Within "harbours" and "harbour areas" the regulations apply essentially to the loading and unloading of dangerous substances onto and from ships and the storage and movement of dangerous substances related to such loading and unloading. They do not, for example, apply to a dangerous substance which is brought into a "harbour" or "harbour area" from inland to be stored or used in a factory there unless it is to be loaded on board a ship in the "harbour" or "harbour area". A number of cases where the regulations do not apply are specified in paragraph (2) of regulation 5.

171. The Dangerous Substances in Harbour Areas Regulations are a detailed and comprehensive code. The following paragraphs deal with the aspects of the regulations which seem most likely to give rise to legal question. They do not cover the whole content of the regulations, much of which consists of practical rules.

172. A feature of the Dangerous Substances in Harbour Areas Regulations is the discretionary powers which in a number of contexts are vested in the harbour master. "Harbour master" is defined in regulation 2 as the "harbour master, dock or other officer duly appointed by the harbour authority to act in such capacity or any person having authority so to act". Generally, no doubt, the harbour master for the purpose of the regulations will be the harbour master in the ordinary sense. But if the exercise of any of the discretions conferred on the harbour master by the regulations appears to a harbour authority to require technical or scientific knowledge which the harbour master would be unlikely to possess it would be possible for the harbour authority to appoint someone else to act as harbour master for the purpose of exercising that particular discretion.

173. Perhaps the most important powers conferred on a harbour master by the Dangerous substances in Harbour Areas Regulations are those contained in regulations 6 and 7. Regulation 6 provides for notice to be given of the entry of a dangerous substance into a "harbour" or "harbour area" in the case of a vessel by the master or agent and in the case of any other mode of transport (usually a lorry from inland) by the "operator" as defined in regulation 4. Notice must be given to the harbour master and, if the substance is to be brought to a berth, the berth operator. The notice may be given up to six months in advance. It must be in writing or in such other form as the harbour master may agree and contain such information as is adequate to evaluate the risk created by the substance to the health

and safety of any person. In the case of a vessel the notice must also contain the information about the vessel specified in regulation 4(3).

**174.** Like the provisions of regulation 7, referred to below, which confers powers of prohibition, removal and regulation on the harbour master, so far as the entry from the sea is concerned regulation 6 overlaps substantially with existing powers, in the case of regulation 6 with requirements for notice of entry contained in harbour authority by-laws and in the Merchant Shipping (Tankers) (EEC Requirements) Regulations 1981 (see paragraphs 151 to 154 and 157 *ante*). Again, like regulation 7, regulation 6 is an important extension of a harbour master's jurisdiction at most harbours in that it applies not only to entry to a "harbour" or "harbour area", as defined in the regulations, from the sea but also to entry from inland.

**175.** Regulation 6 confers quite wide discretions on harbour masters as to the length of notice. Normally, at least 24 hours' notice must be given or such longer time, not exceeding 14 days, as the harbour master may for operational reasons require. If, however, it is not reasonably practicable to give 24 hours' notice, the period of notice may be such shorter time as the harbour master and berth operator may together agree. Regulation 6 also authorizes a harbour master to grant exceptions from the notice requirements where it appears to him that this is necessary for securing the health and safety of any person.

**176.** Regulation 7 authorizes a harbour master to give directions to—
   (a) regulate or prohibit the entry into;
   (b) require the removal from, or
   (c) regulate the handling movement or position within the "harbour" or "harbour area" of:–
      (i) any dangerous substance, if in his opinion its condition is such as to create a risk to the health and safety of any person; or
      (ii) any freight container, portable tank or receptacle containing a dangerous substance or any vehicle or vessel carrying a dangerous substance, if in his opinion the condition of the container, tank or receptacle, vehicle or vessel is such as to create a risk to the health and safety of any person from the substance which it contains or carries.

**177.** To enable a harbour master to give directions under regulation 7 there must therefore be, in his opinion, a risk to health and safety *from a dangerous substance* which may be caused either by the condition of the dangerous substance itself or by the condition of the container, tank or receptacle which contains the substance or of the vehicle or vessel which carries it. In deciding whether to give such directions a harbour master must have regard to all the circumstances of the case and in particular to the safety of any person, whether that person is within or outside the "harbour" or "harbour area". Paragraph (4) of regulation 7 enables the Secretary of State to require a harbour master to substitute different directions for those the harbour master has given, which corresponds to the similar provision of section 3 of the Dangerous Vessels Act 1985. This power for the Secretary of

State to override the harbour master may be exercised only for the purpose of securing the safety of any person.

**178.** As indicated above, the powers conferred on a harbour master by regulation 7 in relation to ships overlap existing powers of harbour masters both under local legislation, including section 52 of the Harbours, Docks and Piers Clauses Act 1847 as incorporated in local Acts and orders, and the Dangerous Vessels Act 1985 (see paragraphs 123 to 147 *ante*). It does not, however, completely duplicate them, in particular because the regulation does not apply to a ship which is not carrying a dangerous substance. The Dangerous Vessels Act is intended to deal with acute emergencies and it would seem that the powers of that Act should generally be used where a harbour master considers that there is a grave and imminent risk of a major disaster.

**179.** Other important discretions conferred on a harbour master by the Dangerous Substances in Harbour Areas Regulations relate to the anchoring and mooring of a vessel carrying, or about to be loaded with, a dangerous substance (regulation 14) and to various operations by vessels in connection with the carriage, loading, unloading or transfer of liquid dangerous substances in bulk (regulations 19–22). Where the vessel is at a berth, the berth operator is also involved in these decisions.

**180.** Regulation 26 of the Dangerous Substances in Harbour Areas Regulations imposes an important new duty on harbour authorities. Before dangerous substances are handled in their "harbour area" a harbour authority must prepare an effective emergency plan for dealing with emergencies which involve, affect, or could affect, dangerous substances that are brought into or are handled in the "harbour area". A harbour authority are required to keep the plan up to date and to consult the emergency services and any other body which appears to them to be appropriate about the preparation of the plan and keeping it up to date. Port users and berth operators are required to cooperate with a harbour authority in preparing the plan if so requested by the authority. A harbour authority must notify the contents of their plan to those responsible for putting it into effect.

**181.** Part IX of the Dangerous Substances in Harbour Areas Regulations deals with explosives. It introduces a new system for licensing the handling of explosives and this applies not only in "harbours" and "harbour areas" but also under regulation 33(1) to the loading on board or unloading from a vessel of any explosive on any part of the coast of Great Britain or in any tidal water or within territorial waters to which sections 1–59 and 80–82 of the Health and Safety at Work, etc. Act 1974 are applied by article 7 of the Health and Safety at Work, etc. Act 1974 (Application outside Great Britain) Order 1977 (i.e., areas designated under the Continental Shelf Act 1964). Regulation 33(2) specifies cases where a licence is not required. These include the case of explosives of less than one tonne in quantity intended for immediate use in connection with harbour works or for wreck dispersal in a "harbour" or "harbour area" if the consent in writing of the harbour master has been obtained and the explosives are carried and used in accordance with any conditions attached to that consent.

**182.** Under regulation 34(1) a person must not—
  (a)  bring any explosive into a "harbour" or "harbour area";
  (b)  carry or handle any explosive within a "harbour" or "harbour area"; or
  (c)  load or unload any explosive outside a "harbour" or "harbour area"
       where the licensing system applies by virtue of regulation 33(1),
unless there is in existence an explosives licence permitting that activity and the
conditions attached to the licence are complied with. However, where by-laws
under the Explosives Act 1875 were in force immediately before the regulations
came into force on 1 June 1987 then, by virtue of regulation 33(2), if an application
for an explosives licence has been made before 6 April 1988, explosives may continue to be handled in accordance with the terms of those by-laws (which, as indicated below, will, in themselves, have been revoked) until the licence is issued or
refused or until 31 December 1991, whichever is the earlier. In the case of the
handling of military explosives the position is the same except that the explosives
must continue to be handled in accordance with the terms of the Conveyance in
Harbours of Military Explosives Regulations 1977.

**183.** The explosives licensing system is administered by the Health and Safety
Executive. An application for a licence, where the explosive is being, or is to be,
handled within a "harbour" or "harbour area" must be made to the Executive by
the harbour authority or by the operator of the berth in question (if the latter he
must inform the harbour authority of his intention). Where the explosive is to be
loaded or unloaded outside a "harbour" or "harbour area" the application must be
made by a person interested in such loading or unloading. The procedure for
explosives licence applications is contained in Schedule 7 to the regulations. On
receipt of an application the Health and Safety Executive may prepare a draft
licence and may require the applicant to publish, in a form approved by the Executive, a notice giving such particulars of the draft licence as the Executive may
require. Such notice must state that any comments or objections to the application
must be sent to the Executive within one month of the publication of the notice.
Within that time, the applicant must give to any interested person such additional
information about the application as the Executive may determine.

**184.** In considering an application for an explosives licence or for any alteration
in the terms of an existing licence the Health and Safety Executive must take into
account any comments or objections received pursuant to the publication of the
notice and may reject the application or may grant the licence or amending licence
subject to such conditions as the Executive thinks fit. An explosives licence may be
with or without limit of time and may be varied or revoked in writing by the Executive at any time. The Health and Safety Executive may grant a provisional explosives licence in cases of urgency which may have effect for a period of up to six
months.

**185.** As indicated above, the Dangerous Substances in Harbour Areas Regulations supersede, and to a considerable extent substantially reproduce, the pre-
existing regime for handling, etc., dangerous goods in harbours. The repeal
provisions of the regulations are contained in regulation 47 and Schedule 8. With

regard to the enabling powers for these repeal provisions, under section 15(3)(*a*) of the Health and Safety at Work, etc. Act 1974, health and safety regulations (a category which includes the Dangerous Substances in Harbour Areas Regulations) may repeal or modify any of the "existing statutory provisions". The existing statutory provisions are defined in section 53 of, and Schedule 1 to, the 1974 Act as meaning, broadly, provisions of specified general statutes relating to health and safety at work and subordinate legislation made thereunder. The provisions in question include most of the Explosives Act 1875, the Explosives Act 1923 and the Petroleum (Consolidation) Act 1928. Under section 80 of the 1974 Act, which is cited among the enabling powers for the Dangerous Substances in Harbour Areas Regulations, the regulations may also repeal any other provision contained in an Act of Parliament or subordinate legislation which was passed or made before the passing of the 1974 Act on 31 July 1974 if it appears to the Secretary of State that the repeal is expedient in consequence of or in connection with any provision of the regulations.

**186.** The Dangerous Substances in Harbour Areas Regulations repealed on the one hand the existing explosives and petroleum by-laws made by harbour authorities under the Explosives Act 1875 and the Petroleum (Consolidation) Act 1928 and also the Conveyance in Harbours of Military Explosives Regulations which were made under the 1875 Act and, on the other hand, local harbour Acts and harbour by-laws passed or made before 31 July 1974 which in the Secretary of State's opinion duplicated or were inconsistent with, or otherwise did not fit in with, the regulations.

**187.** The regulations repealed certain of these provisions when the regulations came into force on 1 June 1987 and other provisions on 31 December 1989. Certain sections of the Explosives Acts, including the by-law making powers, and all by-laws made thereunder and the Military Explosives Regulations were repealed when the regulations came into force. The by-law making powers under the Petroleum (Consolidation) Act 1928 were repealed when the regulations came into force and most of the harbour petroleum by-laws made thereunder ceased to have effect on that date. But under paragraph (3) of regulation 47 the petroleum by-laws specified in Part I of Schedule 8 will continue in force until 31 December 1989. The local Acts and by-laws specified in Part II of Schedule 8, all of which were passed or made before 31 July 1974, were repealed when the regulations came into force. The by-laws specified in Part III of Schedule 8, again being by-laws made before 31 July 1974, will be repealed on 31 December 1989. However, the repeal of these pre-1974 local Acts and by-laws is expressed to be limited to the extent to which they applied within harbour areas in relation to dangerous substances. Insofar as they have a wider application they therefore continue in force.

**188.** The reason why the repeal of some of these provisions was postponed until the end of 1989 was that the provisions concerned relate to particular local circumstances which could not adequately be catered for by the general provisions of the regulations. It was envisaged that before the end of 1989 by-laws will be made under regulation 43 (see paragraph 189 *post*) to deal with these local situations. A statutory harbour authority which has by-laws specified in Part I or Part III of Schedule 8 may apply to the Secretary of State to have them revoked before the end of 1989. Any application for that purpose would usually be coupled with the submission of new by-laws under regulation 43.

**189.** Regulation 43 of the Dangerous Substances in Harbour Areas Regulations authorizes a statutory harbour authority to make by-laws in respect of their "harbour area" prohibiting the entry or regulating the entry, carriage, handling and storage of dangerous substances. This is a wide power and is not intended merely to fill the gaps which will be left when the provisions repealed by the regulations at the end of 1989 cease to have effect. The by-law making power is intended to deal with any local circumstances which are not adequately covered by the general provisions of the regulations but they must not of course conflict with those provisions. In particular, by-laws under regulation 43 may prohibit or regulate the entry of a particular dangerous substance which a statutory harbour authority feel would in itself, and not because of its condition (which is what the harbour master's powers under regulation 7 depend on—see paragraph 176 *ante*) create a danger to health and safety in the circumstances of their harbour.

**190.** Schedule 6 specifies the procedure for making by-laws and bringing them into force. Subject to one unusual provision which is mentioned below, the procedure is broadly similar to that which currently applies in the case of most harbour authority by-laws. The Secretary of State may confirm by-laws submitted to him by a statutory harbour authority with or without modification or may refuse to confirm them, but before reaching a decision he is required to consult the Health and Safety Commission. Where the Secretary of State proposes to confirm a by-law with a modification which appears to him to be substantial he must inform the statutory harbour authority and require them to take any steps he considers necessary for informing persons likely to be concerned with the modification and must not proceed to confirm the by-law until the statutory harbour authority and other persons concerned have had a reasonable opportunity to comment on the proposed modification.

**191.** The by-law procedure in Schedule 6 to the regulations includes one unique provision. Under paragraph 2 by-laws generally do not have effect until they are confirmed by the Secretary of State, which is of course the usual state of affairs. But under the proviso to that paragraph a by-law which prohibits or regulates the entry of a dangerous substance into a harbour area and which has been made after consultation with any berth operator who appears to the statutory harbour authority to be affected by the proposed by-law comes into force when application is made for its confirmation. However, as one would expect, such a by-law ceases to have effect if the Secretary of State subsequently refuses to confirm it. If he confirms it with modifications, then the by-law thereafter has effect as so modified. The purpose of this unusual provision is to enable a harbour authority to take action at short notice to prohibit or regulate the entry of a (new) dangerous substance into their harbour.

**192.** Under regulation 44 of the Dangerous Substances in Harbour Areas

Regulations a statutory harbour authority are responsible for enforcing Part II of the regulations (entry of dangerous substances into harbour areas), Part III (marking and navigation of vessels), regulation 19 (fitness of vessels for carrying, loading or unloading liquid dangerous substances in bulk), regulation 20 (permission for transfer between vessels of liquid dangerous substances in bulk), regulation 32(2) (parking of road vehicles carrying dangerous substances) and regulation 38 (vessels and vehicles loaded with explosives to be taken out of harbour areas) in their harbour area against persons other than themselves. Otherwise, the Health and Safety Executive are responsible for enforcing the Dangerous Substances in Harbour Areas Regulations.

193.  The penalty provisions for failing to comply with the requirements of the Dangerous Substances in Harbour Areas Regulations are contained in the Health and Safety at Work, etc. Act 1974. Under section 33(1)(c) of that Act it is an offence for a person to contravene any health and safety regulations. It is also an offence to contravene any requirement or prohibition imposed under any such regulations and this would appear to include by-laws under regulation 43 of the Dangerous Substances in Harbour Areas Regulations. The maximum penalty which may be imposed for such an offence is a fine of £2,000 on summary conviction or, on conviction on indictment, an unlimited fine. In a few cases, including handling explosives without a licence under Part IX of the regulations, the maximum penalty on indictment may be, or include, imprisonment for a term not exceeding two years.

194.  Regulation 45, however, provides that it is a defence for a person charged with a contravention of the regulations or of by-laws made under regulation 43, to prove that he took all reasonable precautions and exercised all due diligence to avoid the commission of the offence. Regulation 45 excepts proceedings for an offence under regulations 16, 31(a) or 32(1) from the defence which it provides but that is because each of those regulations requires something to be done so far as reasonably practicable or to take all reasonably practicable steps for a specified purpose so that, in effect, the same defence is built into them.

195.  Under section 38 of the Health and Safety at Work, etc. Act 1974 proceedings for a contravention of the regulations in England and Wales can only be brought by an inspector appointed by an enforcing authority under section 19 of the Act or by or with the consent of the Director of Public Prosecutions (in Scotland such proceedings will be brought by the Procurator Fiscal).

196.  Under regulation 46 of the Dangerous Substances in Harbour Areas Regulations the Health and Safety Executive may grant exemption from the provisions of the regulations. The Executive must not grant such an exemption unless it is satisfied that neither the health or safety of any person nor the security of any explosive likely to be affected by the exemption will be prejudiced. The Secretary of State for Defence may also grant exemptions from the provisions of the regulations in the interests of national security.

197.  Apart from the Dangerous Substances in Harbour Areas Regulations, the special legislation of some harbour authorities includes provisions to control the

entry of dangerous goods, including powers to prohibit the entry of such goods, on lines exemplified by sections 67 and 68 of the Forth Ports Authority Order Confirmation Act 1969 which are set out in Appendix H. Provisions of this kind are not repealed by the Dangerous Substances in Harbour Areas Regulations. The Dover Harbour Board, under the Dover Harbour Revision Order 1978, have considerably wider powers for regulating the entry of dangerous goods into their harbour and adjoining land owned or occupied by them which are also not affected by the Dangerous Substances in Harbour Areas Regulations.

**198.** There are other statutory controls in relation to dangerous substances which apply both at harbours and elsewhere but particular reference should perhaps be made to Part IV of the Housing and Planning Act 1986, since it includes special provisions in relation to harbours and harbour authorities (at the time of writing, Part IV of this Act had not been brought into force).

**199.** Part IV of the Housing and Planning Act 1986 provides, by way of amendments to the Town and Country Planning Act 1971 and the Town and Country Planning (Scotland) Act 1972, that a "hazardous substances consent" is required if a specified quantity of a hazardous substance is present on, over or under land. The substances which are hazardous substances for this purpose, and the quantity which is to be the controlled quantity of any such substance, will be specified in regulations made by the Secretary of State (for the Environment). Such regulations may also provide that hazardous substances consent is not required in relation to land of prescribed descriptions or by reason of the presence of hazardous substances in prescribed circumstances.

**200.** Hazardous substances consents will be administered by "hazardous substances authorities" which, in relation to most land, will be local planning authorities in England and Wales and, in Scotland, planning authorities. However, in relation to a harbour authority's "operational land" (see paragraph 93 *ante*), and also any "harbour land" and "wharves", as defined in the Harbours Act 1964 at their harbour (see paragraph 18 *ante*) which are not operational land the hazardous substances authority will be the Secretary of State (in most cases for Transport) who will also, in conjunction with the Secretary of State for the Environment, determine any question as to whether, for this purpose, any land is a wharf or harbour land. This should secure that the whole of any harbour complex falls within the jurisdiction of the Secretary of State as hazardous substances authority.

**201.** Part IV of the 1986 Act also contains provisions to ensure that a harbour authority will not be penalized thereunder because of the deposit on their land of a controlled quantity of a hazardous substance which they could not prevent without being in breach of a statutory duty (e.g., section 33 of the Harbours, Docks and Piers Clauses Act 1847—see paragraph 44 *ante*).

**202.** Part IV of the Housing and Planning Act 1986 provides that the temporary presence of a hazardous substance while it is being transported from one place to another is not to be taken into account *unless it is unloaded.* The words italicized could cause difficulties in the harbour context and it is expected that regulations made under the enabling power referred to above will deal with this matter.

# CHAPTER 8

# PREVENTION OF POLLUTION, ETC.

**203.** Generally, the discharge of oil from ships into the sea is regulated by Part 3 of the Merchant Shipping (Prevention of Oil Pollution) Regulations 1983. These regulations were made by the Secretary of State under powers conferred by the Merchant Shipping (Prevention of Oil Pollution) Order 1983, an Order in Council made under section 20 of the Merchant Shipping Act 1979. These regulations give effect to the International Convention for the Prevention of Pollution from Ships 1973, including Annex 1 to the Convention which relates to pollution by oil, but not the other Annexes to the Convention, as amended by a Protocol of 1978. (The 1973 Convention, as amended by the Protocol of 1978, is usually called, and is hereafter referred to as, "MARPOL"). Regulation 12 regulates the discharge of oil into the sea from ships other than oil tankers and as respects oil tankers regulates such discharges from their machinery space bilges. Regulation 13 regulates other discharges of oil into the sea from oil tankers. The regulations define "sea" as including any estuary or arm of the sea.

**204.** However, by virtue of section 1(2) of the Prevention of Oil Pollution Act 1986 regulations 12 and 13 of the Merchant Shipping (Prevention of Oil Pollution) Regulations 1983 do not have effect in relation to any discharge of oil from ships which occurs landward of the line which for the time being is the baseline for measuring the breadth of the territorial waters of the United Kingdom (this baseline is currently prescribed by the Territorial Waters Order in Council 1964 and the Territorial Waters (Amendment) Order in Council 1979). But this does not affect the operation of so much of regulations 12 and 13 as prohibits the discharge into the sea of chemicals or other substances in quantities or concentrations which are hazardous to the marine environment.

**205.** The discharge of oil from ships into waters (including inland waters) which are navigable by sea-going ships and which are landward of the line which for the time being is the baseline for measuring the breadth of the territorial waters of the United Kingdom is dealt with in subsections (2A) and (2B) of section 2 of the Prevention of Oil Pollution Act 1971. Subsections (2A) and (2B) were inserted in the 1971 Act by the Prevention of Oil Pollution Act 1986 (to reinstate, effectively, provisions which had inadvertently been repealed by the Merchant Shipping (Prevention of Oil Pollution) Order 1983). The waters within the jurisdiction of harbour authorities are in most cases wholly, and in other cases mainly, landward of the baseline mentioned above. Generally, therefore, the relevant provisions for controlling the discharge of oil from ships in harbour are those contained in the Prevention of Oil Pollution Act 1971, as amended by the Prevention of Oil Pollution Act 1986 although regulations 12 and 13 of the Merchant Shipping (Prevention of Oil Pollution) Regulations 1983 are the relevant provisions in relation to such discharges into the outer limits of some harbour authorities.

206. Section 2(2A) of the Prevention of Oil Pollution Act 1971 provides that if any oil or mixture containing oil is discharged from a vessel into waters navigable by sea-going ships landward of the baseline for measuring the breadth of the territorial waters of the United Kingdom then, subject to the qualifications referred to below, the owner or master of the vessel shall be guilty of an offence. If the discharge is from a vessel but takes place in the course of a transfer of oil to or from another vessel or a place on land and is caused by the act or omission of any person in charge of any apparatus in that other vessel or that place, the owner or master of that other vessel or, as the case may be, the occupier of that place, is guilty of an offence.

207. Subsection (2B) of section 2 of the 1971 Act provides that subsection (2A) shall not apply to any discharge which is made into the sea and is of a kind or is made in circumstances for the time being prescribed by regulations made by the Secretary of State. The purpose of this provision is to enable the Secretary of State to exempt from prosecution under the 1971 Act certain discharges which would be permitted under regulations 12 and 13 of the Merchant Shipping (Prevention of Oil Pollution) Regulations 1983 if they applied to the waters in question. These discharges are, in particular, those referred to in regulations 12(3) and 13(3) which contain only very small proportions of oil. No regulations have yet been made under section 2(2B) of the 1971 Act and it is virtually inconceivable that a prosecution under section 2(2A) would be instituted in respect of a discharge of the kind mentioned above.

208. Under section 5 of the 1971 Act it is a defence for the owner or master of the vessel charged with an offence under section 2 of the Act to prove that the oil or mixture was discharged for the purpose of securing the safety of any vessel, or of preventing damage to any vessel or cargo or of saving life, unless the court is satisfied that the discharge of the oil or mixture was not necessary for that purpose or was not a reasonable step to take in the circumstances. Section 7 of the Act also provides that where any oil or mixture containing oil is discharged in consequence of the exercise of certain statutory power by a harbour authority, the authority or person acting on their behalf shall not be convicted of an offence under section 2 unless it is shown that they or he failed to take such steps (if any) as were reasonable in the circumstances for preventing, stopping or reducing the discharge.

209. Section 2(4) of the 1971 Act provides that a person guilty of an offence under section 2 shall be liable on summary conviction to a fine not exceeding £50,000 or on conviction on indictment to a fine. Under section 20(2) the court may order the whole or any part of such fine to be applied towards defraying the expense of removing the pollution attributable to the offence.

59

**210.** Under section 19 of the 1971 Act, proceedings for an offence under section 2 of the Act which consists of the discharge of oil, or a mixture containing oil, into the waters of a harbour in the United Kingdom can, in England and Wales, only be brought by the harbour authority or by or with the consent of the Attorney-General or by the Secretary of State or a person authorized by the Secretary of State (in Scotland all such proceedings are brought by the Procurator Fiscal).

**211.** In the Prevention of Oil Pollution Act 1971—

> "harbour authority" means a person or body of persons empowered by an enactment to make charges in respect of vessels entering a harbour in the United Kingdom or using facilities therein;
>
> "harbour in the United Kingdom" means a port, estuary, haven, dock or other place which fulfils the following conditions:—
>
>> (a) that it contains water to which section 2 of the 1971 Act applies; and
>> (b) that a person or body of persons is empowered by an enactment to make charges in respect of vessels entering that place or using facilities therein.

The reference in paragraph (a) of this definition of harbour to water to which section 2 of the Act applies refers to the waters specified in section 2(2), i.e.

> (a) the whole of the sea within the seaward limits of the territorial waters of the United Kingdom; and
> (b) all other waters (including inland waters) which are within those limits and are navigable by sea-going ships.

**212.** The waters specified in section 2(2) are therefore more extensive than, and include, those specified in the new section 2(2A) mentioned above (to which paragraph (a) of the definition of "harbour" also no doubt refers). The waters specified in section 2(2) are still relevant in relation to the discharges of oil or mixture from land or resulting from operations for the exploration, etc., of the sea-bed referred to in paragraphs (c), (d) and (e) of section 2(1) of the 1971 Act but such discharges are not generally important from the point of view of harbour authorities.

**213.** Regulation 32 of the Merchant Shipping (Prevention of Oil Pollution) Regulations 1983 contains powers for persons appointed by the Secretary of State to inspect ships at United Kingdom ports and terminals. Such inspection is normally to be limited to verifying that there is on board a valid International Oil Pollution Prevention Certificate in the form prescribed by MARPOL or a valid United Kingdom Oil Pollution Prevention Certificate in the form prescribed by the regulations. If, however, there are clear grounds for believing that the condition of the ship or her equipment does not correspond substantially with the particulars of the certificate or if there is no valid certificate on board, the inspector must take such steps as he may consider necessary to ensure that the ship shall not sail until she can proceed to sea without presenting an unreasonable threat of harm to the marine environment. In such a case the Secretary of State may permit the ship to leave port for the purpose of proceeding to the nearest appropriate repair yard. Regulation 33(1) provides that if a harbour master has reason to believe that a ship which he believes proposes to enter the harbour in question does not comply with the requirements of the regulations (i.e., as respects the condition of the ship or her equipment) he must immediately report the matter to the Secretary of State who, if he is satisfied that the ship presents an unreasonable threat of harm to the marine environment, may deny the entry of such ship to United Kingdom ports or off-shore terminals. Regulation 33(2) enables the Secretary of State to detain a ship which is suspected of contravening the requirements of the regulations.

214. Section 10 of the Prevention of Oil Pollution Act 1971 requires notice to be given to the harbour master (or if there is no harbour master to the harbour authority) before oil is transferred between sunset and sunrise to or from a vessel in any harbour. Section 11 provides that if any oil or mixture containing oil is discharged or escapes into the waters of a harbour the occurrence must be forthwith reported to the harbour master (or the harbour authority if there is no harbour master) by, if the discharge or escape is from a vessel, the owner or master of that vessel, or, if the discharge or escape is from a place on land, by the occupier of that place.

215. Section 18(6) of the 1971 Act confers on, *inter alia*, the harbour master at a harbour, certain powers to board and inspect vessels in the harbour for purposes related to the provisions of the Act.

216. Turning to the clearing up of oil spills, harbour authorities do not generally have specific powers for this purpose. However, it seems that the terms in which the general duties of a harbour authority are now commonly expressed (see, for example, the general duties of the PLA set out in Part II of Appendix B) are probably wide enough to cover this. Alternatively, the clearing up of oil spills would appear to be reasonably incidental to the express powers of a harbour authority.

217. The functions of harbour authorities in connection with the clearing up of oil spills overlap with those of local authorities and the Secretary of State. Under section 12 of the Prevention of Oil Pollution Act 1971 the Secretary of State has wide powers to deal with shipping casualties (including those which occur in harbours) where, in his opinion, oil, or, by virtue of the Merchant Shipping (Prevention of Pollution) (Intervention) Order 1980, a substance other than oil, from the ship will or may cause pollution on a large scale. The Secretary of State's powers under section 12 include power to direct that a stricken ship is to be moved to a specified place. The Secretary of State may therefore direct a shipping casualty to be moved to a particular harbour if he considers that this is urgently necessary for the purpose of preventing or reducing pollution or the risk of pollution. If he does so, or if the accident has occurred while the ship is in harbour, it seems that the powers of the Secretary of State under section 12 would override the statutory powers (i.e., to regulate the movement of the ship or in some cases to prohibit entry) of the harbour authority for the harbour or their harbour master. (In practice, no doubt, the officers of the Department of Transport would consult the harbour authority's officers and act in close co-operation with them.)

218. Where a harbour authority incur expenditure in clearing up a major oil

spill they will generally be able to recover the cost from the owner of the ship concerned even in the absence of negligence on the part of the master or crew. Under the Merchant Shipping (Oil Pollution) Act 1971 the owner of a ship constructed or adapted for carrying oil in bulk as cargo is absolutely liable for (*inter alia*) the cost of any measures reasonably taken to prevent or minimize damage caused by contamination resulting from the discharge or escape of oil from the ship unless this—

(a) resulted from an act of war, hostilities, civil war, insurrection or an exceptional, inevitable and irresistible natural phenomenon; or

(b) was due wholly to anything done or omitted to be done by another person, not being a servant or agent of the owner, with intent to do damage; or

(c) was due wholly to the negligence or wrongful act of a government or other authority in exercising its function of maintaining lights or other navigational aids for the maintenance of which it was responsible.

The owner of the ship, however, will be entitled to limit his liability in accordance with the provisions of the Merchant Shipping (Oil Pollution) Act 1971 unless it is proved that the owner was personally responsible, within the terms of section 4 of the Act, for the escape or discharge in question.

**219.** Where a harbour authority cannot recover, or recover in full, the cost of clearing up an oil spill from the owner of the ship because the discharge or escape occurred in circumstances in which, under the Merchant Shipping (Oil Pollution) Act 1971, the owner is not liable (other than war, hostilities, civil war or insurrection) or because the owner cannot meet his obligations in full or because the cost incurred exceeds the statutory limitation on the owner's liability, the harbour authority will usually be entitled, under section 4 of the Merchant Shipping Act 1974, to claim from the fund referred to in that Act (which was established pursuant to an international Convention and funded by contributions from the oil industry).

**220.** Regulation 12 of Annex I and regulation 7 of Annex II of MARPOL require the provision at ports and terminals of reception facilities for the discharge from vessels of residues and mixtures which contain, respectively, oil or "noxious liquid substances" as specified in Appendix II to Annex II. The Prevention of Pollution (Reception Facilities) Order 1984 is an Order in Council made under enabling powers contained in section 20 of the Merchant Shipping Act 1979 to give effect to these requirements. It is hereafter referred to as "the Reception Facilities Order".

**221.** The Reception Facilities Order applies to any "harbour authority" or "terminal operator" whose harbour or terminal in the United Kingdom is used by oil tankers, chemical tankers or other vessels, any of which are carrying residues or mixtures which contains oil or noxious liquid substances. "Harbour" is defined in the order, in similar terms to the definition in the Prevention of Oil Pollution Act 1971, as a "harbour, port, estuary, haven, dock or other place which contains waters which are within—

(a) the sea within the seaward limits of the territorial waters of the United Kingdom; and

(b) all other waters (including inland waters) which are within those limits and are navigable by sea-going ships

but does not include a terminal within the harbour managed by a person other than the harbour authority for the harbour.

**222.** The Reception Facilities Order defines "harbour authority" as "a person or body of persons having for the time being the management of a harbour in the United Kingdom" so it does not appear to be limited to harbour authorities managing harbours under statutory powers. "Terminal" is defined as a "terminal, jetty, pier or mono-buoy" and "terminal operator" as "a person or body of persons having for the time being the management of a terminal in the United Kingdom". "Noxious liquid substance" is defined as "any substance which may be specified by the Secretary of State in regulations made under this Order and any other liquid substance which, when discharged into the sea from tank cleaning or deballasting operations, presents a risk of harm to human health, marine resources or other legitimate uses of the sea equivalent to that presented by any substance so specified".

**223.** The Reception Facilities Order provides that the powers exercisable by a harbour authority in respect of any harbour shall include power to provide reception facilities for the discharge from vessels using the harbour of residues and mixtures which contain oil or noxious liquid substances and that any such powers shall include power to join with any other person in providing such facilities. Such a provision in relation to terminal operators was presumably not thought to be necessary because a terminal operator will usually be a company formed under the Companies Act and not therefore subject to the same limitations of legal power as a statutory corporation.

**224.** The Reception Facilities Order requires each harbour authority in respect of their harbour and each terminal operator in respect of its terminal to ensure that:

(a) if the harbour or terminal has reception facilities for the discharge from vessels of residues or mixtures containing oil or noxious liquid substances, those facilities are adequate to comply with the requirements of regulation 12 of Annex I or regulation 7 of Annex II, as the case may be, of MARPOL;

(b) if the harbour or terminal has no such facilities, such facilities are provided,

for vessels which may be expected to use the harbour for "a primary purpose other than utilizing reception facilities". This means that reception facilities must be provided for vessels which, for example, load or unload cargo at the harbour or terminal or are repaired or broken up there but not for vessels which do not come to the harbour or terminal for a purpose other than discharging mixtures or residues to which the order relates.

**225.** The Reception Facilities Order empowers the Secretary of State, after consultation with any organization appearing to him to be representative of owners of vessels registered in the United Kingdom, the harbour authority and, where appropriate, the terminal operator, to direct a harbour authority or terminal operator to provide or arrange for the provision of such reception facilities as he may specify if it appears to him either that a harbour or terminal has no reception facilities and that such facilities should be provided there, or that any existing reception facilities at the harbour or terminal are inadequate in order to comply, for vessels which in his opinion may be expected "to use the harbour or terminal for a primary purpose other than utilizing the reception facilities", with regulation 12 of Annex I or regulation 7 of Annex II of MARPOL.

**226.** The Reception Facilities Order authorizes a harbour authority or terminal operator providing reception facilities or a person providing such facilities by arrangement with a harbour authority to make reasonable charges for their use and to impose reasonable conditions in respect of their use. Any reception facilities provided by, or by arrangement with, a harbour authority or by a terminal operator must be open to all vessels which in the opinion of the harbour authority or terminal operator "are using the harbour or terminal for a primary purpose other than utilizing the reception facilities" on payment of any charges and subject to compliance with any conditions. The master of a vessel proposing to discharge a residue or mixture containing oil or a noxious liquid substance into a reception facility must first inform in writing the person providing the facility of the quantity and content of the substances to be discharged.

**227.** The Reception Facilities Order provides that it shall be an offence punishable only on summary conviction for a harbour authority or terminal operator to fail to comply with a direction by the Secretary of State under powers conferred on him by the order or for the master of a vessel to provide information about the quantity or content of a proposed discharge to reception facilities which he knows to be false in a material particular or recklessly to provide such information which is false in a material particular, and prescribes maximum penalties for these offences.

**228.** The application of the statutory procedures for the disposal of waste in relation to residues and mixtures containing oil or noxious liquid substances discharged by vessels into reception facilities provided in accordance with the Reception Facilities Order presented some problems which were addressed in the Control of Pollution (Landed Ships' Waste) Regulations 1987. These regulations were made under enabling powers contained in the Control of Pollution Act 1974. The provisions of these regulations refer to a "harbour area" which now, by virtue of the Control of Pollution (Landed Ships' Waste) (Amendment) Regulations 1989, has the same meaning as in the Dangerous Substances in Harbour Areas Regulations 1987. The definition of "harbour area" in the latter regulations is discussed in paragraph 166 *ante*.

**229.** The Control of Pollution (Landed Ships' Waste) Regulations provide that "tank washings", defined as "waste residues from the tanks (other than fuel tanks) or holds of a ship or waste arising from the cleaning of such tanks or holds" is "controlled waste" for the purposes of Part I of the Control of Pollution Act 1974. This means that, subject as mentioned below, persons operating facilities to receive and store tank washings must hold a licence under the 1974 Act. However, the regulations exempt from the requirement to hold a licence the deposit of tank washings at reception facilities provided in accordance with the Reception Facilities Order which are within a harbour area as defined in the regulations except where the deposit is liable to give rise to an environmental hazard within the meaning of section 4(5) of the 1974 Act (that is to say, where the waste has been deposited in such a manner or in such a quantity as to subject persons or animals to a material risk of death, injury or impairment of health or as to threaten the pollution of any water supply). The discharge of residues and mixtures containing oil or noxious liquid substances into reception facilities provided by, or by arrangement with, a harbour authority or by a terminal operator within the area where the harbour authority have statutory jurisdiction does not therefore normally give rise to the need for a licence under the 1974 Act but the final disposal of such waste must be to a site licensed under that Act by a waste disposal authority.

**230.** Residues and mixtures containing noxious liquid substances will often be "special waste" to which the Control of Pollution (Special Waste) Regulations 1980 apply. These regulations provide for a consignment note system and include requirements for producers, carriers and disposers of special waste to keep registers and a requirement for disposers to keep site records.

**231.** The Control of Pollution (Landed Ships' Waste) Regulations modify the application of the Special Waste Regulations. The provisions of the latter relating to consignment notes do not apply as respects the removal of tank washings—

   (a) from a ship to reception facilities, or between reception facilities, provided within a harbour area in accordance with the Reception Facilities Order; or

   (b) by pipeline to any such facilities provided outside a harbour area in accordance with that order.

Where such tank washings as are referred to in (a) above are removed from the harbour area or, such tank washings as are referred to in (b) above are further removed, the provisions of the Special Waste Regulations relating to consignment notes apply as if the person operating the facilities from which the tank washings are removed were the producer of the waste. The Control of Pollution (Landed Ships' Waste) Regulations also modify the procedures prescribed by the Special Waste Regulations to meet the case where tank washings are removed in a harbour area from a ship to a conveyance for transportation directly to reception facilities outside a harbour area or directly for disposal outside such an area.

**232.** Regulation 7 of Annex V of MARPOL requires the provision at ports and terminals of facilities for the reception of garbage from ships. The Merchant Shipping (Reception Facilities for Garbage) Regulations 1988, made under enabling powers contained in the Merchant Shipping (Prevention of Pollution by Garbage) Order 1988, an Order in Council made under section 20 of the Merchant

Shipping Act 1979, give effect to this requirement. They are hereafter referred to as "the Garbage Regulations".

233. The Garbage Regulations require each harbour authority in respect of their harbour and each terminal operator in respect of its terminal to ensure that—

(i) if the harbour or terminal has reception facilities for garbage from ships, those facilities are adequate, or

(ii) if the harbour or terminal has no such facilities, adequate facilities are provided.

234. The Garbage Regulations define—

"harbour authority" as a person or body of persons having for the time being the management of a harbour in the United Kingdom;

"habour" as a harbour, port, estuary, haven, dock or other place used by ships;

"terminal" as a terminal, jetty, pier, wharf or mono-buoy used by ships which is either not within a harbour or, if it is within a harbour is not managed by the harbour authority for that harbour;

"terminal operator" as a person or body of persons having for the time being the management of a terminal in the United Kingdom: and

"garbage" as all kinds of victual, domestic and operational waste excluding fresh fish and parts thereof generated during the normal operation of the ship and liable to be disposed of periodically except sewage originating from ships.

235. The Garbage Regulations enable the Secretary of State if it appears to him, after consultation with a harbour authority or terminal operator that—

(a) if the harbour or terminal has reception facilities for garbage from ships, those facilities are inadequate, or

(b) if the harbour or terminal has no such facilities, such facilities should be provided,

to direct the harbour authority or terminal operator to provide, or arrange for the provision of, such reception facilities as may be specified in the direction. Failure to comply with such a direction is an offence punishable on summary conviction by a fine not exceeding £1,000.

236. A harbour authority or terminal operator providing reception facilities for garbage from ships or a person providing such facilities by arrangement with a harbour authority or terminal operator may make reasonable charges for the use of the facilities and impose reasonable conditions in respect of such use. Reception facilities for garbage from ships provided by, or by arrangement with, a harbour authority or terminal operator are to be open to all ships which in the opinion of the harbour authority or terminal operator are using the harbour or terminal for a primary purpose other than utilizing the reception facilities. Therefore, as in the case of reception facilities for oily and noxious wastes, a ship is not entitled to use a harbour authority's reception facilities if it has no other business in the harbour.

237. By virtue of the Control of Pollution (Landed Ships' Waste) (Amendment) Regulations 1989 the provisions of the Control of Pollution (Landed Ships'

Waste) Regulations 1987 (see paragraphs 228 to 231 *ante*) are applied in relation to garbage discharged by ships into reception facilities provided in accordance with the Garbage Regulations. This means that such garbage is industrial waste for the purposes of the Control of Pollution Act 1974 but that a licence under Part I of the 1974 Act is not required for the deposit of garbage in such reception facilities. With reference to paragraphs 230 and 231 *ante* it would probably be unusual for garbage to be "special waste".

# CHAPTER 9

# HARBOUR AUTHORITY FINANCES

## Charges

**238.** Leaving aside a few special cases, charges made by harbour authorities are essentially of two kinds. There are dues, which pay for the enjoyment of the basic or essential harbour or port works and there are further charges, which pay for the enjoyment, usually optional, of ancillary services. Dues are, to some extent, in the nature of a tax, the amount payable by a user not necessarily being directly related to the service received by that user. However, as indicated below, the distinction between dues and other charges is now often blurred by the levying of combined charges which comprise elements both of dues and other charges. The practice of levying combined charges, which formerly raised some difficult legal questions, was expressly authorized by the Transport Act 1981.

**239.** The Harbours Act 1964 made important changes in the law relating to harbour charges but without departing drastically from basic concepts which had long been embodied in harbour legislation. The scheme of the Act was that, as regards dues, a harbour authority might impose such charges as they thought fit, subject to a right of appeal by users originally to the NCP and, since the abolition of that body pursuant to the Transport Act 1981, to the Secretary of State, but as regards other matters (with immaterial exceptions) they might make only reasonable charges. The greater commercial freedom and flexibility in relation to charges provided by the 1964 Act was emphasized by section 38(1)(c) of the Act which repealed any statutory provision applying to a harbour authority insofar as it prohibited the authority from discriminating in the matter of charges against any person in favour of another.

**240.** The expression "ship, passenger and goods dues" is defined in section 57(1) of the Harbours Act 1964 as comprising three meanings, clearly corresponding to ship dues, passenger dues and goods dues. This definition is as follows—

"ship, passenger and goods" dues means, in relation to a harbour, charges (other than any exigible by virtue of section 29 of this Act) of any of the following kinds, namely,—
    (a) charges in respect of any ship for entering, using or leaving the harbour, including charges made on the ship in respect of marking or lighting the harbour;
    (b) charges for any passengers embarking or disembarking at the harbour (but not

including charges in respect of any services rendered or facilities provided for them); and

(c) charges in respect of goods brought into, taken out of, or carried through the harbour by ship (but not including charges in respect of work performed, services rendered or facilities provided in respect of goods so brought, taken or carried).

(The reference to charges under section 29 of the Act is to charges by a local lighthouse authority who are not a harbour authority.)

**241.** Section 26 of the Harbours Act 1964 removed the limitations (usually in the form of prescribed maxima) which previously applied to harbour authorities' powers under their special legislation to levy ship, passenger and goods dues. The section did not, however, repeal statutory exemptions from dues or provisions which otherwise prohibited the levying of dues. Such provisions therefore remain in force. (Section 26 did not apply to the nationalized harbour authorities—neither did section 27 of the Harbours Act—but, as indicated below, the Harbours Act achieved substantially the same result so far as those authorities were concerned.)

**242.** Section 26(2) confers on harbour authorities the power to demand, take and recover such ship, passenger and goods dues as they think fit subject to the provisions for objections to dues contained in section 31 of the Harbours Act, (the provisions of section 31 are discussed below) and subject also to any express exemptions from, or other prohibitions on levying, dues contained in their special legislation. Section 26 did not repeal powers to levy dues in harbour authorities' special legislation and it therefore appears that a harbour authority may levy dues either under section 26(2) or under their special legislation as amended by section 26. It seems, however, immaterial which of these powers a harbour authority rely on. In practice ship, passenger and goods dues are generally levied under section 26(2). Under section 26(3) of the Harbours Act references in special legislation, including incorporated provisions of the Harbours, Docks and Piers Clauses Act 1847, to charges made under that legislation include references to dues levied under section 26. Section 30 of the Harbours Act requires a harbour authority to keep available at their offices for inspection, and for sale, a list of the ship, passenger and goods dues exigible at their harbour under section 26 (or under section 43 of the Transport Act 1962 mentioned below in the case of a nationalized harbour authority). Under section 30(3) a harbour authority's power to levy dues is conditional on their complying with this requirement. The special legislation of many harbour authorities makes clear that charges reduced by compounding arrangements or rebates need not be included in the harbour authority's list of dues.

**243.** The 1964 Act did not originally contain any power for harbour authorities to levy charges other than ship, passenger or goods dues. Except in the case of the nationalized and formerly nationalized harbour authorities charges other than dues, for example, charges for cargo handling and warehousing and mooring charges, are generally levied under provisions contained in the harbour authority's special legislation. It seems that, in the absence of any statutory power for the purpose, a harbour authority would have implied powers to charge for services which they are authorized to provide. In fact, however, virtually all harbour authorities have express statutory powers to make charges other than dues. The justification for this may be that the statutory power is a peg on which to hang the requirement mentioned below that charges (other than dues) must be reasonable.

**244.** Under section 27 of the 1964 Act where a charge which a harbour authority were authorized to make (other than ship, passenger and goods dues and a few special kinds of charges) was, by virtue of a provision contained in the harbour authority's special legislation, subject to a limitation (other than an express exemption from or other prohibition on the making of, the charge or a requirement that the charge should be reasonable) that limitation was replaced by a requirement that the charge should be reasonable. This section therefore applied the criteria of reasonableness to most harbour charges, other than dues, which were not already subject to it. It does not of course apply in relation to charging powers contained in subsequent legislation but in practice these are nearly always in terms that the charges in question—usually charges for services and facilities provided by the authority—shall be such reasonable charges as the harbour authority may determine. The one common exception to this is a power to make charges for floating plant, which is not a ship as defined in the Harbours Act 1964, entering or leaving the harbour. Provisions for this purpose in the special legislation of harbour authorities effectively equate such charges to ship dues, giving the harbour authority power to levy such charges as they think fit subject to a right of objection to the Secretary of State. Where a charge is subject to a statutory requirement that it shall be reasonable any question of whether or not it is being levied at a reasonable level is for the courts to decide. The author is not however aware of any case where the reasonableness of a harbour charge has been the subject of judicial consideration.

**245.** Section 18(1) of the Transport Act 1981 inserted in the Harbours Act 1964 a new power to make combined charges—section 27A of the 1964 Act as set out in paragraph 8(1) of Schedule 6 to the Transport Act 1981. This power applies where a harbour authority have power to levy ship, passenger and goods dues or equivalent dues ("equivalent dues" are defined as dues exigible in respect of things other than ships for entering, using or leaving a harbour including charges for marking or lighting the harbour) and to make other charges. In such a case the new section 27A authorizes the harbour authority to make a combined charge referable in part to matters for which ship, passenger and goods dues or equivalent dues may be levied and in part to matters for which other charges may be made. However, section 27A provides that a harbour authority may not make a combined charge where the person who would be liable to pay the charge objects to paying a combined charge or, where a number of persons would be jointly and severally liable to pay the charge, any of them objects to paying a combined charge. This limitation on a harbour authority's power to make combined charges means that the power cannot be used to deprive the user of his right to the Secretary of State under section 31 to a ship, passenger and goods dues. If a combined charge comprises, say, a goods due element and a cargo handling element and the customer wishes to object to the former he may object to paying the combined charge and the harbour authority will then have to levy a separate goods due, to which the customer can object under section 31, and make a separate charge for cargo handling which, under the relevant charging power, will in virtually all cases be required to be reasonable. But a customer may not object to paying a combined charge after he has incurred the charge by taking advantage of the service to which it relates or if he has already agreed with the harbour authority to pay it.

**246.** The Transport Act 1981 amends sections 30 and 31 of the Harbours Act 1964 so as to make clear that a combined charge under the new section 27A does not have to be included in the list of dues which a harbour authority is required to keep under section 30 (see paragraph 242 *ante*) and is not open to objection under section 31.

**247.** Prior to the Transport Act 1981 the practice of making combined charges, particularly combined wharfage and cargo handling charges at container terminals, had become fairly common. It was not clear however that harbour authorities had power to make such charges. Also, they sometimes raised difficult problems in relation to objections under section 31. These difficulties have now been removed by the new section 27A.

**248.** As mentioned above, sections 26 and 27 of the Harbours Act 1964 did not apply to the nationalized harbour authorities. The powers of those authorities to levy harbour charges, both dues and other charges, stemmed from section 43(3) of the Transport Act 1962 under which, as amended by the Transport Act 1968, they had power to demand, take and recover or waive such charges for their services and facilities as they saw fit. (It seems that the reference to "services and facilities" in the context of this provision should be widely construed in contrast to the references to "services rendered or facilities provided" in the definition of "ship, passenger and goods dues" in section 57 (1) of the Harbours Act which, in the context, appear to refer to ancillary matters. This is discussed in paragraphs 260 to 266 *post* in connection with the question of whether a wharfage charge is goods due.)

**249.** The powers of the nationalized harbour authorities to charge under section 43(3) of the Transport Act 1962 were, by virtue of section 43(2), subject to any express exemption from, or other prohibitions on the making of, any charge contained in special legislation relating to any of their harbours. By virtue of section 50 of the Transport Act 1962 these powers were also subject to the provisions of the Ninth Schedule to that Act as regards the harbours specified in that Schedule.

**250.** Schedule 9 to the Transport Act 1962 was amended by section 39(3) of the Harbours Act 1964 and much of it was repealed by section 63 of that Act (which also repealed sections 50(3) and 51 of the Transport Act 1962 which related to harbour charges). The result was that, as respects harbour charges, the nationalized harbour authorities were in substantially the same position as other harbour authorities. At the harbours specified in Schedule 9 to the Transport Act 1962 ship, passenger and goods dues were subject to a right of objection under section 31 of the 1964 Act. Other charges at these harbours were required to be reasonable. Section 36(*a*) of the 1964 Act provided that sections 31 and 32 of that

Act should not apply to charges imposed by the nationalized harbour authorities at harbours not specified in Schedule 9 to the Transport Act 1962. However, so far as the BTDB and the BRB were concerned, there were no such harbours.

**251.** Now that the BTDB has been reconstituted under Part II of the Transport Act 1981 as Associated British Ports the charging provisions of the Transport Act 1962 no longer apply to them (see paragraph 29 *ante*). Associated British Ports have power to levy dues under section 26 of the Harbours Act 1964 and paragraph 1(2) of Schedule 4 of the Transport Act 1981 makes clear that sections 26, 27, 30, 31 and 40 of the 1964 Act apply to them (as will the new section 27A). Paragraph 20(1) of Schedule 3 to the Transport Act 1981 confers on Associated British Ports a power to make such reasonable charges (other than ship, passenger and goods dues) as they think fit for services and facilities provided by them or their subsidiaries.

**252.** Now that Sealink has ceased to be a subsidiary of BRB the charging powers of the Transport Act 1962 have also ceased to apply at the harbours managed by Sealink Harbours Limited who like Associated British Ports, now rely on the same general charging provisions as other harbour authorities and in particular, levy ship, passenger and goods dues under section 26 of the Harbours Act 1964. Paragraph 3(1) of Schedule 1 to the Transport Act 1981 authorizes Sealink Harbours Limited to make such reasonable charges as it sees fit for its services and facilities at the harbours which it manages.

**253.** Section 31 of the Harbours Act 1964 enables written objections to be made to the Secretary of State as respects ship, passenger and goods dues imposed by a harbour authority at their harbour. An objector must be a person appearing to the Secretary of State to have a substantial interest (i.e., in the charge in question) or a body representative of persons so appearing and an objection may be made on all or any of the following grounds—

(a) that the charge ought not to be imposed at all;
(b) that the charge ought to be imposed at a rate lower than that at which it is imposed;
(c) that, according to the circumstances of the case, ships, passengers or goods of a class specified in the objection ought to be excluded from the scope of the charge either generally or in circumstances so specified;
(d) that, according to the circumstances of the case, the charge ought to be imposed, either generally or in circumstances specified in the objection, on ships, passengers or goods of a class so specified at a rate lower than that at which it is imposed on others.

**254.** The procedure for making, and dealing with, objections under section 31 is complicated. In each case there can only be one objector (or joint objectors) but other persons, or bodies representative of persons, having a substantial interest may make written representations to the Secretary of State within the period (which cannot be less than 42 days) specified in the notice of the objection which is required to be published. Such representations may be in favour of the charge concerned but usually they are, in effect, additional objections but not necessarily made on the same grounds as the originating objection. The procedure therefore provides an opportunity for all issues relating to a particular charge to be considered and dealt with at the same time.

255. Where there is an outstanding objection or representations under Section 31 the Secretary of State is required to hold an inquiry unless he is satisfied that he can properly proceed to a decision in the matter without holding an inquiry. In practice an inquiry is always held. The Harbours Act does not lay down any specific considerations to which the Secretary of State is to have regard in determining objections under section 31. The considerations which are taken into account depend on the circumstances of particular cases but usually include the costs of the harbour authority in providing the service to which the charge in question relates, the importance to the harbour authority of the revenue from that charge and the burden which the charge imposes on the objector.

256. The Secretary of State may determine a case under section 31 in either of two ways. He may—

(a) approve the charge in question but set a limit (not being later than 12 months from the date on which he approves it) to the period during which the approval is to be of effect, or

(b) give the harbour authority such direction with respect to the charge as would meet objection thereto made on any of the grounds mentioned in paragraphs 253 *ante* (whether or not that was the ground, or was included among the grounds, on which the originating objection was made). Such a direction must specify a date for its coming into operation and the period from that date (not exceeding 12 months) during which it is to have effect. The harbour authority are required to comply with such a direction and are liable, on summary conviction, to a fine not exceeding level 4 on the standard scale (currently £1,000) if they fail to do so.

It seems clear from the terms of section 31 that the Secretary of State does not have power under that section to decide questions of law. However, for the purpose of his functions under section 31 it is sometimes necessary for him to form an opinion on a question of law, most commonly on whether he has jurisdiction under the section, i.e., whether or not the charge in question is a ship, passenger or goods due. Insofar as a determination by the Secretary of State under section 31 is based on the view that he has taken of a legal question it is open to challenge in the courts. And where the Secretary of State has declined to determine a case under section 31 because he has decided that the charge in question is not a ship, passenger or goods due it seems that the decision may also be challenged in the courts. Except on the grounds that the Secretary of State has taken a mistaken view of the law there is no right of appeal against a determination by the Secretary of State under section 31.

257. Where the Secretary of State has determined a case under the section by approving the charge in question no new proceedings may be initiated under section 31 as respects that charge during the period when the approval has effect. There is, however, nothing to prevent the harbour authority from increasing an

approved charge during the period when the approval has effect but if they do the increased charge is open to objection under section 31. Similarly, where the Secretary of State has given a direction, a charge made by a harbour authority in accordance with the direction is immune from challenge under section 31 for so long as the direction has effect.

**258.** A question which has arisen is whether a direction given by the Secretary of State under section 31 can be retrospective. Section 31(7) provides that a direction under section 31(6)(*b*) must specify a date for its coming into operation and the period from that date (not exceeding 12 months) during which it is to have effect. This seems to have a prospective, rather than a retrospective, flavour but it might perhaps be argued that the fact that this provision does not require the period to run from the date when the Secretary of State gave the direction, in contrast to the requirement under section 31(6)(*a*) that the period during which an approval has effect runs from the date of the approval, indicates that the date to be specified under section 31(7) may be in the past. However, the latter part of section 31(10), which provides, in effect, that where a direction has been given under section 31(6)(*b*) a further objection to the charge in question cannot be lodged during the period when the direction has effect, seems to imply that the period envisaged is wholly in the future. Furthermore, to construe section 31(6)(*b*) as authorizing a retrospective direction could lead to absurd results. For example, if the same charge had been imposed by a harbour authority for three years and it was then objected to, it would, on this basis, seem arguable that a direction by the Secretary of State could go back to the beginning of the three-year period and have effect in respect of the dues paid or payable during the first of those years and that further objections could then be lodged in respect of each of the two subsequent past years. The better view therefore seems to be that a direction by the Secretary of State under section 31 cannot be retrospective.

**259.** In proceedings under section 31 of the Harbours Act 1964 questions sometimes arise of whether a particular charge is a ship, passenger or goods due and therefore whether the Secretary of State has jurisdiction under that section. One kind of charge which has been considered from this point of view is a "wharfage charge"—a charge in respect of goods which are placed on a wharf either for loading on, or after unloading from, a ship.

**260.** This question appears to turn upon the meaning of "facilities" in paragraph (c) of the definition of "ship, passenger and goods dues" mentioned above. *Prima facie* the word "facilities" is wide enough to embrace the provision of a wharf or quay for the receipt of goods, and has been so used by the legislature in the past. For example, by section 2(1)(*b*) of the Transport Act 1947, the whole of the British Transport Commission's powers as regards ports and harbours were described as the provision of "port facilities", a term defined in section 125(1) of that Act in the widest possible terms.

**261.** The wide meaning, however, cannot necessarily be applied to the word where used in the definition under consideration. One must look at other provisions of the Harbours Act 1964 and, if need be, to the general circumstances under Parliament's consideration in order to see what meaning must be attached to "facilities" and there are clear indications in the 1964 Act that the meaning is a narrower one. Thus, under subsection (8) of section 32 (repealed by the Transport Act 1981) charges fixed under that section, if at a port specified in Schedule 9 to the Transport Act 1962, were deemed to have been imposed under section 43 of that Act. This was a reference to section 43(3) which empowered *inter alia* the BTDB to make charges "for their services and facilities". Therefore the services and facilities of the Transport Act must have a wider meaning than the work, services and facilities, a charge for which is not a goods due within the definition in section 57(1) of the Harbours Act.

262. Parliament clearly envisaged that goods dues were payable in respect of some consideration and that some other payment might be exigible for the work, services or facilities performed or afforded in respect of the goods. The question resolves itself into an inquiry where the line is drawn and on which side of it wharfage comes. The distinction, long recognized in harbour legislation, that the dues pay for the enjoyment of the basic or essential harbour or port works and further charges pay for the enjoyment, usually optional, of ancillary services has already been referred to. The distinction was very clearly drawn in the BTC (Harbours) Charges Scheme 1948, where the Commission were empowered to levy maximum dues in respect of goods shipped and unshipped, and reasonable charges in respect of the "services and facilities" listed in the Second Schedule to the Scheme. In such a context provision of a wharf or quay is part of the consideration for the dues and is not an ancillary service or facility.

263. Did Parliament intend to move this dividing line so that under the Harbours Act wharfage fell on the other side, among the facilities? At first sight there appear to be indications that it did. The customary reference to "shipping and unshipping" is omitted, and the goods are described as those "brought into, taken out of, or carried through the harbour by ship". The definition, however, makes no mention of the consideration, and the words quoted are words defining what goods are chargeable and give no hint as to what are the harbour works, the enjoyment of which is the reason for the charge. A clue to the strangeness of this phraseology is to be found in the definition of "harbour". In the past there was often in practice a distinction between a harbour authority, who were conservators, and a dock authority, who provided the transhipment facilities. Both are embraced in the definition of "harbour authority" in section 57(1) by virtue of "harbour" being defined as including a dock and a wharf. The draftsman had the task of defining goods dues in a way which would cover the dues imposed by a variety of authorities, from a large conservancy to the statutory operator of a single wharf. This explains part of his phraseology but does not explain the absence of reference to shipping and unshipping, and the absence of that or a similar phrase may point, though not very strongly, towards wharfage being excluded from goods dues.

264. On the other hand, the wording appears to contemplate a well-defined point of demarcation between the goods dues (to be subject to sections 26 and 31) and ancillary charges (to be subject to section 27 and to the jurisdiction of the

courts as to reasonableness). Here the practice as existing at the time of the passing of the 1964 Act is relevant. At the majority of ports there was a tonnage rate on goods expressed to cover shipping or unshipping and to remunerate the authority for the maintenance of the port, and there were ancillary charges for such services as cranage. It would be surprising if the definition of goods dues was intended by Parliament to disturb this practice.

265. Moreover, the practice of goods dues including the use of the wharf corresponds to the legal right of access under section 33 of the Harbours, Docks and Piers Clauses Act 1847: "upon payment of the rates made payable by this and the special Act, . . . the harbour dock and pier shall be open to all persons for the shipping and unshipping of goods . . . ". The rates (or dues) entitle the public to the use of the fixed installation of the port. The shipper may provide his own transport and do his own stevedoring—*LNER* v. *British Trawlers Federation*[1] referred to in paragraph 46 *ante*. If he pays the authority to do the work he is paying for an ancillary service, but he is entitled to the use of the wharf subject to the payment of dues.

266. These arguments appear to outweigh that derived from the absence of any reference to shipping and unshipping in the definition. Weight is lent to this view by the consideration that the words "facilities provided" should be construed *ejusdem generis* with "work performed" and "services rendered", both of which point to some process ancillary to the basic provision of the essential works of the port. The better view therefore appears to be that a wharfage charge is a goods due.

267. Another question which has arisen is whether a mooring charge is a ship due. The question of whether a particular "mooring charge" is within paragraph (a) of the definition of "ship, passenger and goods dues" must always be considered in relation to the facts of the particular case. However, it seems true to say that nearly all "mooring charges" are either—

    (a) a charge made by a harbour authority for the use of a mooring provided by the authority in the harbour, or

    (b) a charge made by a harbour authority for the grant to a person of a licence for that person to lay and maintain his own mooring in the harbour. Such a charge is sometimes made, where the authority own the bed or shores of the harbour, by virtue of that ownership but more often by virtue of a provision in the authority's local enactments—see, for example, sections 16(2)(a) and 24(2) of the Salcombe Harbour Order 1954.

268. It seems that charges of the kind mentioned in (b) of paragraph 267 *ante* are clearly not within paragraph (a) of the definition of ship, passenger and goods dues. A charge made in consideration of a grant to a person of a right for that person to lay, maintain and use a mooring is not a charge "in respect of any ship entering, using or leaving the harbour".

269. In the case of charges made by a harbour authority for the use of their own

1. [1934] A.C. 279.

moorings the position may not be quite so clear. The question appears to turn on whether such a charge is "in respect of any ship for . . . using the harbour". The definition of "harbour" in section 57(1) of the Harbours Act includes wharves, quays and piers in addition to the water area. It does not, however, appear to include a mooring in the ordinary sense of the word.

**270.** It might possibly be argued that a mooring is a facility provided in connection with the harbour; that charges in respect of facilities are expressly excluded in paragraphs (b) and (c) of the definition of "ship, passenger and goods dues" but not in paragraph (a) of that definition, and that this implies that paragraph (a) does include charges for facilities. The answer to this seems to be that the charges described in paragraph (a) of the definition are expressed to be charges "in respect of . . . using the harbour" and that, having regard to the definition of "harbour" in section 57(1), this could not include charges in respect of facilities in the sense mentioned above. There was therefore no need expressly to exclude charges in respect of ancillary matters as there was in paragraphs (b) and (c) where the words "charges for any passengers embarking or disembarking at the harbour" and "charges in respect of goods brought into, taken out of or carried through the harbour" might each, in the absence of the express exclusion, have included charges for ancillary matters.

**271.** It therefore appears that a charge made by a harbour authority for the use of their own moorings will not usually be a charge in respect of "using . . . the harbour" within the meaning of paragraph (a) of the definition of "ship, passenger and goods dues" because (in general at any rate) a mooring is not part of the essential harbour works—the infrastructure of the port—and not within the definition of "harbour" in section 57(1) of the Harbours Act.

**272.** Another question about harbour dues which has arisen on several occasions is whether, or to what extent, a harbour authority can enter into a contract with a user which limits the authority's power under section 26 of the Harbours Act "to demand, take and recover such ship, passenger and goods dues as they think fit". There is a long line of authorities on the general issue of whether a body with a statutory discretion can fetter the exercise of that direction by contract, beginning with the Scottish cases of *Paterson* v. *Provost of St. Andrews*[2] and *Ayr Harbour Trustees* v. *Oswald*.[3] They establish the general principle that a body entrusted with statutory powers cannot by contract fetter the exercise of those powers but some cases indicate that the courts will not press this principle to unreasonable lengths. However, the cases do not lay down precise rules about how far the contractual fettering of the statutory discretion may be permissible. It has been suggested that the test is whether the body concerned is renouncing its "statutory birthright" but the judgments in *British Transport Commission* v. *Westmoreland County Council*[4] indicate that a pragmatic criterion should be applied.

**273.** As to whether a contract by a harbour authority fixing the dues they may

2. *Paterson* v. *Provost of St. Andrews* (1881) 6 App. Cas. 883.
3. *Ayr Harbour Trustees* v. *Oswald* (1883) 8 App. Cas. 623.
4. *British Transport Commission* v. *Westmoreland County Council* [1958] A.C. 126.

charge over a long period is enforceable, the case most clearly in point is *York Corporation* v. *Henry Leetham & Sons Ltd.*[5] In that case the plaintiffs were entrusted by statute with the control of navigation in parts of the rivers Ouse and Fosse with power to charge such tolls as the Corporation deemed necessary to carry on the navigation in which the public had an interest. The Corporation made two contracts with the defendants under which they agreed to accept, in consideration of the right to navigate the Ouse, a regular payment of £600 in place of the authorized tolls. The contract with regard to the navigation of the Fosse was on similar lines. It was held by Russell, J., that the contracts were *ultra vires* and void because under them the Corporation had disabled themselves, whatever emergency might arise, from exercising their statutory powers to increase tolls as from time to time might be necessary. The judge based his decision on the incapacity of a body charged with statutory powers for public purposes to divest itself of such powers or to fetter itself in the use of such powers.

**274.** Russell, J.'s decision was criticized by the House of Lords (and previously by the Court of Appeal) in *Southport Corporation* v. *Birkdale District Electric Supply Co. Ltd.*[6] in which it was held that a contract on the part of the electricity company not to charge higher prices than those charged in the borough of Southport was not *ultra vires*. (The contract had been made with the local authority and not with the company's customers, this being one of the grounds, although not perhaps a very satisfactory one, on which the case was distinguished from *York Corporation* v. *Leetham*.) It was pointed out that the body executing the statutory duties in question was a trading corporation and that the discharge of such duties would be facilitated rather than fettered by a reasonable latitude of discretion in fixing prices (i.e., by contract). However, *York Corporation* v. *Leetham* was distinguished and not overruled. The facts in the *Southport* case were very different and the judgments appear to have turned to some extent on the fact that the undertakers concerned in that case were a limited company rather than a statutory corporation. *York Corporation* v. *Leetham* appears to have been treated as good law by the Court of Appeal in *William Cory & Sons Ltd.* v. *London Corporation*[7] in which it was held that the Corporation could not by contract fetter their statutory duty to make certain by-laws.

**275.** The courts might now be disposed to adopt a more commercial approach. Contracts purporting to fix the level of dues for a particular customer are not uncommon but, in view of the authorities, it seems that a contract by a harbour authority which purported to fetter their discretion under section 26 over a long period would still probably be held to be *ultra vires*. In this connection, section 32 of the Harbours, Docks and Piers Clauses Act 1847, where it is incorporated, authorizes the harbour authority to compound for dues by the year or other shorter period but it seems doubtful whether this extends to the long term fettering of a harbour authority's discretion under section 26. Nor, indeed, does any express power to compound for dues now seem to be necessary since this would appear to

5. *York Corporation* v. *Henry Leetham & Sons Ltd.* [1924] 1 Ch. 557.
6. *Southport Corporation* v. *Birkdale District Electric Supply Co. Ltd.* [1926] A.C. 355.
7. *William Cory & Sons Ltd* v. *London Corporation* [1951] 2 K.B. 476.

be covered by the terms of section 26(2). (It seems, incidentally, that the proviso to section 32, which provides that if the harbour authority agree to dues being compounded in respect of any user all other users are entitled to be treated in the same way, has ceased to have effect by virtue of section 38(1)(*c*) of the Harbours Act 1964.)

**276.** With regard to the recovery of charges by a harbour authority, the authority's special legislation nearly always include a provision to the effect that, in addition to any other remedy under the special legislation or provisions of the Harbours, Docks and Piers Clauses Act 1847 incorporated therewith, the authority may recover any charges payable to them in any court of competent jurisdiction.

**277.** Under section 44 of the Harbours, Docks and Piers Clauses Act 1847, which is incorporated in the special legislation of most harbour authorities, the authority may recover any rates payable to them in respect of a ship by distraint and sale of the ship and its tackle. By virtue of sections 26(3) of the Harbours Act 1964 the rates referred to in section 44 include ship dues levied under section 26.

**278.** Under section 45 of the 1847 Act, which again is incorporated in the special legislation of most harbour authorities, a harbour authority may recover rates payable to them in respect of any goods (again, by virtue of section 26(3) of the Harbours Act 1964 these include goods dues levied under section 26) by distraint and sale of the goods concerned or, if these have been removed from the port premises without payment of the dues, by distraint and sale of other goods on these premises belonging to the person liable for payment of the dues.

**279.** Where sections 44 and 45 of the 1847 Act are not incorporated in a harbour authority's special legislation, such legislation virtually always includes substantive provisions to the same effect. It has been held that a harbour authority may exercise a statutory right to detain a vessel until rates are paid notwithstanding the prior existence of a maritime lien in favour of the master and crew: *The Emilie Millon*.[8]

**280.** Section 43 of the Harbours, Docks and Piers Clauses Act 1847 provides that if the master of any ship or the owner of any goods evades the payment of the rates payable to the harbour authority in respect of the ship or goods (these, again, by virtue of section 26(3) of the Harbours Act 1964 including ship dues or goods dues levied under section 26) he must pay the authority three times the amount of the rates evaded. Section 43 is not usually incorporated in modern local harbour legislation but a substantive provision to the same effect has sometimes been included in recent local harbour Acts and orders.

## Borrowing by harbour authorities

**281.** Virtually all harbour authorities have powers under their special legislation to borrow both for capital purposes and for temporary purposes. The form of port

---

8. *The Emilie Millon* [1905] 2 K.B. 817.

trusts' capital borrowing powers as in force prior to the commencement of section 3 of the Ports (Finance) Act 1985 (whose provisions are described below) varied considerably. In a few cases this was a simple power to borrow with the Secretary of State's consent. In most cases, however, the port trust had power to borrow such sums of money as they thought necessary for capital purposes not exceeding in the aggregate a specified sum and this was usually, although not always, coupled with a provision that the port trust might with the consent of the Secretary of State borrow such further sums of money as they might require. Specified limits on the amount to be borrowed usually applied to the total amount borrowed without regard to repayments (but excluding, in some cases, borrowings for the repayment of amounts previously borrowed). In a few cases the limit was expressed to apply to the amount outstanding from time to time (the limit thus being "ever green").

**282.** The usual power for a port trust to borrow temporarily by way of overdraft or otherwise for meeting or discharging their statutory obligations or functions was usually subject to a specified limit which applied to the total amount borrowed.

**283.** The borrowing powers of statutory harbour companies were usually expressed as a power to borrow up to a specified limit applying to the total amount borrowed. In no case was the Secretary of State's consent required to borrowing by a statutory harbour company.

**284.** These borrowing powers were substantially affected by the provisions of section 3 of the Ports (Finance) Act 1985, which came into force on 1 January 1986. This section applied in relation to any borrowing power contained in an "existing local provision" of a "relevant harbour authority". A "relevant harbour authority" is defined in section 5(1) of the Act as a harbour authority constituted by or under an "existing local provision" for the purpose of managing a harbour. An "existing local provision" is defined in section 5(1) as a provision of a local Act of Parliament, including an Act comprising a provisional order, or a provision of an instrument made under a local Act or of an instrument in the nature of a local enactment made under any other Act, being a provision in force on the date on which section 5 comes into force (1 January 1986). "An instrument in the nature of a local enactment made under any other Act" appears to include a harbour revision or empowerment order or harbour reorganization scheme made under the Harbours Act 1964.

**285.** Section 3 therefore applied in relation to the borrowing powers of port trusts and statutory harbour companies. It did not affect local authorities. Nor did it affect Associated British Ports, Sealink Harbours Ltd. or the British Waterways Board.

**286.** Subsection (1) of section 3 abolished the need for any consent or approval of a Minister of the Crown under the borrowing powers to which section 3 applied.

**287.** Subsection (2) fixed limits to the amounts which may be borrowed under borrowing powers to which section 3 applied where the consent or approval of a Minister of the Crown was required. Where the borrowing power specified a limit, that limit was increased by 20 per cent. Where no limit was specified in the borrowing power, then the limit on the amount which might be borrowed thereunder became an amount equal to the aggregate of the sums specified in the Ministerial consents or approvals given under the provision in question increased by 20 per cent.

**288.** Subsection (3) provided that, where a relevant harbour authority might, by virtue of an existing local provision, borrow any amount without the consent or approval of a Minister of the Crown and, by virtue of that or another such provision, might borrow a further amount with such consent or approval, the amount which might be borrowed without such consent or approval should be increased by 20 per cent.

**289.** Subsection (4) provided that the limit specified in any borrowing power to which section 3 applied should bite on the amount for the time being outstanding in respect of money borrowed under the power in question (instead of, as was formerly the position in most cases, on the total amount borrowed this making the limit "ever green".

**290.** The effect of section 3 on the usual forms of borrowing powers to which it applied seems to be as follows—

(a) If the borrowing power specified a limit to the amount which might be borrowed without any power to borrow further with the consent of a Minister of the Crown, then section 3 did not affect the amount of the limit but the limit became "ever green" if it was not so already.

(b) If the power was simply to borrow with the consent of a Minister of the Crown, the requirement to obtain such consent disappeared but borrowing became subject to an "ever green" limit equal to the aggregate of all the sums the borrowing of which the Minister had consented to before section 3 came into force increased by 20 per cent.

(c) If the power was to borrow with the consent of a Minister of the Crown up to a specified limit, then the requirement to obtain such consent disappeared but borrowing became subject to the former limit increased by 20 per cent which also became "ever green" if it was not so already.

(d) In the most common case, where a port trust had power to borrow up to a specified limit without the consent of a Minister of the Crown and above that with such consent, the requirement to obtain the Minster's consent disappeared and the limit on borrowing became the aggregate of the former limit increased by 20 per cent and any additional amounts to the borrowing of which the Minister had consented before section 3 came into force also increased by 20 per cent, the new limit being, of course, "ever green".

**291.** Since the Ports (Finance) Act 1985 new harbour authority capital borrowing powers have authorized borrowing up to a specified limit on the amount outstanding at any time in respect of borrowed money.

**292.** There is some variation in harbour authority borrowing powers as to the security on which the authority may borrow for capital purposes. In the most recent provisions the security is described in wide terms, e.g., "all or any of the revenues and property of the authority", which would appear to enable the authority to secure a loan on particular property although it is no doubt usually appropriate for borrowings to be charged on the authority's undertaking or revenues as a whole. In some cases the borrowing power describes the authorized security in more limited terms, e.g., "on the security of the revenues of the undertaking".

**293.** With regard to methods of borrowing for capital purposes, modern harbour authority borrowing powers usually authorize the authority to borrow by any method or methods they see fit. Older borrowing powers tend to be more specific, sometimes containing detailed provisions for the issue of bonds or debentures.

**294.** Local authorities have powers to borrow under local government legislation but local authorities which are harbour authorities often have in addition powers under their special harbour legislation to borrow for harbour purposes sometimes without the Ministerial sanction required under local government legislation. The provisions relating to local authority borrowings contained in general legislation usually apply to borrowings under these special powers which are therefore normally charged on all the revenues of the authority concerned.

**295.** In order to avoid possible difficulties arising from the limited terms in which the borrowing powers of some harbour authorities were expressed section 39 of the Docks and Harbours Act 1966 provided that the purposes for which a harbour authority (other than a nationalized harbour authority) might borrow money should include "meeting any expenses properly chargeable to capital, being expenses incurred in connection with the provision or improvement of assets in connection with any activity in which the authority has power to engage". This section also enabled any harbour authority (other than a nationalized harbour authority) to borrow for the purpose of acquiring a harbour business or shares in a harbour business under the powers for those purposes conferred by the Docks and Harbours Act 1966.

**296.** The borrowing powers of Associated British Ports are contained in paragraph 21 of Schedule 3 to the Transport Act 1981. These powers are wide and flexible. They include powers to issue debentures and to mortgage or charge by way of security all or any part of the undertaking, revenues, property or assets (present or future) of Associated British Ports. However, the aggregate amount outstanding at any time of the money borrowed by Associated British Ports and their subsidiaries (and of guarantees given by Associated British Ports and their subsidiaries) must not exceed the limit for the time being set by Associated British Ports Holdings plc.

**297.** Harbour authorities (other than the British Waterways Board who, as the only remaining nationalized harbour authority, may, under the Transport Act 1962, borrow only from the Secretary of State for capital purposes and may borrow temporarily only from the Secretary of State or from someone else with his consent), may borrow from whom they please. Under section 11 of the Harbours Act 1964, as extended by section 40(5) of the Docks and Harbours Act 1966, the Secretary of State with the approval of the Treasury may make loans to a harbour authority in respect of expenses (which he is satisfied are such as ought properly to be regarded as being of a capital nature) incurred by them in respect of a harbour for which they are the harbour authority—

(a) in executing works for the improvement, maintenance or management of an existing harbour or for the construction of a new harbour;

(b) in acquiring plant or equipment required for the carrying out of harbour operations at an existing harbour or at a harbour which the harbour authority are constructing or proposing to construct;

(c) in acquiring land required for the purposes of an existing harbour or an extension thereof or for the construction of a new harbour.

A loan under section 11 may also be made to enable a harbour authority to repay principal or pay interest on a loan previously made to them under that section but not in respect of any part of the principal which does not fall due for repayment until more than five years from the date on which the loan was made nor in respect of interest for any period beginning more than five years from that date.

**298.** A further power for the Secretary of State to make loans to harbour authorities is conferred by the Harbours (Loans) Act 1972. Under that Act the Secretary of State, where it appears to him that a harbour authority are, or are likely to be, unable to pay off a debt when it falls due, and it also appears to him "that the financial prospects of the authority justify making them a loan for the purpose of enabling them to make the payment or repayment", may, with the approval of the Treasury, make the harbour authority concerned a loan to pay off the debt in question which may be either a capital debt or a temporary loan or overdraft. The purpose of this provision is to enable a harbour authority whose financial position is basically sound to be tided over a difficult period.

**299.** Section 43 of the Harbours Act 1964, which is also applied by the Harbours (Loans) Act 1972 for the purposes of that Act, provides that loans which the Secretary of State makes to harbour authorities shall be repaid to him at such times and by such methods, and interest thereon shall be paid to him at such rates and at such times as he may, with the approval of the Treasury, from time to time direct. This seems to mean that the terms of the relevant mortgage deeds could, in theory, subsequently be varied from time to time but it is believed that in practice this has never happened.

**300.** Under section 4 of the Harbours (Loans) Act 1972 the aggregate amount of loans made after the passing of that Act under that Act and under section 11 of the Harbours Act 1964 is not to exceed £200 million or, if the House of Commons so resolve, £300 million. This limit does not take account of loan repayments. In recent years few loans to harbour authority's have been made under the Harbours Act 1964 and none under the Harbours (Loans) Act 1972.

**301.** What are the remedies of the secured creditors of a harbour authority if the authority should default in making payments to them or their security should be in jeopardy? As indicated in paragraphs 48 to 50 *ante*, it seems probable that in general a harbour authority cannot be wound up except by means of an Act of Parliament. With regard to the remedies of a secured creditor of a port trust in England and Wales, it may often be doubtful whether the powers of a mortgagee under section 101 of the Law of Property Act 1925, where the mortgage is made by deed, are available. This is because, according to the terms of the harbour authority's special legislation, the creditors' security may be created by statute rather than by mortgage deed. But in any case, it appears from the old cases of *Gardner* v. *London, Chatham and Dover Railway Company*[9] and *Blaker* v. *Herts and Essex Waterworks Co.*[10] that where, as is usually the case with port trusts, security holders have a charge on the revenue and/or the undertaking of statutory undertakers section 101 of the Law of Property Act 1925 will not apply so as to enable the security holders to sell assets (and therefore, presumably, the right to appoint a receiver under section 101 will not arise). This is because a charge of this nature is essentially a charge on "the fruit of the fruit bearing tree" represented by the complete undertaking. In the course of his judgment in the former case Lord Cairns said:

Whatever may be the liability to which any of the property or effects connected with [the Railway Company's undertaking] may be subjected through the legal operations and consequences of a judgment recovered against it, the undertaking, so far as these contracts of mortgage are concerned, is, in my opinion, made over as a thing complete or to be completed; as a going concern, with internal and Parliamentary powers of management not to be interfered with; as a fruit-bearing tree, the produce of which is the fund dedicated by the contract to secure and to pay the debt. The living and going concern thus created by the Legislature must not, under a contract pledging it as security, be destroyed, broken up or annihilated. The tolls and sums of money *ejusdem generis*—that is to say, the earnings of the undertaking—must be made available to satisfy the mortgage; but in my opinion the mortgagees cannot, under their mortgages, or as mortgagees—by seizing, or calling on this Court to seize, the capital, or the lands, or the proceeds of sales of land, or the stock of the undertaking—either prevent its completion, or reduce it into its original elements when it has been completed.

**302.** A secured creditor of a port trust in England and Wales may commence proceedings and obtain judgment for unpaid principal or interest due to him and could then levy execution on the assets of the port trust. However, it seems that assets necessary for the carrying on of the port trust's undertaking could not be taken in execution. There does not appear to be direct authority for this proposition but it seems to follow from the established principle that a body on which Parliament has imposed duties may not dispose of assets necessary for carrying out those statutory duties: *Re Woking Urban Council (Basingstoke Canal) Act 1911.*[11]

**303.** The secured creditors of such a port trust might also apply to the court for the appointment of a receiver on the grounds either that payments of principal or interest were in arrear or that their security was in jeopardy. It appears from *Gardner* v. *London, Chatham and Dover Railway* that such a receiver could not be appointed also as manager. In the course of his judgment Lord Cairns said:

When Parliament, acting for the public interest, authorizes the construction and maintenance of a railway . . . it confers powers and imposes duties and responsibilities of the largest and most important kind, and it confers and imposes them upon the company which Parliament has before it, and upon no other body or person. These powers must be executed and those duties discharged by the company. They cannot be delegated or transferred.

9.  *Gardner* v. *London, Chatham and Dover Railway Company* (1867) L.R. 2 Ch. App. 201.
10.  *Blaker* v. *Herts and Essex Waterworks Co.* (1889) L.R. 41 Ch. 399.
11.  *Re Woking Urban Council (Basingstoke Canal) Act 1911* [1914] 1 Ch. 300.

However, the Port of London Authority (Borrowing Powers) Revision Order 1971 contains provisions for the appointment by the court on the application of security holders of a receiver and manager of the PLA's undertaking if that authority are in default as mentioned in that order.

**304.** With regard to the remedies of secured loan creditors of harbour authorities in England and Wales which are statutory companies, the relevant principles are substantially the same as in the case of port trusts but incorporated provisions of the Companies Clauses Consolidation Act 1845 may be relevant. In the case of the Mersey Docks and Harbour Company, the Mersey Docks and Harbour Act 1971 contains special provisions for the appointment of a receiver and manager by the court on the application of secured creditors in the circumstances specified in that Act.

**305.** Paragraphs 301 to 304 *ante* refer to the law in England and Wales. The remedies of secured loan creditors of port trusts in Scotland are a matter of technical Scottish law and the author is not qualified to deal with them.

### Other financial assistance to harbour authorities

**306.** Under section 2 of the Fisheries Act 1955 the Minister of Agriculture Fisheries and Food has power to make grants or loans to (*inter alia*) a harbour authority towards expenses incurred by the authority for the provision of fishery harbour works. Since the section describes the bodies to which financial assistance may be given thereunder as "not trading for profit" it would seem that a loan or grant under the section could probably not be made to a harbour authority with share capital.

**307.** The powers of the Secretary of State to give special financial assistance to the PLA and the Mersey Docks and Harbour Company under the Ports (Financial Assistance) Act 1981 and the Ports (Reduction of Debt) Act 1983 are described in paragraph 18 *ante*.

### Accounts of harbour authorities

**308.** Under the new section 42 of the Harbours Act 1964, substituted for the original section by the Transport Act 1981 and set out in paragraph 10 of Schedule 6 to that Act, the legal requirements as respects the accounts of harbour authorities are closely assimilated to those which apply to companies under the Companies Act 1985.

**309.** Section 42 requires every harbour authority (with a few exceptions referred to below) to prepare an annual statement of accounts relating to "harbour activities" and to any "associated activities" carried on by them. "Harbour activities" are defined as activities involved in carrying on a statutory harbour undertaking or in carrying out harbour operations (as to which see paragraph 17 *ante*). "Associated activities" in relation to any harbour activities mean such activities as may be prescribed by regulations made by the Secretary of State. The Statutory

Harbour Undertakings (Accounts, etc.) Regulations 1983 made by the Secretary of State under powers conferred by section 42 provide that, in relation to harbour authorities other than local authorities and natural persons, all activities other than harbour activities and the activities of a pilotage authority[12] are associated activities. The accounts prepared by a port trust or a harbour company will therefore relate to all the activities carried on by that body. With regard to the inclusion of pilotage revenue and expenditure in a harbour authority's statement of accounts see paragraphs 484 and 485 *post*.

310. Where a harbour authority have subsidiaries, for example subsidiary companies carrying out cargo handling activities, section 42 requires that, in addition to the statement of accounts mentioned above relating to their own activities, the harbour authority must prepare an annual statement of accounts relating to the harbour activities and associated activities carried on by them and their subsidiaries.

311. The requirements mentioned above are not satisfied by the preparation of a statement of accounts which relates to other matters in addition to harbour activities and associated activities.

312. Any provision for the auditing of a harbour authority's accounts applies to a statement of accounts prepared by that authority under section 42.

313. A harbour authority by whom a statement of accounts is prepared pursuant to section 42 is required to send a copy of the statement, together with a copy of the auditor's report on it, to the Secretary of State. They must also prepare and send to the Secretary of State a report on the state of affairs disclosed by the statement. This corresponds to a director's report under the Companies Act 1985.

314. Section 42(6) provides that, subject to any regulations made by the Secretary of State under section 42—

(a) the provisions of the Companies Act 1985 relating to company accounts shall apply to a harbour authority's annual statement of accounts relating to the harbour activities and any associated activities carried on by them;

(b) the provisions of those Acts relating to group accounts shall apply to an annual statement of accounts relating to the harbour activities and associated activities carried on by a harbour authority and its subsidiaries; and

(c) the provisions of those Acts relating to the director's report required to be attached to a company's balance sheet shall apply to the report which a harbour authority is required to prepare and send to the Secretary of State on the state of affairs disclosed by their statement or statements of accounts.

315. The Secretary of State may by regulation prescribe cases in which the provisions of the Companies Act 1985 referred to above are not to apply. The Statutory Harbour Undertakings (Accounts, etc.) Regulations 1983 provide that those provisions shall not apply in the case of a person who carries on a statutory harbour undertaking where the annual turnover is less that £250,000. The regulations

12. As indicated in Chapter 12, *post*, pilotage authorities have now been abolished and pilotage has become a function of harbour authorities.

define the circumstances in which the annual turnover of a statutory harbour undertaking is to be treated as being less than that amount.

**316.** The Secretary of State may also by regulations modify the relevant provisions of the Companies Act in their application to harbour authority accounts. The regulations mentioned above provide that provisions of the Companies Act 1985 that small or medium-sized companies shall be entitled to the benefit of certain exemptions in relation to accounts shall not apply in relation to the accounts and reports required to be prepared under section 42.

**317.** The Secretary of State may also prescribe by regulations requirements additional to those imposed by the provision of the Companies Act. The regulations mentioned above provide that, where an annual statement of accounts prepared under section 42 relates to associated activities, then, in addition to complying with the requirements of the Companies Act 1985, the statement of accounts must include a statement of the gross revenue for the period in question in relation to those associated activities.

**318.** Section 42 does not apply to harbour authorities for nationalized harbours. Their accounts are governed by the provisions of section 24 of the Transport Act 1962 which requires that their accounts must be in such form, contain such particulars and be compiled in such manner, as the Secretary of State may from time to time direct. As mentioned above the only remaining nationalized harbour authority is the British Waterways Board.

**319.** Section 42 also does not apply to a statutory harbour undertaker of a class exempted from the section by regulations made by the Secretary of State. The Statutory Harbour Undertakings (Accounts, etc.) Regulations 1983 provide that section 42 shall not apply to a statutory harbour undertaker in respect of any undertaking carried on by him which is used wholly or mainly for ships resorting to the harbour in question wholly or mainly for the purpose of bringing or receiving goods which have been manufactured or produced by the statutory harbour undertaker or which are to be used by him for the manufacture or production of goods or electricity. For this purpose the activities of manufacture or production carried on by a holding company or subsidiary of the statutory harbour undertaker, or by members of a consortium who between them own more than half the issued share capital of the statutory undertaker, are to be treated as carried on by the statutory harbour undertaker in question.

## Auditors of harbour authority accounts

**320.** Virtually all harbour authorities have provisions in their local Acts and orders for the appointment of auditors. The form of these varied somewhat but section 4 of the Ports (Finance) Act 1985 provided that any requirement of an "existing local provision" (see paragraph 284 *ante*) that the auditor of a "relevant harbour authority" (see paragraph 284 *ante*) should be appointed, or that his appointment must be approved, by a Minister of the Crown should cease to have effect, any former Ministerial power of appointment being exercisable instead by the harbour authority. Section 4 also provided that notwithstanding anything to the contrary in any existing local provision a person should be qualified for appointment as auditor of a relevant harbour authority only if he would be qualified for the appointment under section 389 of the Companies Act 1985 if the authority were a company to which that section (other than subsection (2) which relates to unquoted companies) applied. This means that the auditor of a port trust or a statutory harbour company must be a member of—

    (a) the Institute of Chartered Accountants in England and Wales,

    (b) the Institute of Chartered Accountants of Scotland,

    (c) the Chartered Association of Certified Accountants, or

    (d) the Institute of Chartered Accountants in Ireland,

or be authorized by the Secretary of State as mentioned in section 389(1)(*b*) of the Companies Act 1985.

# CHAPTER 10

# SUBORDINATE LEGISLATION UNDER THE HARBOURS ACT 1964

**321.** The Harbours Act 1964 includes important provisions for subordinate legislation which were intended to be a simpler and cheaper alternative to private Bills so far as harbour legislation was concerned. These provisions of the Act deal with three different types of circumstances as mentioned below.

**322.** Under section 14 of the Harbours Act a harbour authority may apply to the Secretary of State for Transport for a "harbour revision order" for the purpose of achieving in relation to their harbour all or any of the objects specified in Schedule 2 to the Harbours Act, or in the new subsection (2A) inserted in section 14 of that Act by the Transport Act 1981. In addition to the harbour authority for a harbour, any other person who appears to the Secretary of State to have a substantial interest in a harbour, or a body representative of such persons, may also apply for a harbour revision order in relation to the harbour in question. And, as mentioned below, in certain circumstances the Secretary of State may promote a harbour revision order himself.

**323.** The objects specified in Schedule 2 to the Harbours Act for which a harbour revision order may be made cover a wide field. They include, in particular, reconstituting a harbour authority, establishing a new harbour authority (either an existing body or one constituted for the purpose) for a harbour in place of the existing one, varying the powers of a harbour authority for managing or operating their harbour or for regulating the activities there of other persons and conferring new powers for these purposes on a harbour authority, altering a harbour authority's limits of jurisdiction, authorizing a harbour authority to purchase land compulsorily and empowering a harbour authority to borrow money. At the end of the Schedule there is a "sweeping up" provision under which a harbour revision order may be made for "any object which, though not falling within any of the foregoing paragraphs appears to the Secretary of State to be one the achievement of which will conduce to the efficient functioning of the harbour".

**324.** In addition to these main objects for which a harbour revision order may be made such an order may also, by virtue of section 14(3) of the Harbours Act (as slightly extended by the Transport Act 1981) include all such provisions as appear to the Secretary of State to be

requisite or expedient for rendering of full effect a provision of the order framed to achieve any of the said objects and any supplementary, consequential or incidental provisions appearing to him to be requisite or expedient for the purposes of the order, including, but without prejudice to the generality of the foregoing words, penal provisions and provisions incorporating with or without modifications, any provision of the Lands Clauses Acts or any other enactment and provisions for repealing or amending any statutory provision of local application to which the order relates . . . .

325. Section 14(3) of the Harbours Act prescribes the maximum penalties which may be imposed by a penal provision contained in a harbour revision order. The relevant part of the subsection was amended by section 18 of, and paragraph 14 of Schedule 6 to, the Transport Act 1981 and by the Criminal Justice Act 1982 and must now be read with section 52 of the Criminal Justice Act 1988. In the result, the maximum fine which may be provided for in the case of an offence triable only summarily is level 4 on "the standard scale" introduced by the Criminal Justice Act 1981 which is currently £1,000 or, in the case of a continuing offence, a daily fine not exceeding £50 for each day on which the offence continues after conviction. Under section 52 of the Criminal Justice Act 1988 where the maximum fine on conviction for a summary offence specified in a harbour revision order made after 30 April 1984 and before the commencement of section 51 on 12 October 1988 is an amount shown in the second column of the standard scale the amount of the maximum fine is to be construed as a reference to the level in the first column of the standard scale corresponding to that amount. In the case of an offence triable either summarily or on indictment the maximum fine on summary conviction which may be provided for is "the prescribed sum" within the meaning of section 32 of the Magistrates' Courts Act 1980 or section 289B of the Criminal Procedure (Scotland) Act 1975—currently £2,000. By virtue of section 51(1) of the Criminal Justice Act 1988 the maximum fine for such an offence under any harbour revision order made before the commencement of section 51 on 12 October 1988 became "the statutory maximum" which is the same as "the prescribed sum" referred to above. A penal provision of a harbour revision order may not provide for a penalty other than a fine where a person is convicted on indictment.

326. Although the power to make harbour revision orders is a wide one it is, like other powers to make subordinate legislation, subject to certain constitutional limitations. For example, a harbour revision order cannot be retrospective and, being delegated legislation, such an order cannot on the basis of the maxim *delegatus non potest delegare*, confer a legislative power on any person except insofar as this is expressly authorized by the Harbours Act, which does indeed provide, in paragraph 4 of Schedule 2, that a harbour revision order may confer powers to make by-laws on a harbour authority.

327. It is also considered that it would probably be *ultra vires* for the Secretary of State to reserve to himself in a harbour revision order anything in the nature of a legislative power, although the reservation, within reason, of an administrative discretion may be permissible.

328. The view is also taken, both on grounds of constitutional principle and also, having regard to the express powers in section 14(3) of, and paragraph 3 of

Schedule 2 to, the Harbours Act which enable a harbour revision order to repeal or amend a statutory provision of local application, on the basis of the maxim *expressio unius, exclusio alterius*, that a harbour revision order cannot repeal, or directly amend, a statutory provision of general application (except in one case mentioned below where this is expressly authorized—such authorization of course tending to confirm the view expressed above). However, in appropriate cases it seems that it is permissible for a harbour revision order to include provisions which supplement those of a statutory provision of general application. For example, it is not uncommon for harbour revision orders to supplement the powers of a harbour authority to deal with wrecks under sections 530 and 532 of the Merchant Shipping Act 1894. Also, as indicated above, a harbour revision order may, under section 14(3), incorporate, with or without modifications "any provision of . . . any . . . enactment" (including, presumably a statutory provision of general application) where this appears to the Secretary of State to be requisite or expedient either for rendering of full effect a provision of the order framed to achieve any of the objects specified in Schedule 2 to the Act or as a supplementary, consequential or incidental provision of the order.

**329.** There is one case in which a harbour revision order may directly repeal or amend general legislation. By virtue of section 43(3) of the Docks and Harbours Act 1966 a harbour revision order may repeal or amend such legislation for the purpose of securing the welfare of the officers or servants of the harbour authority and empowering that authority to provide, or secure the provision, for or in respect of their officers and servants, of pensions, gratuities and other like benefits (this being the purpose specified in paragraph 15 of Schedule 2 to the Harbours Act).

**330.** Under the terms of section 14(2)(*b*) of the Harbours Act the Secretary of State cannot make a harbour revision order unless he is satisfied that this is desirable in the interests of securing the improvement, maintenance or management of the harbour in question in an efficient and economical manner or of facilitating the efficient and economic transport of goods or passengers by sea. Doubts were expressed as to whether, in view of this condition precedent, the harbour revision order procedure could be used for revising and modernizing a harbour authority's special legislation without changing the substance of it. These doubts have been removed by the new subsection (2A) inserted in section 14 by section 18 of, and paragraph 2 of Schedule 6 to, the Transport Act 1981. This subsection provides expressly that a harbour revision order may be made with the objects of repealing or consolidating statutory provisions of local application affecting a harbour and that section 14(2)(*b*) does not apply to an order insofar as it is made for such objects.

**331.** Section 15 of the Harbours Act enables the Secretary of State to promote a harbour revision order himself if he is satisfied that a harbour revision order ought to be made to reconstitute a harbour authority or alter their constitution and/or to regulate (in whole or to a less extent) the procedure of, or of any committee of, the authority and to fix the quorum at a meeting of, or of any committee of, the authority. Before making an order under this section the Secretary of State must be satisfied that the making of the order is desirable as mentioned in section 14(2)(*b*) of the Act referred to in the preceding paragraph.

332. The second kind of subordinate legislation provided for in the Harbours Act as an alternative to private Bills is authorized by section 16 of the Act and enables the Secretary of State for Transport to make "harbour empowerment orders" to authorize the construction and/or improvement, maintenance or management of harbours (including docks and wharves) where no sufficient powers for the purpose already exist. Such an order can be made only on the application of a person desirous of securing the achievement of any of the objects specified in section 16(1). The application may ask for the requisite powers to be conferred on the applicant or a designated person other than the applicant or a body to be constituted for the purpose by the order.

333. A harbour empowerment order may include all such powers, including power to acquire land compulsorily and to levy charges other than ship, passenger and goods dues (if the order comes into force the new harbour authority will have power to levy such dues by virtue of section 26 of the Harbours Act) as are requisite for enabling the object of the order—the construction of an artificial harbour or a dock or wharf and its subsequent improvement, maintenance or management or, as the case may be, the improvement, maintenance or management of an existing harbour, whether natural or artificial—to be achieved. Under section 16(6) a harbour empowerment order may include such ancillary provisions as appear to the Secretary of State to be requisite or expedient. This subsection is in similar terms to section 14(3), which authorizes the inclusion of such provisions in harbour revision orders, except that it does not refer to provisions for repealing or amending statutory provisions of local application (presumably because, *ex hypothesi*, there are no such provisions relating to a harbour which is the subject of a harbour empowerment order). The position as respects the penalties which may be provided for by penal provisions of a harbour empowerment order is the same as in the case of a harbour revision order.

334. Before making a harbour empowerment order the Secretary of State must be satisfied that the making of an order is desirable in the interests of facilitating the efficient and economic transport of goods or passengers by sea. This is narrower than the corresponding requirement relating to harbour revision orders referred to in paragraph 330 *ante*. It means that harbour empowerment orders are directed towards commercial ends and cannot be used to establish or secure the regulation of recreational harbours.

335. In addition to harbour revision and empowerment orders the Harbours Act also contains, in section 18, powers for the grouping together of harbours by means of "harbour reorganization schemes". Section 18 provides that "with a view to securing the efficient and economical development of a group of harbours each of which is being improved, maintained or managed by a harbour authority in the exercise and performance of statutory powers and duties" a harbour reorganization scheme with respect to the group may be submitted to the Secretary of State by all or any of the harbour authorities for the harbours in question. Section 18, as

amended by the Transport Act 1981, further provides that if the Secretary of State is of opinion that, with a view to securing the efficient and economical development of a group of harbours each of which is being improved, maintained or managed by a harbour authority in the exercise and performance of statutory powers and duties, a harbour reorganization scheme ought to be made, he may by order make such a scheme.

336. What is a group of harbours for this purpose? It seems that section 18 envisages two or more harbours in close geographical proximity although not necessarily contiguous to each other. Perhaps the typical group are the harbours in an estuary and the five harbour reorganization schemes which have been made each of which amalgamated the harbours in a major estuary—the Forth, Tyne, Medway, Humber and Southampton. It seems probable however that a scheme under section 18 could almagamate harbours on the coast within, say 15 or 20 miles of each other—but probably not harbours 50 miles apart and certainly not an arbitrary group of harbours scattered around the coastline.

337. A harbour reorganization scheme may provide for the transfer either to one of the harbour authorities concerned or to a new body constituted by the scheme (whichever is to be the harbour authority for the amalgamated group of harbours) of powers and duties conferred by statutory provisions of local application on the harbour authority for any of the harbours in question for the purposes of that harbour, together with that authority's interests in property related to such powers and duties.

338. A scheme may also provide for appropriate transfers of other powers and duties under statutory provisions of local application and interests in property. In particular, a harbour reorganization scheme may provide for the transfer of the statutory powers and duties and the interests in property of a local lighthouse authority (not being a harbour authority) relating to any of the harbours in the group and of interests in property used by a person other than one of the harbour authorities concerned for carrying out harbour operations at any of those harbours (if a scheme does provide for the transfer of interests in property used for the purposes last mentioned it must also provide for the payment of compensation in respect of the transfer).

339. A harbour reorganization scheme may also provide for transferring staff and preserving or otherwise securing pension rights (and by virtue of section 43(3) of the Docks and Harbours Act 1966 may for the latter purpose repeal or amend general legislation) and may include such ancillary provisions as appear to the Secretary of State to be necessary or expedient, including provisions repealing or amending any statutory provision of local application affecting all or any of the harbours concerned. By virtue of section 42 of the Docks and Harbours Act 1966 a harbour reorganization scheme may include provisions for most of the purposes for which provision may be made by a harbour revision order.

340. The procedure for making harbour revision and empowerment orders is prescribed by Schedule 3 to the Harbours Act (Schedule 3 has been substantially amended by the Transport Act 1981—see in particular paragraph 14(4) of

Schedule 5 and paragraphs 4 and 12 of Schedule 6 to the 1981 Act) and by the Harbour Works (Assessment of Environmental Effects) Regulations 1988 made under section 2 of the European Communities Act 1972 to implement the European Communities Directive on Environmental Assessment in relation to works authorized by harbour revision and empowerment orders in England and Wales. The main features of this procedure are as follows—

(a) In the case of an order for which application is made to the Secretary of State the application must be accompanied by not less than six copies of a draft of the proposed order and not less than six copies of any map or maps which, if the order is made in the form of the draft, will be required to be annexed to it. If the Secretary of State considers that an application for an order relating to a harbour in England or Wales is made in relation to a project which falls within Annex 1 to the European Communities Directive on Environmental Assessment (the construction of a trading port which permits the passage of vessels of over 1,350 tonnes) or Annex 2 to that Directive (the construction of any other harbour or the modification of a project included in Annex 1) and, in the latter case, that the characteristics of the project require that an environmental impact assessment should be made, he must direct the applicant to carry out such an assessment and supply him with the relevant information in accordance with the new paragraph 1A inserted in Schedule 3 by the Harbour Works (Assessment of Environmental Effects) Regulations 1988. (Since all Scottish harbour revision and empowerment orders are subject to special parliamentary procedure it was considered that this automatic parliamentary scrutiny excluded the application of the Directive in their case.) The applicant is required, as a condition precedent to the Secretary of State taking further steps in the matter, to publish and serve notices in accordance with paragraph 3 of Schedule 3 and to comply with the requirements of paragraph 1A if they are applicable. If an environmental assessment is required the Secretary of State must furnish such bodies appearing to him to have environmental responsibilities as he thinks fit with any information supplied to him under paragraph 1A and to consult such bodies. In the case of an order which the Secretary of State proposes to make of his own motion the Secretary of State must publish and serve notice in accordance with paragraph 7 of Schedule 3. In either case there is a right to object to the Secretary of State within the period of 42 days from the date of the first publication of the advertisement or of the service of the notice as the case may be.

(b) If an objection is made and not withdrawn, the Secretary of State, unless he decides that the application shall not proceed further, is required to cause an inquiry to be held unless he considers that it is frivolous or too trivial to warrant the holding of an inquiry. If an objection relates only to a provision authorizing the compulsory acquisition of land the Secretary of State may, instead of causing an inquiry to be held, give the objector an opportunity of appearing before, and being heard by, a person appointed by the Secretary of State (affording the like opportunities to the applicant for the order and any other person to whom he considers it expedient to do so). The Secretary of State may disregard an objection to an application for, or proposal to make, a harbour revision or empowerment order unless it states the grounds on which it is made and may also disregard an objection so far as regards the inclusion in the draft order of a provision authorizing the compulsory acquisition of land if he is satisfied that it relates exclusively to matters which can be dealt with by the tribunal by whom compensation in respect of the acquisition will fall to be assessed in default of agreement.

(c) After considering the objections (if any) made and not withdrawn, any information supplied under paragraph 1A and the report of any person who held an inquiry and of any person appointed to hear an objector, the Secretary of State, unless he decides not to make the order, may make it in the form proposed or applied for or subject to such modification as he thinks fit. If he proposes to make an order with modifications which appear to him substantially to affect the character of the order he is required to take such steps as appear to him to be reasonably practicable for informing persons likely to be concerned (and in particular, if the order has been applied for, the applicant) and must not make the order until such period for consideration of, and comment upon, the proposed modifications as he thinks reasonable has elapsed. The Secretary of State is precluded from modifying an order so as to authorize the compulsory acquisition of land that was not described in the draft submitted to him unless all persons interested consent.

(d) When a harbour revision or empowerment order has been made the applicant or, in the case of an order made by the Secretary of State of his own motion, the Secretary of State is required to publish and serve notice stating that the order has been made, whether it is potentially subject to special parliamentary procedure as mentioned in paragraph 343 *post* and, if not, the date on which it came, or will come, into operation. The notice must name a place where a copy of the order may be inspected at all reasonable hours. Where an order which was potentially subject to special parliamentary procedure does not, in the event, become so, the Secretary of State must publish a notice stating that the order is not so subject and indicating the date on which it came, or will come, into operation. If works authorized by a harbour revision order have been the subject of an environmental assessment the Secretary of State must, as soon as may be after the order has been made, publish in any such manner as he thinks fit his decision whether or not to make the order.

**341.** The procedure for the submission and confirmation of harbour reorganization schemes is prescribed by Schedule 4 to the Harbours Act as amended by section 42(2) and (3) of the Docks and Harbours Act 1966 and paragraph 6(6) and (7) of Schedule 6 to the Transport Act 1981. The main features of this procedure are as follows—

(a) In the case of a scheme submitted to the Secretary of State by a harbour authority or authorities the first step after the submission of the scheme is for the Secretary of State to decide whether or not it should proceed. If he decides that the scheme should proceed he is required to publish and serve notices in accordance with paragraph 2 of Schedule 4 as he is also required to do where he proposes to make a scheme of his own motion.

(b) The provisions as respects objections, inquiries and hearings are substantially the same as those contained in Schedule 3 in relation to harbour revision and empowerment orders. The Secretary of State may disregard an objection so far as regards the inclusion in the scheme of a provision transferring interests in property if he is satisfied that the objection relates exclusively to matters in respect of which compensation falls to be provided under the scheme and the scheme is so framed as to enable those matters to be properly dealt with.

(c) The Secretary of State, after considering any outstanding objections and the report of any person who held an inquiry, may, if he then decides to make, or as the case may be, confirm, the scheme, make or confirm it by order either without modifications or with such modifications as he sees fit. If the Secretary of State proposes to make or confirm the scheme with modifications which appear to him substantially to affect the character of the scheme similar provisions apply as in a case where he proposes to make a harbour revision or empowerment order with modifications which appear to him substantially to affect its character. The Secretary of State cannot make or confirm a scheme subject to a modification which provides for the transfer of an interest of a person in property which was not described in the scheme as proposed to be made or submitted as being property in which interests of that person were subject to be transferred unless the person in question gives his consent.

(d) As soon as may be after a harbour reorganization scheme has been confirmed or made by the Secretary of State he must publish notice that it has been confirmed or made naming a place where a copy of the scheme as confirmed or made may be inspected at all reasonable hours and must serve a copy of the scheme as confirmed or made on each harbour authority on whom a copy of the scheme as submitted to, or proposed to be made by, the Secretary of State was served under paragraph 2 of Schedule 4.

342. In relation to harbour revision and empowerment orders and harbour reorganization schemes dealing with harbours in Scotland, the Secretary of State, under section 47(3) of the Harbours Act, may direct that any inquiry which may be required under Schedule 3 or Schedule 4 to the Harbours Act, as the case may be, shall be held by Commissioners under the Private Legislation Procedure (Scotland)

Act 1936. Section 2, as read with section 10 of the Statutory Orders (Special Procedure) Act 1945, requires such an inquiry to be held in any case if there are outstanding objections so unless the Secretary of State gives a direction under section 47(3) in relation to a Scottish harbour revision or empowerment order or harbour reorganization scheme to which there are outstanding objections, it seems that two inquiries would have to be held. In practice, such a direction is always given. If the Secretary of State is not prepared to accept recommendations made by Commissioners who hold an inquiry into objections to a Scottish harbour revision or empowerment order or harbour reorganization scheme that the order or scheme should not be made or confirmed or should be modified he may present to Parliament a Bill for the confirmation of the order or scheme. The procedure on such a Bill is the same as that provided by section 9 of the Private Legislation Procedure (Scotland) Act 1936 in relation to the Confirmation Bills referred to in that Act.

343. Originally, harbour revision and empowerment orders and harbour reorganization schemes, after being made or confirmed, were in all cases subject to special parliamentary procedure. This is still the position as respects harbour revision and empowerment orders relating to harbours in Scotland and all harbour reorganization schemes. But, by virtue of section 18 of, and paragraph 4 of Schedule 6 to, the Transport Act 1981, a harbour revision or empowerment order relating to a harbour in England or Wales is now subject to special parliamentary procedure only if—

    (a) at the time when the order is made there is an outstanding objection to the order (including for this purpose a comment on a proposed modification of the order which, in the Secretary of State's opinion, would, if duly raised in connection with a provision of the original draft order, have amounted to an objection); and

    (b) following the service of notice of the making of the order by the Secretary of State on the outstanding objector, the objector, within 28 days after the date of the notice, gives notice to the Secretary of State that he maintains his opposition to the order.

Corresponding provision was not made for Scottish orders. Having regard to the Scottish provisions of the Statutory Orders (Special Procedure) Act 1945, including section 2 as read with section 10 of that Act referred to in the preceding paragraph, the amendments required for the purpose would have been long and complex.

344. Special parliamentary procedure is prescribed by the Statutory Orders (Special Procedure) Acts 1945 and 1965. The first step in this procedure is for the Secretary of State to lay before Parliament the order as made by him, after publishing the requisite notice of his intention to do so. Within the period of 21 days beginning with the day on which the order is laid before Parliament petitions may be presented against it and these stand referred to the Lord Chairman of Committees and the Chairman of Ways and Means ("the Chairmen"). Such a petition may pray for particular amendments to be made in the order ("a petition for

amendment") or may be a prayer against the order generally ("a petition of general objection").

**345.** As soon as practicable after the expiration of the period of 21 days during which petitions may be presented the Chairmen consider all petitions and, if they are satisfied with respect to any petition that the provisions of the Statutory Orders (Special Procedure) Acts and of the Standing Orders of each House have been complied with, they are required to certify that the petition is proper to be received and is a petition for amendment or a petition of general objection as the case may be.

**346.** The next step is for the Chairmen to report to Parliament whether any petitions have been presented against the order and, if so, which of them have been certified as proper to be received and as petitions for amendment and petitions of general objection respectively. Their report is required to be laid before both Houses of Parliament.

**347.** If either House, within the period of 21 days beginning with the date on which the Chairmen's report is laid before it ("the resolution period") resolves that the order be annulled it thereupon becomes void. If within the resolution period no such resolution is passed then (subject to what is said below about Scottish orders) any petitions which have been certified as proper to be received stand referred to a joint committee of both Houses except that either House may resolve within the resolution period that a petition of general objection shall not be so referred. If neither House resolves that the order be annulled and no petitions stand referred to a joint committee as mentioned above the order comes into operation at the expiration of the resolution period or on such later date, if any, as may be specified in the order.

**348.** In the case of a Scottish order a petition certified as proper to be received does not stand referred to a joint committee of both Houses unless either House orders that it shall be so referred. This provision has regard to the fact that the order will already have been considered by a panel of Commissioners consisting wholly or mainly of Members of Parliament.

**349.** Where a petition against an order stands referred to a joint committee of both Houses the order in question also stands so referred for the purpose of the consideration of the petition. The committee may report the order either without amendment or with such amendments as they think expedient to give effect, either in whole or in part, to the petition and with such consequential amendments as they think proper. Where the petition is a petition of general objection the committee may nevertheless report the order with amendments if they think it right to do so but if in their opinion the order ought not to take effect they must report that it be not approved.

**350.** The report of the joint committee is laid before both Houses of Parliament. If the order is reported without amendment it comes into effect on the date on which it is so laid or on such later date if any as may be specified in the order.

**351.** If the order is reported with amendments it comes into effect on such date as the Secretary of State may by notice determine unless he considers it inexpedient for the order to take effect as amended by the committee. In that event he may either withdraw the order or may present to Parliament a Bill for the confirmation of the order.

352. If the joint committee report that the order be not approved it is also open to the Secretary of State to present to Parliament a Bill for the confirmation of the order.

353. The procedure on the Bills referred to in paragraphs 350 and 351 *ante* is of a special character and is prescribed by section 6(4) and (5) respectively of the Statutory Orders (Special Procedure) Act 1945.

354. Under section 44 of the Harbours Act 1964 as amended by section 44 of the Docks and Harbours Act 1966 and set out in Schedule 2 to that Act (and as further amended by the Transport Act 1981), a harbour revision or empowerment order or a harbour reorganization scheme, unless confirmed by Act of Parliament under the provisions of the Statutory Orders (Special Procedure) Act, may, within six weeks from the date when the order or scheme becomes operative, be challenged in, as the case may be, the High Court or the Court of Session on the ground that there was no power to make the order or confirm the scheme, or that a requirement of the Harbours Act 1964 (which is deemed to include Part III of the Docks and Harbours Act 1966) was not complied with in relation to the order or scheme. The court may suspend the operation of the order or scheme or of any provision thereof either generally or so far as may be necessary for the protection of the interests of the applicant until the final determination of the proceedings and, if satisfied that there was no power to make the order or confirm the scheme or that the interests of the applicant have been substantially prejudiced by a failure to comply with a requirement of the Harbours Act, may quash the order or scheme or any provision thereof either generally or so far as may be necessary to protect the applicant's interests. Section 44 provides the only method for challenging the legality of a harbour revision or empowerment order or harbour reorganization scheme. The section states that, except as therein provided, such an order or scheme shall not, either before or after it is made or confirmed, be challenged in any legal proceedings whatever. It appears from the case of *Smith* v. *East Elloe RDC*[1] in which the effect of the similar provisions limiting the right to question compulsory purchase orders were considered, that this means that an order or scheme cannot even be challenged on the ground of bad faith, at any rate after the six weeks period has expired.

355. Comparing the procedure for subordinate legislation under the Harbours Act with the Private Bill procedure, the former has the advantage that, since a harbour revision or empowerment order or harbour reorganization scheme may be initiated at any time, it is not tied to the same extent to the parliamentary timetable (although this of course is relevant to special parliamentary procedure). The Harbours Act procedure should also be quicker and sometimes is. An unopposed harbour revision order can go through, from submission to coming into operation, in

1. *Smith* v. *East Elloe RDC* [1956] A.C. 736.

about six months. Often however, and usually when the order or scheme is opposed, the Harbours Act procedure takes longer than a Private Bill and the timing is certainly much less predictable. It is clearly easier for many people to object and put forward their arguments under the Harbours Act procedure, which provides for a local inquiry, than it is in relation to a Private Bill.

**356.** The Transport Act 1981 conferred a new power on the Secretary of State to make orders about appointments to the boards of port trusts. Section 15A of the Harbours Act 1964, inserted in that Act by section 18 of, and paragraph 5 of Schedule 6 to, the Transport Act 1981, authorizes the Secretary of State by order, where he is required to appoint a member or members of a port trust, to abolish any such power of appointment, except where this is a power to appoint the chairman of the harbour authority in question, or provide for the power of appointment to be exercised by someone else. An order under section 15A may not, however, be made with respect to the constitution of a port trust where all the members, apart from *ex officio* and co-opted members, are appointed by the Secretary of State. This power to reduce Ministerial appointments does not, therefore, in practice apply in relation to major port trusts. Before making an order under section 15A of the Harbours Act the Secretary of State must consult the harbour authority concerned and such other persons affected, or bodies representative of such persons, as he thinks fit. The Transport Act 1981 extends to orders under section 15A of the Harbours Act the provisions of section 44 of that Act limiting the right to challenge orders, etc., in legal proceedings and applies to such orders the provisions of section 54(2) of the Harbours Act so that they are subject to annulment by either House of Parliament.

# CHAPTER 11

# CARGO HANDLING, ETC.

357. The "harbour operations" (defined in section 57(1) of the Harbours Act 1964) which a harbour authority are authorized by section 38(2) of the Docks and Harbours Act 1966 to carry out, include—

(a) the warehousing, sorting, weighing or handling of goods on harbour land (defined in section 57(1) of the Harbours Act 1964 as land adjacent to a harbour and occupied wholly or mainly for the purposes of activities there carried on) or at a wharf (defined in section 57(1) as any wharf, quay, pier, jetty or other place at which sea-going ships can ship or unship goods or embark or disembark passengers);

(b) the movement of goods or passengers within the limits within which the harbour authority have jurisdiction or on harbour land;

(c) in relation to a harbour other than a wharf (i.e., the water area)—
  (i) the loading or unloading of goods, or the embarking or disembarking of passengers, in or from a ship which is in the harbour or the approaches thereto, and
  (ii) the lighterage or handling of goods in the harbour;

(d) in relation to a wharf, the loading or unloading of goods, or the embarking or disembarking of passengers, at the wharf in or from a ship.

358. Many harbour authorities already possessed powers for these purposes under their special legislation before the commencement of the Docks and Harbours Act 1966 but cargo handling activities, and particularly the loading and unloading of goods at wharves, have in recent years become a much more important activity of harbour authorities.

359. Section 37 of the 1966 Act authorized harbour authorities (other than harbour authorities for nationalized harbours which already had powers for the purpose under the Transport Act 1962) to acquire by agreement any business or undertaking consisting wholly or mainly of the carrying out of harbour operations or so much of any business as consists of the carrying out of such operations. The section also authorized harbour authorities to subscribe for or acquire any securities of a body corporate wholly or mainly engaged, or proposing to become wholly or mainly engaged, in carrying out harbour operations. The special legislation of some harbour authorities already included similar powers. Associated British Ports

101

has somewhat wider powers under paragraphs 24 and 25 of Schedule 3 to the Transport Act 1981.

360. Section 37 relates, in practice, mainly to companies carrying out cargo handling and warehousing activities. In recent years a number of harbour authorities have acquired all or most of the share capital in such companies and many cargo handling companies, particularly at major harbours, are now therefore subsidiaries of the harbour authority.

361. Most harbour authorities provide some warehousing or storage facilities. In carrying out this activity a harbour authority have the same common law duty as any other bailee for reward to exercise reasonable care in respect of the goods and the burden of proof that they have complied with this duty rests on them. This common law duty may be modified by contract and most harbour authorities make their acceptance of goods for storage subject to terms and conditions. However, under the Unfair Contract Terms Act 1977, any such terms and conditions must be fair and reasonable within the meaning of that Act.[1]

362. The special legislation of many harbour authorities provides that the authority shall not be responsible for the safety of any goods deposited in any part of their docks or land adjoining the harbour which is not specifically set apart by the authority for the purpose of warehousing. Such a provision would exclude liability as bailee on the part of the harbour authority but it seems doubtful whether it would exclude liability for damage to goods caused by the negligence of the harbour authority's employees (although the onus would then of course be on the owners of the goods to prove negligence).

363. A unique feature of the ports industry is the Dock Labour Scheme originally introduced to ameliorate, and in its latest form, coupled with Part 1 of the Docks and Harbours Act 1966 referred to below, to abolish the old casual system of employing dock workers. The Dock Labour scheme at present in force is the Dock Workers Employment Scheme 1967 made by the (then) Minister of Labour under the Dock Workers (Regulation of Employment) Act 1946. If and when the new Dock Labour Scheme made under the Dock Work Regulation Act 1976, is, in accordance with that Act, approved in draft by resolution of each House of Parliament, the 1946 Scheme will gradually be replaced by the new Scheme in accordance with the provisions of the 1976 Act.

364. The Dock Workers Employment Scheme 1967 applies to a number of specified ports which include most major commercial harbours, but a significant number of harbours, including several important commercial ports, are not within the Scheme. At each port to which the Scheme relates it applies to classes or descriptions of dock work and dock worker defined by reference to the provisions of certain former dock labour or port registration schemes. The work to which the current Scheme applies is therefore by no means uniform as between the ports to

---

1. For a recent case in which a harbour authority's conditions for bailment of goods were discussed see the *Singer Company (UK) Limited and Singer do Brazil Industria Comercio Ltda.* v. *Tees and Hartlepool Port Authority* [1988] 1 F.T.L.R. 442.

which it relates. But the Dock Workers Employment Scheme 1967 provides (consistently with the definition of "dock worker" in the Dock Workers (Regulation of Employment Act 1946)) that the Scheme shall not apply to a dock worker at any port unless he is employed or registered for employment in, or in the vicinity of, that port on work in connection with the loading, unloading, movement or storage of cargoes, or work in connection with the preparation of ships or other vessels for the receipt or discharge of cargoes or for leaving port.

**365.** The Dock Workers Employment Scheme 1967 is administered by the National Dock Labour Board (NDLB) which has now been reconstituted on a somewhat wider basis than previously under the Dock Work Regulation Act 1976. The Board now consists of 14 members, eight of whom are representative members appointed by the Secretary of State for Employment on the nomination of the National Joint Council for the Port Transport Industry, four to represent dock employers (who are now to a large extent, although by no means exclusively, harbour authorities) and four to represent dock workers. The chairman, vice-chairman and four other members are appointed by the Secretary of State for Employment after consultation with the National Joint Council, the TUC and the CBI. Also participating in the administration of the 1967 Scheme are the Local Dock Labour Boards established under that Scheme which consist of equal numbers of representatives of dock employers and dock workers and are mainly responsible for the administration of the Scheme at port level.

**366.** The objects of the Scheme are stated to be to ensure greater regularity of employment for dock workers and to secure that an adequate number of dock workers is available for the efficient performance of dock work. At each port to which the Scheme applies the local board keeps a register of dock workers and dock employers. Only an employer whose name is on the register (and the NDLB) may employ persons to do work which is dock work at the port in question and, generally, a registered employer is prohibited from employing on dock work anyone who is not a registered dock worker. However, the Scheme provides for the local board to authorize a registered employer to employ a person who is not a registered dock worker to do dock work in special circumstances.

**367.** The Scheme requires the local boards to allocate registered dock workers to registered employers as permanent workers. Any registered dock worker who is not so allocated is known as a temporarily unattached worker and is employed and controlled, on behalf of the NDLB, by the local board who may allocate him for temporary employment by a registered dock employer. Where there is no work available with a registered employer for a temporarily unattached worker the Scheme provides that he is to be paid by the NDLB (via the local board) the amounts agreed for the time being between representatives of workers and employers. However, in practice, it has been agreed that a registered dock worker will always be allocated to a registered employer. The temporarily unattached worker is therefore now a rarity. Many dock employers have been compelled to employ more dock workers than they need or can afford. Where the harbour authority at a port is a registered dock employer it has been the practice for the local board to allocate any surplus dock workers to them. The Scheme enables dock workers to be transferred from one dock employer to another with the consent of the local board and, with a view to ensuring the fullest possible use of the workers available, for temporary transfers under the supervision of the local board.

**368.** The Scheme requires both registered dock workers and registered dock employers to comply with the obligations of the Scheme. If a registered employer fails to carry out the provisions of the Scheme the NDLB may suspend him from the Scheme for such period as the Board may specify in a written notice given to the employer in question and his name is removed from the register during the period of suspension. A registered employer who has been given notice that he will be suspended from the Scheme may appeal to the NDLB who are required to refer the matter to the Secretary of State for determination.

**369.** The Scheme authorizes a registered employer, in a case where a registered dock worker who has been allocated to him has, in the employer's view, been guilty of misconduct which is sufficiently serious to warrant his summary dismissal, to terminate the worker's contract without notice. The dock worker concerned thereupon becomes a temporarily unattached worker in the employment of the NDLB and the local board is required to investigate the matter. After doing so, the local board may—

(a) dismiss the worker summarily;

(b) give him written notice to determine his employment (the length of such notice depends on how long he has been a registered dock worker);

(c) suspend him from the Scheme for a period not exceeding five consecutive working days and thereafter return him to his former employer; or

(d) reinstate him with his former employer and, if they think fit, also direct the former employer to pay such sums in respect of the worker's wages since his dismissal as the local board may determine, either to the worker or to the local board or to both.

If the local board decides to dismiss the worker summarily or give him notice to terminate his employment or suspend him from the Scheme as mentioned above the worker may appeal to an appeal tribunal. Such a tribunal consists of not less than three and not more than five persons, not being members or deputy members of the local board, appointed by the local board from persons nominated by the Local Joint Committee or Committees of the National Joint Council for the Port Transport Industry. In determining the appeal, the tribunal has the same powers as respects the dock worker in question as the local board had except that the tribunal cannot impose on him a penalty which is more severe than that imposed by the local board. A registered employer may also, where in his opinion a registered dock worker who has been allocated to him has been guilty of misconduct which is not sufficiently serious to merit summary dismissal, suspend the dock worker for up to five consecutive working days. The worker may appeal against such suspension to the local board.

**370.** The Scheme provides that (even in the absence of misconduct) a registered dock employer may, *with the consent of the local board*, terminate the employment of a registered dock worker who has been allocated to his employment by giving him in writing not less than the appropriate period of notice. This is one week's notice if the worker has been a registered dock worker for less than two years, two weeks' notice if he has been a registered dock worker for at least two, but less than five, years, and four weeks' notice if he has been a registered dock worker for five years or more. Where a registered dock worker is dismissed in this way he either becomes a temporarily unattached worker employed by the NDLB or has his name removed from the register at the discretion of the local board. A registered dock worker who receives notice to terminate his employment as mentioned above may, however, appeal to an appeal tribunal unless the notice was given on the ground that he falls within a class or description of dock workers whose names are to be removed from the register in order to reduce its size. In such a case, however, he may still appeal on the ground that he does not belong to the class or description in question.

**371.** An important function of the NDLB under the Scheme, and one which cannot be delegated to local boards, is "determining and keeping under review in consultation with local dock labour boards the size from time to time of the registers of dock workers and the increases or reductions to be made in the numbers in any such registers having regard to all the circumstances in the port in relation to which the registers are kept". It is not, however, clear that the NDLB have any power to terminate the employment of registered dock workers who are employed by registered employers. As indicated above, such termination requires notice to be given by the employer with the consent of the local board (except that a registered dock worker may himself terminate his employment with the NDLB or with a registered employer as the case may be by giving at least seven days' notice in writing to the local board or his employer as the case may be). No doubt the absence of a right to appeal to an appeals tribunal in a case where notice has been given on the ground that the dock worker falls within a class or description of dock workers whose names are to be removed from the register in order to reduce its size envisages that an initiative has been taken by the NDLB. The NDLB or local board may terminate the employment of a temporarily unattached worker by giving him not less than the appropriate period of notice as indicated above.

**372.** Other important functions of the NDLB under the Scheme, which may be delegated to local boards, include making provision for the training and welfare of registered dock workers, administering pension schemes and compensating under the terms of any national or local agreement dock workers whose names are removed from the register of dock workers either at their own request or otherwise. The administration of the Scheme is financed by a levy imposed by the NDLB on registered dock employers. Under the Dock Work Regulation Act 1976 as amended by the Ports (Financial Assistance) Act 1981 the NDLB may borrow such sums as they require for performing their functions from the Secretary of State or with his consent from other persons. The aggregate amount outstanding by way of principal of money borrowed by the NDLB must not exceed £50 million (which figure may be increased up to £90 million by an order made by the

Secretary of State; before such an order can be made the draft must be laid before, and approved by a resolution of, the House of Commons).

**373.** Under the Dock Work Regulation Act 1976 the NDLB have the general duty of keeping under review various matters relevant to what work should be classified as dock work and to the appropriate size and deployment of the dock labour force and of submitting reports and proposals for action to the Secretary of State for Employment. In respect of these and cognate matters the NDLB are required to maintain regular consultation with persons appearing to the NDLB to be concerned. The NDLB are also responsible for advising the Secretary of State on the matters in question.

**374.** The Dock Work Regulation Act 1976 provides for the classification of work as dock work for the purposes of the new Dock Labour Scheme which under that Act is to be brought into force (port by port). It is anticipated that the application of the new Scheme, if it comes into force, will be considerably wider, both as respects the ports, and the nature of the work, to which it will relate, than the current Scheme. However, the 1976 Act generally limits the application of the new Scheme (except in relation to premises where the 1967 Scheme applies or is treated as applying by custom and practice) to places within half a mile (in a direct line) of a harbour or the nearest harbour land adjacent to a harbour ("harbour" and "harbour land" having the same meaning as in the Harbours Act 1964). The Act also excludes certain important categories of work, including the unloading of most fishing vessels and the loading, unloading and storage of oil and oil-derived liquids, natural gas, liquid chemicals and liquified gases, from classification as dock work. The NDLB are required to make recommendations to the Secretary of State for Employment about what work should be classified as dock work. In relation to the classification of work which is not dock work for the purposes of the 1967 Scheme (or treated as such) they must have regard to certain specified considerations and consider representations from employers and trade unions. The activation of the provisions of the Dock Work Regulation Act 1976 and the bringing into operation of the new Dock Labour Scheme under that Act have now been in suspense for a number of years.

**375.** Part I of the Docks and Harbours Act 1966 established a licensing system for employers of dock workers at ports specified in the Act which corresponded to the ports to which the Dock Workers Employment Scheme 1967 applied. The licensing authorities under the Act are harbour authorities for such ports. In most cases the licensing authority at a port are the harbour authority for that port but in a few cases the licensing authority are the harbour authority for a neighbouring (larger) port.

**376.** Part I of the Docks and Harbours Act 1966 prohibits the employment of dock workers at any port to which the Act applies (except by the NDLB or the licensing authority) unless a licence for the purpose has been granted by the licensing authority. A licence must be granted for a period of not less than three years and not more than seven years and may impose conditions for various specified purposes which include restricting the employment of dock workers by the applicant to a specified berth or a specified part of the port and restricting the operations in which the applicant may engage. Before reaching a decision on an application for a licence a licensing authority are required to consult the NDLB. A licensing authority are prohibited from employing dock workers at a port for which they are the licensing authority unless they have made a proposal for the purpose.

**377.** The Act specifies certain considerations to which a licensing authority are required to have regard in deciding whether or not to grant a licence and the terms of a licence. These include the desirability of securing that the number of employers of dock workers (including the licensing authority) in the port in question is brought or kept within a limit which in the opinion of the licensing authority is the maximum number which is compatible with the efficient working of the port.

**378.** The Act includes provisions for licensing authorities to renew licences subject to the same procedure as applies in relation to the granting of a licence and to transfer, vary, and, in certain circumstances, revoke, licences. There are rights of appeal to the Secretary of State against decisions of a licensing authority under the Act in relation to the licensing of port employers and against a proposal by a licensing authority to employ dock workers if they have not previously done so or to employ dock workers in a part of the port where they were not previously entitled to do so. Under section 52 of the 1966 Act the Secretary of State must direct an inquiry to be held in connection with the consideration and determination by him of appeals and objections under Part I of the Act unless he obtains consent in writing to dispense with the inquiry from all persons who, by regulations made under section 52, are entitled to appear at the inquiry. These persons are currently prescribed by the Licensing of Port Employers (Inquiries Procedure) Regulations 1967 and comprise the employer whose appeal occasioned the inquiry, the licensing authority and the NDLB.

**379.** A person whose application for renewal of a licence has been refused is entitled to be compensated by the licensing authority. The measure of compensation is any diminution in the value of the assets of his dock business in the port in question (being the difference between their market value immediately before the refusal and their market value immediately after) and any expenditure, other than certain tax payments, incurred in winding up that business which is directly attributable to the refusal. In order to qualify for compensation a person must have employed dock workers in the port in question for the minimum time specified in section 14 of the 1966 Act. Where a licensing authority pay compensation for refusing to renew a licence they may recover the whole or part of the amount by means of a levy on other licensed employers at the port.

**380.** Section 12(1) of the Dock Work Regulation Act 1976 provides that an order by the Secretary of State for Employment bringing the new Dock Labour Scheme into force at any port to which Part I of the Docks and Harbours Act 1966 applies shall comprise an order removing that port from the scope of the 1966 Act. If and when the new Dock Labour Scheme has been approved in draft by each House of Parliament the licensing provisions of Part I of the 1966 Act will therefore, subsequently, over a period cease to have effect. As soon as the Secretary of

State is satisfied that the 1967 Dock Labour Scheme is no longer in operation for any part of Great Britain he may by order repeal, *inter alia*, Part I of the Docks and Harbours Act 1966.

**381.** With regard to the safety of cargo handling, the Docks Regulations have been the principal legislation by which health and safety in ports and harbours in Great Britain, particularly in relation to cargo handling, has been regulated for the greater part of this century.

**382.** In 1899 two factory inspectors surveyed conditions in the nation's docks and wharves and their report led to the adoption of the first set of Docks Regulations in 1904. Made under the Factory and Workshop Act 1901, they were almost certainly the first such provisions adopted anywhere in the world.

**383.** The regulations of 1904 were superseded by the Docks Regulations 1925 which had a wider scope and included first-aid provisions.

**384.** Dock safety was one of the first matters considered by the International Labour Organization (ILO) which was established to deal with international matters concerned with employment. Convention 32, which was adopted in 1932, was concerned with the protection of dockers against accidents and it was quickly ratified by the United Kingdom Government and reflected in a further set of Docks Regulations which were made in 1934.

**385.** Like their predecessors, the new regulations applied to Great Britain and in 1936 were reflected in a similar set of regulations covering Northern Ireland (no such provisions have been made in respect of the Channel Islands or the Isle of Man).

**386.** Each of the sets of regulations was principally a set of work rules covering cargo handling and the lifting machinery then in use, both on the ship and on shore. The nature of such work was based to a large extent on manual operations and had changed very little over the years. Thus, the legal provisions equally had changed only in the light of experience.

**387.** However, the rapid mechanization and extensive changes in cargo packaging and handling which took place from the 1960s onward resulted in a revolution in port operations which had the effect of rendering the old laws obsolete, more because of what was not covered rather than because the actual provisions had become obsolete.

**388.** This situation was recognized by ILO, who adopted a new Convention, Number 152, in 1979. This Convention, "Health and Safety in Dockwork", not only reflected the new conditions and methods, but, in recognition of the fact that change was continuing, was drafted in more general terms, thus making it more flexible for the future.

**389.** With regard to the implementation of this Convention in Great Britain, it was decided that, contrary to what had been the position before, the new legislation would be split between a new set of Docks Regulations dealing with activities on the shore and use of equipment on the ship and Merchant Shipping Regulations which would cover the provision of safety equipment, plant, etc., on the ship.

**390.** The main new shoreside provisions, the Docks Regulations 1988, were made under the Health and Safety at Work, etc. Act 1974 and deal comprehensively with modern-day port operations. They are drafted with the future as well as present operations in mind, and cover such facets as planning, lighting, access by land and by water, rescue and emergency arrangements, hatches, training, fitness and competence of drivers, maintenance and use of vehicles, testing, examination, marking and use of lifting plant, records, confined spaces and protective equipment. These regulations are health and safety regulations within the meaning of the Health and Safety at Work, etc. Act 1974 and are enforceable as such under the provisions of that Act.

**391.** In accordance with section 16 of the 1974 Act, an approved code of practice and a guidance note were also published at the same time to make the intentions clear and to detail how the regulatory requirements can be applied in the complex circumstances of a modern port. With a few exceptions, the Docks Regulations 1988 came into force on 1 January 1989, replacing the 1934 regulations (except for Part I of those regulations mentioned below).

**392.** Also made and coming into force at the same time, the Loading and Unloading of Fishing Vessels Regulations 1988, deal with the landing of wet fish across quays and the fuelling, provisioning and icing of vessels. They replace the previous provisions of Part I of the 1934 regulations.

**393.** The Docks Regulations 1988 are complemented by regulations under the Merchant Shipping Act 1979 dealing with the provision of safe equipment and working conditions on board ship.

# CHAPTER 12

# PILOTAGE

## Introduction

**394.** On 1 October 1988 Part I of the Pilotage Act 1987 came into force. 1 October 1988 is therefore "the appointed day" for the purposes of that Act. On that day the legal structure of the marine pilotage service based on the Pilotage Act 1913 which had lasted, with a few changes made by the Merchant Shipping Act 1979, for more than 60 years, was swept away and pilotage became a function of harbour authorities.

**395.** The introduction of a basically different, and much simpler, legal structure means that some of the legal authorities on marine pilotage are no longer relevant or must be treated with caution.

**396.** Before discussing the new Act it seems pertinent to say a little about the statutory definition of "pilot" which remains the same. It also seems necessary to describe briefly the legal structure of pilotage which existed before 1 October 1988, since the Pilotage Act 1987 refers to this in a number of contexts.

**397.** The expression "Pilot" is defined in section 742 of the Merchant Shipping Act 1894. That definition is applied for the purposes of the Pilotage Act 1987 by section 31(1) of that Act and it applied for the purposes of the pilotage legislation in force before 1 October 1988.

**398.** A pilot is "any person not belonging to a ship who has the conduct thereof". This definition re-enacted verbatim that contained in the repealed Merchant Shipping Act 1854. Prior to that Act no statutory definition of the word "pilot" existed, but an authoritative opinion as to its meaning was given by Baron Tenterden, an eminent 18th century authority on maritime law, in a treatise on that subject. In it he stated:

The name of a pilot, or steersman, is applied either to a particular officer, serving on board a ship during the course of a voyage, and having the charge of the helm and the ship's route; or to a person taken on board at a particular place for the purpose of conducting a ship through a river, road, or channel, or from or into a port.[1]

---

1. Charles Abbott, *A Treatise of the Law relative to Merchant Ships and Seamen* (2nd edn., London, 1804), p. 167.

The second part of this definition was considered and held to be accurate by Hill, J., in *The Andoni*.[2]

399. In 1916 a case was brought under the Defence of the Realm (Consolidation) Regulations 1914. A Notice to Mariners made under those regulations stated that "all ships . . . whilst navigating in the waters from Gravesend to London Bridge, or vice versa, must be *conducted* by pilots licensed by the London Trinity House". In giving judgment, Bargreave Deane, J., interpreted the verb "to conduct" as follows:

> She took her pilot on board at Gravesend for the purpose of being "conducted" by him to London. I think the word "conducted" means that the pilot is in charge under the old system—that is in full charge—and entitled to all the assistance he can get from the master and crew. He is in command.[3]

In a later case brought under the same regulations this interpretation was reaffirmed by Pickford, L.J., who said:

> A regulation having a statutory force which provides that a ship is to be conducted by a pilot does not mean that she is to be navigated under his advice; it means she must be conducted by him . . . .[4]

The statutory definition of the word "pilot" was alluded to in a more recent case in the House of Lords. Counsel for the respondent had claimed that a vessel which under certain specified circumstances was "not deemed to be navigating in the District", was not therefore being piloted. Lord Widgery, C.J., concurred:

> . . . he [counsel for the respondent] contends that if a ship is not navigating then no question of her being piloted can arise. This part of his argument does not derive specifically from the terms of the statute but derives from a common and normal use of language. He says that before anyone can be a pilot, who is defined in section 742 of the Merchant Shipping Act, 1894, as "a person not belonging to a ship who has the conduct thereof", the ship must be navigating. The ship must be in a condition in which the pilot has some function to perform. Accordingly he argues that if by virtue of the byelaw this particular ship is not deemed to be navigating in the district at all, then no person in charge of her, be it the master or anyone else, can be a pilot within the meaning of legislation . . . I have come to the conclusion that Mr Stone's [counsel for the respondent] argument upon this is right.[5]

It would appear from these judgments, therefore, that a person can only come within the statutory definition of a pilot if he actually has the conduct of the vessel, the verb "to conduct" being synonymous with the verb "to navigate".

A definitive interpretation of the word "pilot" is also contained in the report of a Royal Commission published in 1968, which investigated all aspects of pilotage in Canada. The definition contained in the Canada Shipping Act 1952 is expressed in words identical to the definition contained in the Merchant Shipping Act 1894 and the Royal Commission's Report concurs with the general import of the

---

2. *The Andoni* (1918) 14 Asp. M.L.C. 326, at p. 328.
3. *The Nord* (1916) 13 Asp. M.L.C. 606, at p. 608.
4. *The Mickleham* [1918] P. 166 (C.A.), at p. 169.
5. *Babbs* v. *Press* [1971] 2 Lloyd's Rep. 383, at pp. 387, 388.

judicial pronouncements stated above. The report analyses the statutory definition of the word "pilot" as follows:

This is composed of two elements:
  (a) having the conduct of the ship, that is the action of navigating the ship;
  (b) not belonging to the ship, that is the relationship towards the ship.
The expression "having the conduct of the ship" is not defined and, therefore, it should be construed in its normal meaning, that is to have charge and control of navigation; in other words, of the movement of the vessel. Hence the substansive "pilot" is synonymous with "navigator" and the verb "to pilot" is equivalent to "to navigate" . . . The verb "to pilot" and the noun expressing the action of piloting, i.e. "pilotage" are synonymous with "to navigate a ship" and "the action of navigating a ship" . . . Therefore, to be a pilot as defined in the Act is not a question of qualification, profession, certificate or licence; it is the fact of actually navigating a vessel (and not of being capable or authorized to navigate a vessel). A pilot, whether licensed or not, ceases to be "pilot" when, for any reason, he is superseded by the Master or by the person in command. Similarly, if anyone is merely used as an adviser and is not entrusted with the navigation of the ship, he is not the pilot of that ship. Therefore the general provisions concerning pilots do not apply to him under such circumstances. The first component of the definition is, therefore, the ordinary sense of the term, i.e. the person who at a given moment is navigating the ship is the pilot at that time. It is by the second component of the definition that the legislature has restricted the general meaning of the term to those navigators who are not part of the normal complement of the crew. Therefore, a "pilot" as defined in the Act in addition to navigating the ship must also be a stranger as far as that ship is concerned.[6]

**400.** A clear understanding of the statutory definition of the word "pilot" is important when the subject of the master-pilot relationship is considered in Chapter 13.

### The legal structure of pilotage under the Pilotage Act 1983

**401.** The Pilotage Act 1983, most of which was repealed by the Pilotage Act 1987 on 1 October 1988 and the remaining provisions of which will be repealed when the Pilotage Commission has completed its functions under the Act of 1987 and is dissolved, consolidated the Pilotage Act 1913, the Pilotage Authorities (Limitation of Liability) Act 1936 and the pilotage provisions of the Merchant Shipping Act 1979.

**402.** The Pilotage Act 1983 reproduced most of the provisions of the Pilotage Act 1913 (which was implemented by pilotage orders made under that Act in the early 1920s). However, the Merchant Shipping Act 1979 has made some changes and modernized certain provisions. It made clear that pilots licensed by a pilotage authority (as to which see below) could also be employed by the authority although very few were, the great majority being self-employed on the rather special basis subsisting under the Pilotage Act 1983 and the orders and by-laws made thereunder.

**403.** The Merchant Shipping Act 1979 had established the Pilotage Commission, comprising representatives of licensed pilots, shipowners, harbour

6. CANADA. *Report of Royal Commission on Pilotage.* Ottawa, 1968, Part 1, pp. 23, 24.

authorities and pilotage authorities and other persons of relevant experience. It was mainly an advisory body but also had the important functions of considering pilotage charges and powers in certain circumstances to promote pilotage orders and by-laws to bring about changes in the organization of the pilotage service.

**404.** Under the Pilotage Act 1983 the local administration of pilotage was carried out by pilotage authorities. Each pilotage authority administered a pilotage district. Some pilotage authorities administered more than one district and one authority, London Trinity House, was responsible for over 40. There were in total 94 pilotage districts.

**405.** Each pilotage district was established by a pilotage order made under the Pilotage Act 1913 or the Pilotage Act 1983. Each pilotage order designated or constituted the pilotage authority for the district. A pilotage order might include a number of other provisions and might, in particular, provide whether and in what circumstances pilotage was to be compulsory in the district, although this also depended to some extent on the provisions of section 31 of the Pilotage Act 1983 and of by-laws made by the pilotage authority.

**406.** A pilotage order was made by the Secretary of State under provisions latterly contained in section 9 of the Pilotage Act 1983, on the application of any person interested in the pilotage of any pilotage district or in the operation or administration of the laws relating to pilotage in that district or, in certain circumstances, on the application of the Pilotage Commission. The related procedure was contained in the Pilotage Orders (Applications) Regulations 1980 and could be lengthy. After a pilotage order had been made it was subject to a parliamentary control. If there were no outstanding objections to the order it was subject to annulment in pursuance of a resolution by either House of Parliament. If there were outstanding objections the order was subject to special parliamentary procedure.

**407.** There were, broadly speaking, three different types of pilotage authorities, as follows:

(a) London Trinity House, which was by far the largest pilotage authority, administered the London Pilotage districts and over 40 other districts (known as "outport districts"). The administration of the London districts was to a considerable extent delegated to the London Pilotage Committee which included, in addition to five elder brethren of Trinity House, representatives of shipowners, pilots and harbour authorities. In every other Trinity House district, Trinity House's pilotage functions were to some extent delegated to Sub-Commissioners who, according to the provisions of the pilotage order for the district, generally included representatives of pilots, shipowners and any harbour authority whose harbour was within the district. Mention should also be made of Trinity House, Newcastle, which was the pilotage authority for several small pilotage districts in the North East of England.

(b) In a number of pilotage districts, the relevant pilotage order constituted the local harbour authority as the pilotage authority for the district.

Where a harbour authority was also a pilotage authority, the pilotage order usually provided for the establishment of a pilotage committee on which pilots and shipowners as well as the harbour authority were represented, and for certain functions of the authority to be delegated to the committee.

(c) In some pilotage districts the pilotage authority was a body constituted for the purpose by the pilotage order. These *ad hoc* pilotage authorities usually included representatives of local pilots, shipowners and the local harbour authority or authorities.

**408.** The most important functions of a pilotage authority were the licensing of pilots for its district and, where pilotage was compulsory, granting pilotage certificates to masters and first mates (who were Commonwealth citizens, citizens of the Republic of Ireland or nationals of another Member State of the EEC) to enable them, in effect, to pilot a specified ship or ships in the compulsory area. The granting of pilotage licences and certificates was regulated to some extent by the provisions of pilotage by-laws made by the pilotage authority. There were also a number of related provisions in the Pilotage Act 1983, including the right for a licensed pilot to appeal to a court against the suspension or revocation of his licence by the pilotage authority or the refusal or failure of the authority to renew his licence.

**409.** In practice it was very rare for a licensed pilot to lose his licence. There were also rights of appeal to the Secretary of State against the action, or lack of it, by pilotage authorities in relation to the granting of pilotage licences and certificates and the renewal, suspension or revocation of pilotage certificates.

**410.** Other important functions of pilotage authorities were—

(a) The making and enforcement of pilotage by-laws which provided for detailed matters regarding the adminstration of pilotage within the framework laid down by the Pilotage Act 1983 and the relevant Pilotage order.

(b) The making of pilotage charges.

(c) The approval and licensing of pilots' boats.

**411.** The numerous purposes for which pilotage by-laws might be made included determining the qualifications required by candidates for pilots' licences, providing for the "good government" of pilots and apprentices and ensuring their "good conduct and constant attendance to and effectual performance of their duties whether at sea or on shore". Pilotage by-laws had to be submitted to the Secretary of State for confirmation and the procedure could sometimes take a considerable time.

**412.** In most pilotage districts, the by-laws provided for pilotage charges to be collected by the pilotage authority and distributed to the pilots. Under the Pilotage Act 1983, a pilotage authority might make charges to be paid by persons who made use of the services of pilots licensed for the district. These included charges for the services of a pilot and charges in respect of the cost of providing, maintaining and operating pilot boats, and of other costs in respect of providing and maintaining the local pilotage organization. The Act provided that objections to such charges might be made to the Pilotage Commission by the majority of the pilots licensed for the district, three or more shipowners whose ships navigated in the district, a harbour authority whose area lay within the district or any other person who appeared to the Pilotage Commission to have a substantial interest in the charges. Upon such an objection, the Commission might cancel or alter the pilotage authority's charges.

413. The history of the law of Pilotage prior to the Pilotage Act 1913 is summarized in Appendix I to this book.

## THE PILOTAGE ACT 1987

### Which harbour authorities are responsible for pilotage?

414. The primary responsibility for the provision of a pilotage service on and after the appointed day (which, as mentioned above, was 1 October 1988) is imposed on a class of harbour authorities described in section 1 of the Act, perhaps a little invidiously, as "competent harbour authorities". For a harbour authority to fall within this class:

(a) they must be a harbour authority as defined in the Harbours Act 1964 or, in Northern Ireland, the Harbours Act (Northern Ireland) 1970, i.e., an authority who manage their harbour under statutory powers;

(b) they must have statutory powers in relation to the regulation of shipping movements and the safety of navigation within their harbour; powers vested in the harbour master, for example, his power to give directions to ships under section 52 of the Harbours, Docks and Piers Clauses Act 1847, are deemed for this purpose to be powers exercised by the harbour authority, and the harbour authority's harbour is the area or areas inside the limits of which their statutory powers and duties as a harbour authority are exercisable; and

(c) their harbour must fall within a so-called active former pilotage district, that is to say a pilotage district designated by a pilotage order made under the Pilotage Act 1983, or the legislation which it consolidated, where at least one act of pilotage was performed in 1984, 1985, 1986 or 1987, or in respect of which a pilotage certificate authorizing a master or first mate to pilot his ship in circumstances in which pilotage was compulsory was in force at any time in any of those years.

415. That then is the class of competent harbour authorities described by section 1 of the Act but the clause excludes from that class:

(a) regional water authorities and certain other drainage and river authorities (unless they have special powers under local statutes);

(b) a Queen's harbour master, that is to say the harbour master for a Dockyard Port (within the meaning of the Dockyard Ports Regulation Act 1865), or

(c) any own account operator, that is to say a body which manages a harbour under statutory powers wholly or mainly for the purpose of goods which it, or an associated body, manufactures or produces, for example, an oil company which manages its own jetty under statutory powers.

**416.** This class is not, however, immutable. A harbour authority who manage their harbour under statutory powers but are not within the class, for example, because the harbour does not fall within a former pilotage district, may apply to the Secretary of State to be added to it and the Secretary of State may by order provide accordingly. The Secretary of State may, again by order, provide that a competent harbour authority shall exercise pilotage functions in an area additional to their own harbour. Such an additional area may be outside the limits of any competent harbour authority or it may comprise another competent harbour authority's harbour. In the latter case, the Secretary of State's order may provide that the other harbour authority shall be excluded from the class of competent harbour authorities. The Secretary of State may only provide under this enabling power for a competent harbour authority to exercise pilotage functions in an additional area if he considers that this is in the interests of efficiency and safety of navigation.

**417.** Before the Secretary of State makes an order under section 1 either to add a harbour authority to the class of competent harbour authorities or to provide for a competent harbour authority to exercise pilotage functions in an additional area, he must inform the persons he considers may be affected by the terms of the proposed order and specify a reasonable time within which they may object.

**418.** If a person objects to an order under section 1 and does not withdraw his objection, then if the Secretary of State makes the order substantially in the form originally proposed, the order as made is subject to special parliamentary procedure. Otherwise the order as made is subject to the negative resolution procedure—annulment by a resolution of either House of Parliament.

**419.** Still on the subject of which authorities are to be responsible for pilotage, reference is now made to section 11, subsections (2) and (3) and to sections 12 and 13. Under section 11(2), a competent harbour authority may arrange for another competent harbour authority to exercise on their behalf all or any of their pilotage functions, except the primary duty under section 2(1) of keeping under consideration what pilotage services need to be provided and whether and how far pilotage should be compulsory. Arrangements under section 11(2) could therefore provide for one competent harbour authority to stand substantially in the shoes of another, although they could also provide for something short of that.

**420.** Under section 11(3) two or more competent harbour authorities may arrange to discharge any of their pilotage functions jointly. This would enable two or more competent harbour authorities to establish a joint committee which would, in effect, operate as the competent harbour authority to provide pilotage services for their combined harbours and approaches. Joint arrangements under section 11(3) could stop short of complete integration, and, for example, could be limited to the provision and operation of pilot boats.

**421.** Arrangements made under section 11(2) or (3) may be terminated by the giving of reasonable notice to the other party or parties by a competent harbour authority who entered into the arrangements.

**422.** Section 12 enables the Secretary of State to intervene in certain cases where joint arrangements might, *prima facie*, seem appropriate. In particular he may do so where the harbours of two or more competent harbour authorities fall wholly or partly within a single former pilotage district, or where access for ships to the harbour of one competent harbour authority is through the harbour of another.

**423.** He may also intervene where a person other than the competent harbour authority carries on harbour operations within their harbour (for example, a terminal operator); where a person other than the harbour authority carries on harbour operations in a harbour which is not that of a competent harbour authority, access to which is through the harbour of a competent harbour authority; and where the harbour of a competent harbour authority and a dockyard port fall within the same former pilotage district.

**424.** Also under section 12, the Secretary of State may require the competent harbour authorities concerned to provide him with any information he requests about arrangements made or proposed for the provision of pilotage services in the sort of cases mentioned above. If no arrangements have been made or proposed and the Secretary of State considers that these are necessary, he may direct the authorities concerned to make such arrangements—for example, for the harbour authorities in an estuary to establish a joint committee to discharge pilotage functions in their harbours and approaches. If he considers that any arrangements actual or proposed are unsatisfactory, he may direct either that they must be modified in such ways as he may specify, or that the authorities concerned must make different arrangements. Section 12(4) makes clear that the right mentioned above to withdraw from joint arrangements entered into by agreement does not apply to arrangements made or modified pursuant to a direction by the Secretary of State.

**425.** Section 13 provides for the Secretary of State to determine disputes between competent harbour authorities concerning, among other things, joint arrangements for the discharge of pilotage functions.

**426.** Usually, the authority responsible for the provision of pilotage services at a harbour will be the harbour authority for that harbour, if they are a competent harbour authority, as is the case with most important commercial harbours. But it may be another competent harbour authority by virtue of arrangements under section 11(2), or a joint board or committee by virtue of arrangements under section 11(3).

**427.** If the body managing a harbour are not a competent harbour authority, for example, if they are a company which manages the harbour otherwise than under statutory powers, the Secretary of State may by order provide for a competent harbour authority to provide pilotage services there. Even where the harbour authority for a harbour are a competent harbour authority, the Secretary of State may appoint another competent harbour authority to provide pilotage services there if he considers that somewhat drastic step to be necessary in the interests of efficiency and safety of navigation.

### General duties for provision of pilotage services

**428.** The general duties for the provision of pilotage services are contained in section 2. Under section 2(1) each competent harbour authority are required to keep under consideration whether any and if so what pilotage services need to be provided to secure the safety of ships navigating in or in the approaches to their harbour and whether, in the interests of safety, pilotage should be compulsory in any part of that harbour or its approaches. If so, the authority must consider for what ships and in which circumstances pilotage is necessary, and what services should be provided.

**429.** This general duty applies to a competent harbour authority in relation to any additional area for which they have been made responsible by an order under section 1. It cannot be delegated by arrangements under the Act to anyone else—not even another competent harbour authority—but only to a joint committee or board established to carry out the pilotage functions of two or more competent harbour authorities. A question which may arise under subsection (1) of section 2 is what area is comprised in the approaches to a particular harbour. The answer is that this is a question of fact and depends on the circumstances of each case.

**430.** In performing their duty under section 2(1), each competent harbour authority is required by subsection (2) to have particular regard to the hazards involved in the carriage of dangerous goods or hazardous substances by ship.

**431.** Subsection (3) of section 2 imposes on each competent harbour authority the duty of providing such pilotage services as they consider necessary. Under section 11 this duty of providing the pilotage services which a competent harbour authority consider necessary may be the subject of arrangements for the services to be provided on behalf of the competent harbour authority by another competent harbour authority or by an agent such as Trinity House (although as described in paragraphs 454 and 455 *post* in the latter case certain powers must be reserved to the competent harbour authority).

**432.** A case which may still be relevant in this context is *Anchor Line (Henderson Bros.) Ltd.* v. *Dundee Harbour Trustees*[7] in which it was held that an authority which failed to maintain an adequate service of pilots might incur liability to the owner of a ship which had sustained damage in consequence of the absence of the pilot.

**433.** The duties imposed on a competent harbour authority by section 2 of the 1987 Act probably mean that the courts would hold that a competent harbour authority are engaged in the business of piloting ships in a sense which the former pilotage authorities were not. In the case of *Fowles* v. *Eastern and Australian Steamship Co. Ltd.*[8] the question was posed: "Was it the duty of the Government (of Queensland) to undertake with due care and skill the pilotage of . . . vessels or was it only a duty to supply qualified pilots to those who were bound to accept the services of such officers?" In relation to the Government of Queensland it was held

7. *Anchor Line (Henderson Bros.) Ltd.* v. *Dundee Harbour Trustees* [1922] 38 T.L.R. 299.
8. *Fowles* v. *Eastern and Australian Steamship Co. Ltd.* [1916] A.C. 556.

in the *Fowles* case that only the latter duty applied and in the recent case of *Esso Petroleum Co. Ltd.* v. *Hall, Russell & Co.*,[9] it was held that this was also the position as respects pilotage authorities under the Pilotage Act 1913. It may well be, however, that under the Pilotage Act 1987 competent harbour authorities have the duty first mentioned in the question referred to above. If this is correct it has implications for the legal relationship between the owner of a ship and the pilot.

## The authorization and engagement of pilots

**434.** Perhaps the most interesting, and certainly the most complicated, part of the 1987 Act is the complex of inter-related provisions dealing with the authorization of pilots, the arrangements under which pilots are to provide their services and, if they are employed, the terms of their employment. These provisions are contained in sections 3, 4 and 5 and subsection (1) of section 11 and also in paragraph 2 of Schedule 1.

**435.** The power for competent harbour authorities to authorize persons to act as pilots in their harbours and approaches clearly has analogies with the former power for pilotage authorities under the Pilotage Act 1983 to license pilots for their districts. In each case the purpose is to ensure that pilots have the necessary skill and experience. The difference is that, whereas under the former system a licence in itself enabled a pilot to provide his services as a pilot in the district for which he was licensed, authorization under section 3 must be coupled with arrangements under a contract of employment or otherwise to enable him to act as an authorized pilot in the harbour in question.

**436.** A competent harbour authority's power to authorize pilots for their harbour and the approaches cannot be exercised on their behalf by an agent under section 11(1) (although, as mentioned above it may be exercised by another competent harbour authority or a joint committee pursuant to arrangements under subsections (2) or (3) of section 11).

**437.** Under subsection (1) of section 3, a competent harbour authority may authorize such persons to act as pilots in or in any part of their harbour or the approaches to the harbour as they consider are suitably qualified to act in that capacity. An authorization must specify the area within which it has effect. It may, for example, authorize the pilot to act only in part of the harbour. It may also authorize him to pilot only ships of a particular description and, if so, the authorization must specify that too.

**438.** The authority may determine the qualifications in respect of age, physical fitness, time of service, local knowledge, skill, character and other qualities required from persons applying for authorization. That gives a competent harbour authority a wide discretion as to the qualifications on which they may insist in authorizing pilots, but it is hardly necessary to add that that discretion must be

9. *Esso Petroleum Co. Ltd.* v. *Hall, Russell & Co., Shetland Islands Council and others* (1st Div.) 1988 S.L.T. 33; [1988] 3 W.L.R. 730 (H.L.).

exercised reasonably and with relevant—but only relevant—considerations in mind. A competent harbour authority may require different qualifications from persons who immediately before the appointed day were licensed pilots for any district or who were time-expired apprentice pilots, or recognized assistant pilots. The purpose of that provision is of course to enable a harbour authority's general requirements to be relaxed or modified for people who have had substantial recent experience of piloting ships, but a competent harbour authority are not obliged to relax their requirements for such persons, though they may do so on a selective basis.

**439.** During the period of four years beginning on the appointed day a competent harbour authority's discretion as to whom they authorize as pilots is limited by subsections (3) and (4) of section 3. During that period they must not, in the first place, authorize any persons who were not licensed pilots immediately before the appointed day, unless the number of former licensed pilots applying to be authorized and who have the qualifications required by the authority (which may be modified for former licensed pilots) fall short of the number of pilots considered necessary by the authority. In the second place, if during that period the number of suitably qualified persons who were licensed pilots immediately before the appointed day does fall short of the required number, the competent harbour authority must not authorize any persons who were not immediately before the appointed day time-expired apprentice pilots or recognized assistant pilots, unless the number of apprentice and assistant pilots who have the requisite qualifications also falls short of the number required. After that the field is open for suitably qualified people.

**440.** A "time-expired apprentice pilot" is defined as a person who had served the full term of his apprenticeship but was not the holder of a licence under section 12 of the Pilotage Act 1983. A "recognized assistant pilot" is defined as a person who acted as an assistant to pilots in a pilotage district and was recognized as such an assistant by the pilotage authority but was not the holder of a pilot's licence.

**441.** Turning to subsection (4) of section 4, we see that a competent harbour authority may refuse to authorize any person who is not willing to provide his services as a pilot in accordance with the arrangements made for the provision of such services in its area. What those arrangements might be is discussed below but this subsection means, for example, that if the arrangements are that pilots are to be employed by the competent harbour authority, the authority may refuse to authorize a former licensed pilot who insists that he will only provide pilotage services on a self-employed basis.

**442.** Returning to section 3, a competent harbour authority may under subsection (5) suspend or revoke an authorization which they have granted if it appears to them:

    (a) that the authorized person has been guilty of any incompetence or misconduct affecting his capability as a pilot;

    (b) that the authorized person has ceased to have the qualifications required of persons applying for authorization, or has failed to provide evidence that he continues to have the qualifications—and that includes qualifications in respect of physical fitness;

(c) that the number of persons for the time being authorized by it exceeds the number required to be authorized; or

(d) that it is appropriate to do so by virtue of any alteration in or the termination of any contract or other arrangement under which the services of pilots are provided at the harbour.

**443.** However, the Act provides that a competent harbour authority may not revoke the authorization of a pilot who provides his services under a contract for services (as distinct from a contract of employment) on the grounds that there are too many authorized pilots, except where the authority gave the pilot notice before the appointed day that they proposed in the first place to authorize more pilots than were needed (in order to give surplus pilots who do not wish to retire the opportunity to transfer to another authority), and that they intended to revoke his authorization after allowing him a reasonable period to seek authorization by another competent harbour authority.

**444.** Before suspending or revoking an authorization on the grounds either that a pilot has been guilty of any incompetence or misconduct or that he has ceased to have the required qualifications or has failed to provide evidence that he still has them, a competent harbour authority must give written notice of their intention to the pilot concerned, stating their reasons, and must give him a reasonable opportunity of making representations.

**445.** Where a competent harbour authority suspend or revoke an authorization either on the grounds that there are too many authorized pilots or because of the termination of any contract or other arrangement, they must give the pilot concerned a notice in writing stating the grounds of the suspension or revocation and specifying the length of time for which he had been authorized as a pilot by that authority. This is intended, as a formal testimonial to his professional competence.

**446.** Subsection (7) of section 3 makes it an offence for a person who is not an authorized pilot for an area to hold himself out as an authorized pilot. The maximum penalty on summary conviction is a fine at level 5 of the standard scale which is currently £2,000.

**447.** Again, under section 4, which deals with such matters as the employment of authorized pilots, subsection (2) imposes a duty on a competent harbour authority to offer themselves to employ under a contract of employment any person they authorize as a pilot (apart from pilots who are already employed by them) unless (a) a majority of the "relevant licence holders" have agreed during the period beginning six months and ending three months before the appointed day that the authority need not offer to employ them; or (b) a majority of the "relevant authorized pilots" have agreed on or after that day that the authority need not do so. A competent harbour authority's duty under section 4(2) cannot be exercised on their behalf by an agent under section 11(1), although it could be exercised by another competent harbour authority or by a joint committee. Subsection (3) of section 4 defines "relevant licence holders" and "relevant authorized pilots".

*"Relevant licence holders"*

    (a) If the competent harbour authority's harbour falls within more than one former pilotage district (it is believed that the only case of that kind is the harbour of the Tees and Hartlepool Port Authority), "relevant licence holders" means the persons who at the time of the agreement that the competent harbour authority need not offer to employ them were holders of pilotage licences for the district which includes the area for which the authorizations covered by the agreement were granted.

    (b) If the competent harbour authority's harbour falls within a former pilotage district in which another competent harbour authority's harbour also falls (as for example in the case of the harbours in the London district), then the relevant licence holders are the persons who at the time of the agreement that the competent harbour authority need not offer to employ them were holders of pilotage licences for the district and, in the opinion of the Pilotage Commission, were at that time regularly providing their services as pilots within the part of the district in which the harbour in question is situated.

    (c) In any other case, the relevant licence holders are all the persons who at the time of the agreement that the competent harbour authority need not offer to employ them, were the licensed pilots for the former pilotage district in which the competent harbour authority's harbour falls.

*"Relevant authorized pilots"*

These are the people who on and after the appointed day may agree that the competent harbour authority need not offer employment to a pilot whom it authorizes:

    (a) If the competent harbour authority's harbour falls within more than one former pilotage district, the relevant authorized pilots are the persons who at the time of the agreement are authorized for the area for which the pilot or pilots concerned are authorized.

    (b) In any other case, the relevant authorized pilots are the persons who at the time of the agreement are authorized pilots for the harbour of the competent harbour authority.

    **448.** Section 4(1) provides that, subject to subsection (2) (i.e., subject to the competent harbour authority's obligation to offer to employ the pilots whom they authorize unless that obligation is removed by an agreement on the part of a majority of the local pilots), a competent harbour authority may make such arrangements as they consider appropriate for the provision of the services of authorized pilots in their harbour and the approaches, whether under a contract of employment or a contract for services.

    **449.** Functions under section 4(1) are not among those which are excluded by section 11(1) from the functions which may be exercised by an agent on behalf of a competent harbour authority. If, therefore, a competent harbour authority make arrangements with a company for that company to exercise pilotage functions on their behalf, these could include giving the company the discretion of deciding under section 4(1) whether to employ the pilots, or to enter into contracts with them under which they would provide their services as self-employed contractors. That situation could, of course, only arise if the majority of the local pilots had agreed to release the competent harbour authority from their obligation under subsection (2) to offer to employ them.

**450.** It should be noted that under section 4(1), a competent harbour authority may employ the pilots they authorize, even where a majority of the local pilots have agreed that the authority need not employ them and would prefer some other arrangement.

**451.** A point which may not be completely clear is whether the obligation to offer to employ an authorized pilot implies a continuing obligation to employ him so long as he remains an authorized pilot, in the absence of an agreement to the contrary by a majority of the relevant authorized pilots. It is thought that the better view is that it does.

**452.** The distinction between a contract of employment and a contract for services can be a fine one. One test which the courts have applied is whether the employer has the right to control the manner of doing the work but that test is not always correct: *Cassidy* v. *Ministry of Health.*[10] It would not seem to be the appropriate test to apply in the case of marine pilots. An analogous case appears to be that of a master of a ship who is clearly employed by his shipping company. His employer can tell him where to go but not how to navigate (*Gold* v. *Essex County Council*[11]). With regard to the distinction between a contract of employment and a contract for services Stevenson, L.J., said in *Cassidy* v. *Ministry of Health*: "One perhaps cannot get much beyond this: Was the contract a contract of service (i.e., of employment) within the meaning which an ordinary person would give under the words?"

**453.** Subsection (5) of section 4 enables a competent harbour authority to pay into a pilots' benefit fund (which includes the Pilots' National Pension Fund to which most pilots belong) such contributions as may be required by the rules governing the fund in respect of any authorized pilot providing his services under such arrangements as are mentioned in subsection (1).

**454.** Under subsection (1) of section 11, a competent harbour authority may arrange for certain of their pilotage functions to be exercised on their behalf by such other persons as they think fit. A competent harbour authority may also establish such companies as they think fit to exercise those functions on their behalf. The subsection, however, excludes from such arrangements a competent harbour authority's basic statutory functions in relation to pilotage.

10. *Cassidy* v. *Ministry of Health* [1951] 2 K.B. 343.
11. *Gold* v. *Essex County Council* [1942] 2 K.B. 293.

**455.** The functions which cannot be exercised by an agent or by a company established by a competent harbour authority are:

(a) the general duty contained in section 2(1) to keep the need for pilotage services under review;

(b) the authorization of pilots under section 3(1);

(c) determining the qualifications to be required from applicants for authorization under section 3(2);

(d) the obligation to offer to employ authorized pilots under section 4(2);

(e) the licensing of pilot boats operated by persons other than the authority under section 6(1)(*b*);

(f) directing that pilotage shall be compulsory under section 7(1);

(g) granting pilotage exemption certificates under section 8(1);

(h) making charges under section 10; and

(i) making payments required by a pilots' compensation scheme under section 28.

As mentioned above, the arrangements which can be made with other competent harbour authorities are more comprehensive.

**456.** Section 5 and paragraph 2 of Schedule 1 provide for a temporary arbitration procedure for resolving disputes between competent harbour authorities and authorized pilots whom they employ. Pilots already employed before the passing of the Act are excluded from this procedure. Section 5 relates to the position after the appointed day. It provides that where any dispute arises between a competent harbour authority and an authorized pilot or a person wishing to be authorized:

(a) as to what the terms of any provision in any contract of employment which is to be entered into between them should be; or

(b) whether the terms of any provision in any existing contract of employment between them should be modified,

and that dispute cannot be resolved by negotiation between them, the authority or a majority of the authorized pilots for the harbour may refer the dispute to an arbitration panel. The arbitration panel is to consist of three members, one appointed by the Secretary of State, who is the Chairman; one appointed by a body appearing to the Secretary of State to be representative of harbour authorities throughout the United Kingdom; and one appointed by a body appearing to him to be representative of pilots throughout the United Kingdom.

**457.** When a dispute is referred to them the panel are required to determine what the terms of the provision in dispute should be, and the kinds of contracts of employment between the authority and authorized pilots to which their determination is to apply. In making a determination the panel must have regard to any general guidance issued by the Secretary of State as to the matters to be considered by them. The Secretary of State has issued the following guidance:

The arbitration panel should in making their determination have regard as appropriate to the following considerations where disputes relate to levels of earnings. Other matters may also be taken into account as appropriate where disputes relate to other issues.

1. The previous earnings of pilots in the port, taking account both of actual earnings and the levels of earnings recommended under the former Letch agreement (suitably updated).
2. The work rate, the volume of work (number of ships to be piloted) and the mix of work (for example, range of sizes and types of vessels covered).
3. Earnings of pilots in comparable ports elsewhere in the country.
4. The physical conditions under which pilotage is undertaken in the port.
5. The physical and geographical characteristics of the port, particularly including those relevant to navigational hazards.
6. The earnings, conditions of employment and working patterns of senior staff of the harbour authority, including those of marine officers, in comparison with the working conditions and work patterns applied to pilots.
7. Any national guidelines agreed between representatives of the harbour authorities and of the pilots regarding the employment of pilots by the harbour authorities.

(The Letch agreement referred to in paragraph 1 of the Secretary of State's guidelines was an agreement reached between pilots and shipowners in 1957 under which the more important pilotage districts were ranked in groups for earnings purposes. Those earnings, as the Agreement provided, were subsequently reviewed from time to time in the light both of National Maritime Board awards to Merchant Navy officers and of changes of trade in the districts.)

**458.** Where the arbitration panel make a determination, then subject to any agreement to the contrary between the harbour authority and the authorized pilots and to the effect of any subsequent determination:

(a) on and after the date on which the determination is made, any contracts of employment between the harbour authority and the pilots of the kinds to which the panel have decided their determination is to apply, which have been entered into before the date of the determination have effect with the substitution of a provision in the terms determined by the panel for any inconsistent provision; and

(b) any such contracts entered into on or after the date of the determination must contain a provision in the terms determined by the panel.

**459.** Section 5 contains a power for the Secretary of State to make regulations about the referral and determination of disputes under the section. Pursuant to that power he has made the Terms of Employment of Pilots (Arbitration) Regulations 1988. These provide, *inter alia*, that the arbitration panel must seek to determine a dispute through a unanimous decision of the panel, and if this proves impossible through a majority decision; but if it proves impossible for any two members of the panel to agree to a decision the panel may act through the decision of the Chairman alone.

**460.** Section 5(7) provides that the arbitration procedure shall come to an end on such date as the Secretary of State may by order prescribe, but not earlier than the expiry of the period of three years, beginning with the appointed day. An order prescribing the date on which the procedure terminates is not to affect the terms of any contract continuing in force at that date.

**461.** Paragraph 2 of Schedule 1 adapts the procedure under section 5, and applies it to disputes before the appointed day between a competent harbour authority and any person who wishes to be authorized by the authority on or after that day. Under the procedure as adapted and applied by paragraph 2, such a dispute could be referred to the panel by the harbour authority or by any person or organization which represents the majority of licensed pilots for a pilotage district in which the authority's harbour falls.

## Compulsory pilotage

**462.** Sections 7, 8 and 15 of the Act deal with the important subject of compulsory pilotage. On the appointed day all existing requirements for pilotage to be compulsory in the Pilotage Act 1983, pilotage orders and pilotage by-laws were abrogated. Instead, under section 7, if a competent harbour authority consider that in the interests of safety they should do so, then they have a duty to direct that pilotage shall be compulsory for ships navigating in, or in any part, of their harbour or the approaches. This power is flexible and discriminating. A pilotage direction:

    (a) may apply to all ships (except ships of less than 20 metres in length, fishing boats of less than 47.5 metres in length and, by virtue, respectively, of Crown and Sovereign Immunity, British and foreign warships) or all ships of a description specified in the direction (subject to any specified exceptions);

    (b) shall specify the area and circumstances in which it applies;

    (c) may specify the circumstances in which an authorized pilot in charge of a ship to which the direction applies is to be accompanied by an assistant who is also an authorized pilot; and

    (d) may contain such supplementary provisions as the authority consider appropriate.

**463.** Among other things, it is possible under this power for a competent harbour authority to direct that any ship which has a defect in its hull, machinery or equipment which might materially affect its navigation should be subject to compulsory pilotage (*cf.* the former section 30(3) of the Pilotage Act 1983).

**464.** Where a competent harbour authority consider that pilotage should be compulsory in part of the approaches to their harbour, the limits of their harbour must be extended by a harbour revision order under section 14 of the Harbours Act 1964 to include the area in question before a pilotage direction can become effective in that area. By virtue of provisions of the Interpretation Act 1978 which enabled anticipatory action to be taken in certain circumstances, it was possible for a competent harbour authority who intended to give a pilotage direction in respect of an area outside their harbour on or after the appointed day, to apply before that day for a harbour revision order to extend their limits. If they did so, then if pilotage was already compulsory in the area concerned by virtue of a pilotage order, the harbour revision order had the benefit of an expedited procedure as specified in paragraph 3 of Schedule 1 to the 1987 Act.

**465.** A pilotage direction is not subject to appeal, but before giving such a direction a competent harbour authority must consult the owners of ships which customarily navigate in the area which would be affected and any other persons who carry on harbour operations within the harbour, or, in either case, the appropriate representative bodies. A competent harbour authority must arrange for any pilotage direction given by them to be published in such a manner as to bring it to the notice of those persons likely to be interested.

**466.** Section 9 of the 1987 Act requires a competent harbour authority to secure that any ship owned or operated by them in the exercise of their functions otherwise than under the 1987 Act (that is, craft operated by the authority other than pilot boats) is subject to the same obligations as respects pilotage while navigating within their harbour as any other ship.

**467.** It may be pertinent to refer here to section 16 of the 1987 Act which provides that the fact that a ship is being navigated in an area and in circumstances in which pilotage is compulsory for it shall not affect any liability of the owner or master of the ship for any loss or damage caused by the ship or by the manner in which it is navigated. This section re-enacts in a slightly different form the provisions originally contained in section 15(1) of the Pilotage Act 1913 which abolished the defence of compulsory pilotage. For the history of, and the background to, this provision reference should be made to the notes to section 15 of the 1913 Act in Temperley, *Merchant Shipping Acts* (7th edn.) (*British Shipping Laws*, Vol. 2), pp. 362–63. Section 16 is referred to in paragraph 492 *post* in the context of liability for damage caused by a ship under compulsory pilotage.

### Pilotage exemption certificates

**468.** Section 8 of the Act provides in effect that where pilotage is compulsory the competent harbour authority must, on application by the master or first mate of a ship, grant him a certificate enabling him to navigate that ship (and any other ships specified in the certificate) in the area concerned without a pilot if they are satisfied (by examination or by reference to such other requirements as they may reasonably impose) that his skill, experience and local knowledge are sufficient for the purpose and, if it appears to be necessary in the interests of safety, that he has sufficient knowledge of English.

**469.** However, under section 8(2) a competent harbour authority's requirements for the grant of a certificate must not be unduly onerous having regard to the difficulties and danger of navigation in the harbour. They must not be more onerous than those which the authority require from persons applying to be authorized as pilots (other than former licensed pilots, time-expired licensed pilots, etc., in respect of whom a competent harbour authority may require different qualifications from those upon which they generally insist).

**470.** If the Secretary of State is satisfied on application made to him by a competent harbour authority that it is appropriate for him to do so by reason of the unusual hazards involved in shipping movements within their harbour, he may direct that during such period (not exceeding three years) as he may specify, the competent harbour authority may refuse to grant pilotage exemption certificates, even in cases where they are satisfied as regards the applicants' skill, experience and local knowledge. If such a direction is given then pilotage exemption certificates already in force in the harbour cease to have effect.

**471.** A pilotage exemption certificate is not to remain in force for more than one year, but may be renewed annually on application by the holder, if the competent harbour authority continue to be satisfied that he is qualified to navigate the ship or ships in question in its harbour. It may be altered so as to refer to different ships if the competent harbour authority are satisfied that the holder is also suitably qualified to navigate those other ships in the harbour.

**472.** Section 8 enables a competent harbour authority to revoke or suspend a pilotage exemption certificate if it appears to them that the holder has been guilty of any relevant incompetence or misconduct. Before doing so, and before refusing to grant or renew a pilotage exemption certificate, a competent harbour authority must give the holder written notice and give him a reasonable opportunity of making representations.

**473.** A competent harbour authority may charge such fees as they consider reasonable to meet their administrative costs in connection with granting, renewing or altering of pilotage certificates and conducting examinations for the purpose.

**474.** Under paragraph 5(1) of Schedule 1 to the 1987 Act where immediately before the appointed day a pilotage certificate granted by a pilotage authority under section 20 of the Pilotage Act 1983 is in force that certificate continues in force for the period for which it was granted (even, it would seem, if that period exceeds one year) as if it had been granted under section 8 by the authority or authorities which are the competent harbour authorities as respects the area in relation to which the certificate was granted.

### Failure to comply with pilotage directions

**475.** Section 15 provides that a ship being navigated in an area and in circumstances where pilotage is compulsory by virtue of a pilotage direction must be under the pilotage of an authorized pilot, accompanied by an assistant if that is required by the direction, or under the pilotage of a master or first mate possessing a pilotage exemption certificate for the ship. If any ship is not under such pilotage after an authorized pilot has offered to take charge of the ship, the master is guilty of an offence and liable on summary conviction to a fine not exceeding level 5 on the standard scale which is currently £2,000.

**476.** Under subsection (3) of section 15, if the master of a ship navigates in an area and in circumstances in which pilotage is compulsory without notifying the competent harbour authority that he proposes to do so, he is guilty of an offence and liable on summary conviction to a fine not exceeding level 2 on the standard scale (which is currently £100). This is a new provision. It is still not an offence in itself for a master without a pilotage exemption certificate to navigate his ship without a pilot where pilotage is compulsory unless and until an authorized pilot offers to take charge,[12] but he must now notify the competent harbour authority before doing so.

**477.** With regard to what constitutes an offer by an authorized pilot to take charge of a ship, the cases on what constituted an offer by a licensed pilot under the Pilotage Act 1913 and the Pilotage Act 1983 would still appear to be relevant. In *Babbs* v. *Press*[13] it was claimed that a flag displayed at the Trinity House pilot station at Gravesend constituted an offer of pilotage on the part of the pilots stationed there. Lord Widgery, C.J., did not agree. He said:

An offer to provide pilotage for the purpose of the Pilotage Act (1913) section 30(3) must be an offer made or communicated in relation to the particular movement of the vessel in question . . . Whether or not in a given case an offer has been made relative to the particular movement of the vessel is a question of fact . . . in many instances an offer may be made simultaneously to a number of vessels at the same time . . . On the facts of this case I think the Justices were wholly justified in reaching the conclusion that the presence of the pilot station and its flag two miles down river were not a sufficient offer to the master of the *Matilde* of a licensed pilot at the time when she set off on this short two-mile voyage.

**478.** In *Jenkin* v. *Godwin*[14] it was held that the refusal of a licensed pilot to take charge of a ship in the evening (because he considered it unsafe to proceed on the flood tide 20 minutes before sunset) but to take charge the following morning did not constitute a reasonable offer by the pilot.

**479.** In modern circumstances the normal practice is for the master to ask for a pilot by radio. Failing that, notification (by radio) under section 15(3) that the master proposes to navigate in a compulsory pilotage area will no doubt prompt the speedy dispatch of a pilot to take charge of the ship.

## Charges by competent harbour authorities

**480.** Section 10 of the 1987 Act authorizes a competent harbour authority to make reasonable charges in respect of the pilotage services provided by them and such charges may include:

   (a) charges for the services of a pilot authorized by the authority;
   (b) charges in respect of any expenses reasonably incurred by a pilot in connection with the provision of his services as a pilot;
   (c) charges by way of penalties payable in cases where the estimated time of arrival or departure of a ship is not notified as required by the authority or the ship does not arrive or depart at the notified time;

12. See *Muller (W. H.) & Co.* v. *Trinity House (Deptford Strond)* [1925] 1 K.B. 166; 16 Asp. M.L.C. 458, although the decision in that case is now in some respects out of date.
13. *Babbs* v. *Press* [1971] 2 Lloyd's Rep. 383.
14. *Jenkin* v. *Godwin* (1983) 81 L.S.G. 482.

(d) charges in respect of the cost of providing, maintaining and operating pilot boats for the area; and

(e) charges in respect of any other costs involved in providing and maintaining the pilotage organization provided by the authority.

**481.** Where pilotage is compulsory, a competent harbour authority may also make reasonable charges in respect of a ship which is being navigated by a master or first mate with a pilotage exemption certificate. It was held in *W. H. Muller & Co.* v. *Trinity House (Deptford Strond)*[15] that the reference in the Pilotage Act 1913 to rates of payments to be made in respect of the services of a licensed pilot meant payments for "services rendered" and that a pilotage authority could not therefore impose a charge (by by-law under section 17(1)(*f*) of the 1913 Act) upon a ship when in fact no pilotage charges had been performed. This principle may still apply but does not, of course, affect the express power to make reasonable charges in respect of a ship which is being navigated by a master or first mate with a pilotage exemption certificate.

**482.** Section 10 applies section 31 of the Harbours Act 1964 (see paragraphs 253–59 *ante*) with modifications to enable:

(a) the owners of ships which customarily navigate in the harbour in question;

(b) any persons who carry on harbour operations within the harbour; and

(c) any other harbour authority to whose harbour ships obtain access through that harbour,

or, in any of those cases, persons representatives of them, to object to the Secretary of State against pilotage charges on the grounds:

(i) that the charge ought to be imposed at a rate lower than that at which it is imposed; or

(ii) that, according to the circumstances of the case, the charge ought to be imposed (either generally or in circumstances specified in the objection) on ships of a class so specified at a rate lower than that at which it is imposed on others.

**483.** Section 10 differs from the charging provisions of the Harbours Act 1964 in that it combines, in respect of the same charges, a requirement that charges must be reasonable with a statutory objection procedure. The existence of this procedure might be held to exclude application to the courts for a declaration as to whether a charge was reasonable[16] but it seems likely that a shipowner, in addition to his right to object to the Secretary of State, could refuse to pay pilotage charges on the grounds that they were unreasonable with a view to the issue of reasonableness being tested in the court when the harbour authority instituted proceedings to recover the charges.

---

15. [1925] 1 K.B. 166; 16 Asp. M.L.C. 458.
16. See *Gillingham Corporation* v. *Kent County Council* [1953] Ch. 37.

## Accounts

**484.** Section 14 of the new Act relates to the accounts of competent harbour authorities. This section extends the Secretary of State's power to make regulations under section 42 of the Harbours Act 1964 about a statutory harbour undertaker's accounts (as to which see paragraphs 308–19 *ante*) so as to enable the Secretary of State to require a competent harbour authority's statement of accounts relating to pilotage functions to be made available for inspection by the public. The Statutory Harbour Undertakings (Pilotage Accounts) Regulations 1988 made by the Secretary of State under section 42 of the Harbours Act 1964 as extended by section 14 of the 1987 Act:

(a) Prescribe a competent harbour authority's activities in relation to pilotage as "associated activities" for the purposes of section 42 which must therefore be included in the authority's statement of accounts to be prepared under that section but excludes pilotage activities from the scope of regulation 5 of the Statutory Harbour Undertakings (Accounts, etc.) Regulations 1983, which provide that where a statement of accounts prepared under section 42 relates to associated activities it must include a statement of gross revenue in relation to (all) those activities.

(It seems arguable that a competent harbour authority's pilotage activities are in fact "harbour activities" as defined in section 42, i.e., activities involved in carrying on the authority's statutory harbour undertaking, and should be included in their statement of accounts on that basis, but with the amendment of regulation 5 of the 1983 Regulations. The point is academic.)

(b) Require a competent harbour authority to show pilotage income and expenditure separately in their accounts.

(c) Require copies of any statement of accounts identifying pilotage revenue and expenditure to be made available for inspection by the public at all reasonable hours at the registered office of the competent harbour authority and require that authority to make copies available for purchase by members of the public at a reasonable charge.

**485.** Section 14(3) provides that where a competent harbour authority's pilotage functions are discharged by an agent, the statement of accounts under section 42 of the Harbours Act must still relate to these activities, and the agent must furnish the authority with the requisite information.

## Limitation of liability

**486.** It may be helpful to begin by referring briefly to the statutory limitations of liability which formerly applied in relation to pilots and pilotage authorities under the Pilotage Act 1983:

(a) Under section 17 of the Pilotage Act 1983, a pilotage authority had no vicarious liability for any loss occasioned by any act or default of a pilot whom it had licensed.

(b) Under section 42 of the 1983 Act a pilot's liability, and that of an authorized assistant, for neglect or want of skill was limited to £100 and the amount of the pilotage charges in respect of the voyage during which the liability arose.

(c) Also under section 42, the vicarious liability of a pilotage authority for neglect or want of skill on the part of a pilot, or assistant, whom it employed was similarly limited to £100 and the pilotage charges in respect of the relevant voyage.

(d) Under section 55 of the 1983 Act, a pilotage authority had a general right to limit its liability for loss or damage to vessels, goods and other property arising on one distinct occasion, which did not result from its personal act or omission made with intent to cause such loss or recklessly and with the knowledge that such loss would probably result, to the amount of £100 multiplied by the number of licensed pilots for the district at the time when the loss or damage occurred.

(e) Section 58 of the 1983 Act made clear that none of these specific rights to limit liability prejudiced the right of a pilotage authority to limit its liability as a shipowner under section 17 or 18 of the Merchant Shipping Act 1979, e.g., for damage caused by a pilot boat.

487. Under section 22 of the 1987 Act:

(a) Subsection (8) provides that a competent harbour authority shall not be liable for any loss or damage caused by any act or omission of a pilot authorized by them by virtue only of that authorization. That corresponds to section 17 of the 1983 Act.

(b) Subsection (2) limits the liability of any authorized pilot for any loss or damage caused by any act or omission of his while acting as such a pilot to £1,000 and the amount of the pilotage charges in respect of the voyage during which the liability arose. So that corresponds, as far as pilots are concerned, to section 42 of the 1983 Act with a reasonable escalation in the amount of the limitation.

(c) Subsection (3) limits the liability of a competent harbour authority for loss or damage to any ship, to any property on board any ship or to any property rights of any kind caused, without the personal act or omission of the authority, by an authorized pilot whom they employ, to £1,000 multiplied by the number of authorized pilots employed by the authority at the date when the loss or damages occurs. Subsection (3) is therefore adapted from the right for pilotage authorities to limit their liability generally contained in section 55 of the 1983 Act, but applies only to vicarious liability for damage to property caused by employed pilots. Subsection (4) limits in the same way the liability of persons providing pilotage services as agents for competent harbour authorities for loss or damage caused by authorized pilots employed by such agents.

(d) Subject to these specific provisions, a competent harbour authority's general right to limit their liability for loss or damage to ships or to property on board ships under sections 2 and 3 of the Merchant Shipping (Liability of Shipowners and Others) Act 1900 as amended by the Merchant Shipping Act 1979 applies in relation to pilotage functions. (The amount of that limitation depends on the tonnage of the largest British ship which, at the relevant time, is, or within the past five years has been, within the harbour, with certain qualifications.)

**488.** With regard to liability arising from the operation of pilot boats, it appears that a competent harbour authority are entitled to limit their liability as shipowners under the Merchant Shipping Act 1979. Subsection (7) of section 22 makes clear that the special right to limit vicarious liability for loss or damage caused by an employed pilot does not affect a competent harbour authority's right to limit their liability as shipowners.

**489.** In the Scottish case of *Esso Petroleum Co. Ltd.* v. *Hall, Russell & Co. Ltd., Shetland Islands Council and others*[17] which related to events which occurred on 30 December 1978 in an area where pilotage was compulsory, it was held (*inter alia*) that Shetland Islands Council, the pilotage authority for the district, were not vicariously liable for the negligence of a pilot licensed by them whom (unusually) they also employed. This decision appears to have rested on the following two grounds:

(1) By virtue of section 15(1) of the Pilotage Act 1913 (which provided that the owner or master of a vessel navigating in circumstances in which pilotage was compulsory was answerable for any loss or damage caused by the vessel or by any fault of the navigation of the vessel in the same manner as he would if pilotage were not compulsory) the pilot (piloting the ship in an area where pilotage is compulsory) falls to be regarded as the servant of the shipowner at the time of his alleged act of negligence and cannot, accordingly, at the same moment, be regarded as being also the servant of the pilotage authority (even if it employed him).

(2) The pilotage authority for the district is not engaged in the business of piloting ships. The pilot is carrying out independent legal duties imposed upon him by his licence and is not in the employment of the pilotage authority in the sense of carrying out work which the pilotage authority itself is required to perform.

**490.** A number of authorities were cited in support of these propositions and in particular the case of *Fowles* v. *Eastern and Australian Steamship Co. Ltd.*[18] in which it was held by the Privy Council that the Government of Queensland were not

---

17. (1st Div.) 1988 S.L.T. 33, *supra* fn.9. The decision of the Court of Session on the pilotage issue was upheld on appeal by the House of Lords, [1988] 3 W.L.R. 730.
18. [1916] A.C. 556, *ante* fn.8.

vicariously liable for the negligence of a marine pilot whom they employed. It was said by Lord Emslie in the Inner House decision:

As in *Fowles* the true position of the council appears to be that they have the obligation to license qualified pilots and to ensure that a sufficient number of licensed pilots are available to meet the needs of the port. It is for that latter purpose that they employ licensed pilots and there is no material in this case to support the proposition that they undertake the quite different obligation to shipowners to pilot their ships safely into harbour.

**491.** Section 42 of the Pilotage Act 1983, which seems to have implied that a pilotage authority would be vicariously liable for the negligence of an employed pilot (although the authority's liability was limited to a very small amount), was not in force at the time of the incident which led to the case of *Esso Petroleum Co. Ltd.* v. *Hall, Russell* and was not considered by the court.

**492.** Whether or not consideration of that section might have affected the decision in that case, it is submitted that the duty imposed on a competent harbour authority by section 2 of the Pilotage Act 1987 to provide a pilotage service, coupled with the clear implication contained in section 22 of the 1987 Act that a competent harbour authority is vicariously liable for the negligence of a pilot whom they employ, means that *Esso Petroleum Co. Ltd.* v. *Hall, Russell* is now of doubtful authority—although section 15(1) of the Pilotage Act 1913, which was re-enacted in the Pilotage Act 1983, is again re-enacted, in substance although in a different form, in section 16 of the 1987 Act.

**493.** If the view suggested in paragraph 433 *ante* that competent harbour authorities, unlike the former pilotage authorities, are in the business of piloting ships is correct then, where pilotage is on a voluntary basis, there would appear to be a direct contractual relationship between a competent harbour authority and the owners of a ship under the pilotage of an authorized pilot in their harbour or the approaches at least where the competent harbour authority employ the pilots they authorize. Where the harbour authority has arranged, under section 11 of the 1987 Act, for their pilotage functions to be exercised to a substantial extent by an agent there would similarly appear to be a contractual relationship between the agent and shipowners if the agent employs the pilots.

**494.** The statement by Lord Atkinson in *The Beechgrove*[19] that there exists between the shipowner and the non-compulsory pilot "a contractual relationship to which the maxim *respondeat superior* applies" and the decision in *Thom* v. *J. & P. Henderson*[20] that section 15 of the Pilotage Act 1913 resulted in the same relationship being created between the shipowner and the compulsory pilot may therefore no longer hold good where the pilot is employed by the competent harbour authority or agent. Where the pilot is not employed but provides his services under a contract for services the position may be more doubtful.

19. *The Beechgrove* [1916] 1 A.C. 364.
20. *Thom* v. *J. & P. Henderson*, 1925 S.C. 386.

**495.** Given the limitations of liability provided for in section 22 of the 1987 Act these interesting questions may not however be of critical importance to pilots, harbour authorities and agents providing pilotage services on behalf of harbour authorities (except, in the case of harbour authorities and their agents, where the liability is in respect of loss of life or personal injury).

## Rights of authorized pilots

**496.** Sections 17 to 20 of the 1987 Act apply to pilots authorized under that Act provisions similar to those of the Pilotage Act 1983 which related to the rights of licensed pilots and the obligations of masters of ships in relation to such pilots.

**497.** Under section 17(1) an authorized pilot may, within the harbour for which he is authorized, supersede as the pilot of a ship any unauthorized person who has been employed to pilot it. This right does not, however, apply in the approaches to a harbour, even though the competent harbour authority may be obliged to provide pilotage services in them. Similarly, subsections (2) and (4) which, respectively, make it an offence for a master to navigate his ship in any part of a harbour under the pilotage of an unauthorized person without first notifying the competent harbour authority that he proposes to do so, or to knowingly employ or continue to employ an unauthorized person to pilot his ship after an authorized pilot has offered to pilot it, do not apply in the approaches to a harbour, and neither does subsection (3) which makes it an offence for an unauthorized person to pilot a ship within a harbour knowing that an authorized pilot has offered to pilot it.

**498.** So far as pilotage in the approaches to a harbour is concerned the position is, therefore, that, although the competent harbour authority may be providing a service, authorized pilots may be competing with deep sea pilots.

**499.** Subsections (7) and (8) of section 17 enable a competent harbour authority to direct that the rights of authorized pilots and the related obligations of masters shall not apply to certain ship movements for the purpose of changing a ship from one mooring to another or taking it into or out of dock. The circumstances in which such a direction can be given, and the area to which it may apply, are narrowly limited. The effect is to enable harbour authorities to allow dock pilots and watermen to continue to operate where they do so already.

**500.** Under section 18 a pilot may require the master of a ship which he is piloting to declare its draught of water, length and beam and to provide him with other relevant information. This provision is not limited to authorized pilots or to a particular area. It would, therefore, seem to apply to deep sea pilots and indeed to an unauthorized person who pilots a ship within a harbour.

**501.** Section 19 re-enacts the former prohibition on a master taking a pilot out of his area but in terms that an authorized pilot must not, without reasonable excuse, be taken without his consent beyond the point up to which he has been engaged to pilot the ship. This recognizes that the approaches to a harbour are not usually a clearly defined area.

**502.** Section 20 requires the master of a ship to give a pilot facilities for boarding, and subsequently leaving, his ship. Failure to comply with this requirement is an offence punishable on summary conviction by a fine not exceeding level 4 on the standard scale (currently £1,000).

### Misconduct by pilots

**503.** Under section 21 of the 1987 Act if the pilot of a ship:

(a) does any act which causes or is likely to cause the loss or destruction of, or serious damage to, the ship or its machinery, navigational equipment or safety equipment or the death of, or serious injury to, a person on board the ship; or

(b) omits to do anything required to preserve the ship or its machinery, navigational equipment or safety equipment from loss, destruction or serious damage or to preserve any person on board the ship from death or serious injury,

and the act or omission is deliberate or amounts to a breach or neglect of duty or he is under the influence of drink or a drug at the time of the act or omission he is guilty of an offence and liable:

(a) on summary conviction, to imprisonment for a term not exceeding six months or a fine not exceeding the statutory maximum (currently £2,000) or both; or

(b) on conviction on indictment, to imprisonment for a term not exceeding two years or a fine or both.

### Winding up of pilotage authorities and Pilotage Commission

**504.** Sections 24 to 29 of the 1987 Act deal with the winding up of the former pilotage structure. The Act provides for the Pilotage Commission to play a central role in this process. To fit it for these important duties, the Commission has been re-constituted with a drastically reduced membership in accordance with section 27.

**505.** On the appointed day every pilotage authority within the meaning of the Pilotage Act 1983 ceased to exist as such an authority. Of course, if a body which was a pilotage authority also had other capacities—if it was, for example, also a harbour authority—it continues to exist in that capacity and if, indeed, it is a competent harbour authority within the meaning of the Act, continues to perform pilotage functions, but in its capacity as a harbour authority. And Trinity House of course continues to exist.

**506.** Perhaps the most important duty imposed on the Pilotage Commission was that contained in sections 24 and 25 of the 1987 Act to prepare and submit to the Secretary of State proposals for a scheme or schemes for the transfer of property, rights and liabilities of pilotage authorities, including liabilities in respect of pensions payable in respect of staff and former staff, and including arrangements as regards pilotage authority staff. A scheme might also make arrangements for staff employed by licensed pilots if the Commission considered that that would be appropriate.

**507.** In a case where one competent harbour authority became responsible for pilotage functions in the harbours in the former pilotage district or districts of a pilotage authority, the scheme had to provide for the vesting in the harbour authority of the property rights and liabilities of the pilotage authority which, in the opinion of the Commission, had been used, had accrued, or had been incurred exclusively in connection with the pilotage functions of the abolished pilotage authority.

**508.** In a case where more than one competent harbour authority became responsible for pilotage functions in the harbours in the former pilotage district or districts of a pilotage authority, which of course includes the case of Trinity House, then the scheme:
  (a) had to provide for the vesting of the property, rights and liabilities of the pilotage authority which in the opinion of the Commission had been used, had accrued or had been incurred exclusively in connection with the pilotage functions of the abolished pilotage authority in any competent harbour authority the Commission considered appropriate or in the Commission;
  (b) might, if the Commission thought fit, make similar provision as to any property, rights or liabilities of the pilotage authority which in the opinion of the Commission had been used, had accrued or had been incurred substantially but not exclusively in connection with its pilotage functions; and
  (c) might require any competent harbour authority the Commission considered appropriate to make provisions to secure that the future payment of any pension which was payable in respect of staff or former staff of the pilotage authority and which was calculated by reference to remuneration paid and service given before the appointed day was properly funded or guaranteed. That would appear to extend to staff who were not transferred by the scheme.

**509.** With regard to the staff of pilotage authorities, a scheme submitted by the Pilotage Commission had to apply to all the staff of a pilotage authority which would cease to exist as a corporate body or, where the authority would continue to exist in another capacity, to such of the staff as the authority determined were not required by it for its functions in that other capacity.

**510.** In a case where one competent harbour authority became responsible for pilotage functions in the harbours in the former pilotage district or districts of a pilotage authority, then the scheme had to provide for the staff of the pilotage authority to which it applied to be transferred to the competent harbour authority.

**511.** In a case where more than one competent harbour authority became responsible for pilotage functions in the former pilotage district or districts of a pilotage authority, then the scheme had to provide for the staff of the pilotage authority to which it applied to be transferred to such competent harbour authority as the Commission thought fit or to the Commission.

**512.** The Act provides that where staff of a pilotage authority are transferred by a scheme, their contracts of employment are not terminated but continue in force in all respects with the competent harbour authority or, as the case may be, the Commission, stepping into the shoes of the pilotage authority. For the purposes of the Employment Protection (Consolidation) Act 1978, the period of employment with the pilotage authority counts as a period of employment with the competent harbour authority or, as the case may be, the Pilotage Commission. Also, a scheme might provide for compensation for any loss of employment which is attributable to any provision made by or under the Act, but without prejudice to any other rights to compensation. A scheme might therefore provide, and the schemes under sections 24 and 25 did provide, for members of a pilotage authority's staff who were transferred to a competent harbour authority and were shortly afterwards made redundant to be compensated on a special basis in addition to the ordinary statutory redundancy payments.

**513.** The Secretary of State was required to make a scheme or schemes giving effect to the proposals submitted to him by the Commission with such modifications as he considered appropriate. Schemes under sections 24 and 25 of the 1987 Act transferring to competent harbour authorities the property, rights, liabilities and staff of the former pilotage authorities have been duly made by the Secretary of State after appropriate consultation.

**514.** Section 26 of the 1987 Act provides for the abolition of the Pilotage Commission. It is to cease to exist on such day as the Secretary of State may by order appoint, and no later than six months before that day the Commission must submit to the Secretary of State a scheme for its winding up. The Secretary of State is required to provide by order for the transfer of the property, rights and liabilities of the Pilotage Commission, and for arrangements to be made regarding its staff in accordance with the scheme submitted by the Commission, with or without modification.

**515.** Under section 27, in addition to its other specific duties after the Act becomes law, the Pilotage Commission, until it is abolished, will be responsible for advising the Secretary of State on matters connected with the reorganization of pilotage services.

**516.** Section 28 of the 1987 Act requires the Secretary of State to make a scheme or schemes (to be known as "pilots' compensation schemes") to compensate pilots for any loss of employment which they may suffer in consequence of the reorganization of pilotage services under the Act. In accordance with that section the Secretary of State has made a pilots' compensation scheme. It provides that, subject to certain qualifications, any pilot aged between 50 and 65 on the appointed day who was a licensed pilot immediately before that day and who either—

(i) has no arrangements offered to him (whether by way of employment under a contract of employment or otherwise) for the provision of his services as an authorized pilot after the appointed day; or

(ii) has such arrangements made with him which are terminated within three years from the appointed day,

is entitled to a compensation payment calculated in accordance with the scheme (broadly, one year's earnings for pilots aged between 50 and 60 with a progressive reduction in the amount for those aged over 60).

517. Payments are made by competent harbour authorities via the Pilotage Commission which plays an important part in the administration of the scheme and is responsible for determining any disputes as to entitlement to a payment under the scheme.

518. Competent harbour authorities liable for payments under the scheme are, in the case of a pilot who has no arrangements offered to him immediately after the appointed day, the authority or authorities whose harbour or harbours were situated in the former pilotage district for which the pilot was licensed and, in the case of a pilot who has arrangements made with him which are terminated within three years from the appointed day, the authority who terminated those arrangements. The scheme provides for the amount of such payments to be apportioned by the Pilotage Commission where more than one harbour authority is involved.

519. The scheme provides for the repayment of compensation, or a proportion thereof, if a pilot, after receiving compensation is subsequently authorized by a competent harbour authority within the periods specified in the scheme (but occasional authorization for short periods is permitted without repayment).

520. The scheme enables a competent harbour authority to require the whole or part of any existing fund constituted for the purpose of making payments for loss of employment to pilots working in their harbour to be applied towards payments required to be made by the harbour authority under the pilots' compensation scheme.

521. Section 29 of the 1987 Act provides for the funding of the reorganization arrangements. It enabled the Secretary of State, on application by the Pilotage Commission, to make a scheme for the recovery of the Commission's expenses in performing its functions under the Act and any sums required by the Commission by virtue of the Act. Such a scheme might provide for a charge to be imposed on any competent harbour authority and for the amount of the charge to be determined by reference to such factors as the Secretary of State might determine. In accordance with section 29 the Secretary of State has made the Pilotage Commission (Recovery of Expenses) Scheme 1988 which requires each competent harbour authority to pay to the Pilotage Commission one per cent of its revenue from rates charged for the provision of pilotage services (excluding boarding and

landing charges) received by the authority from 1 October 1988 to 31 March 1989 inclusive.

**522.** Under subsection (5) of section 29, a competent harbour authority may recover:

(a) any charges imposed on them by a scheme to meet the costs of, and the expenses of winding up, the Pilotage Commission;

(b) any sums required to meet obligations or liabilities transferred to or imposed on them by a scheme transferring the property, liabilities and staff of a former pilotage authority; and

(c) any payments they are required to make under a pilots' compensation scheme;

by increasing any charges, dues or fees payable to them.

### Pilot boats

**523.** Section 6 of the 1987 Act provides that pilot boats—"ships regularly employed in pilotage services provided by or on behalf of any competent harbour authority"—shall—

(a) if they are operated by the authority be approved by the authority; and

(b) otherwise (i.e., if they are operated by an agent on behalf of the authority pursuant to arrangements made under section 11) be licensed by the authority.

Section 6 also requires a competent harbour authority to make such other provisions as it considers necessary for the operation of pilot boats.

**524.** It is expected that the Secretary of State, under enabling powers contained in sections 21 and 22 of the Merchant Shipping Act 1979, will make regulations to secure the safety of pilot boats.

### Deep sea pilotage certificates

**525.** A deep sea pilotage certificate relates to the competence of a person to act as a pilot in respect of any part of the sea falling outside the harbour of a competent harbour authority. It is a recommendation to masters of ships but does not entitle the holder to supersede any other person as the pilot of a ship. In short, it has no legal force. Section 23 of the 1987 Act enables the Secretary of State to authorize any body appearing to him to be competent to do so to grant deep sea certificates in respect of such part of the sea falling outside the harbour of any competent harbour authority as he may specify. Any body for the time being so authorized may grant a deep sea certificate to any person on application by him if they are satisfied (by examination or by reference to such criteria as they may reasonably impose) that he is qualified to act as a pilot of a ship for the area in respect of which the body is authorized to grant deep sea certificates.

**526.** Since, as indicated in paragraph 497 *ante*, an authorized pilot is not entitled to supersede any other person piloting a ship in the approaches to a harbour as distinct from the harbour itself authorized pilots and deep sea pilots could, at least in theory, be competing with each other in the approaches to a harbour.

**527.** The pilots' compensation scheme described in paragraphs 516 to 520 *ante* disqualifies from entitlement to compensation thereunder a pilot who, at the relevant time, is the holder of a deep sea pilotage certificate.

**528.** Before the appointed day for the coming into force of the main provisions of the 1987 Act deep sea pilotage certificates had been granted by such pilotage authorities as were authorized to do so by pilotage orders made under the Pilotage Act 1913 or the Pilotage Act 1983 and related to parts of the sea outside a pilotage district. Paragraph 6 of Schedule 1 to the 1987 Act requires the Secretary of State, on application by any body which immediately before the appointed day was authorized, as mentioned above, to grant deep sea pilotage certificates, to authorize that body to grant such certificates under section 23. This would, in particular, relate to Trinity House. Paragraph 6 also provides that any deep sea pilotage certificate granted to any person pursuant to a pilotage order which is in force immediately before the appointed day in respect of any area shall continue in force during the period for which it was granted and may, on application by him, be renewed by any body authorized under section 23 to grant deep sea pilotage certificates in respect of the whole or part of the area concerned.

# CHAPTER 13

# DIVISION OF CONTROL BETWEEN
# MASTER AND PILOT

**534.** Before 1913 the owner or master of a ship being navigated in circumstances in which pilotage was compulsory was not answerable for any loss or damage occasioned by the fault of a compulsory pilot. This situation led to a profusion of cases coming before the courts where an almost unending stream of litigants attempted to attach either blame or exculpation to pilots in order to avoid the payment of costly damages. The result was that hardship was frequently inflicted on innocent persons whose property had received damage, and the Departmental Committee of 1911 strongly recommended that the defence of compulsory pilotage should be abolished.

**535.** The Pilotage Act 1913 achieved this purpose by making the shipowner answerable for any loss or damage "caused by the vessel or by any fault of the navigation of the vessel" whether pilotage was compulsory or not[1], and as a consequence since the shipowner had to meet the cost in either event, the question as to whether either the master or the pilot was responsible for damage has, since 1913, been largely academic. Now that many pilots have become employees of the harbour authorities, however, it may well be that in future cases the courts will consider harbour authorities whose pilots are under contracts of employment to be principals and as such to be vicariously responsible for any damage caused by them. If this is so then the question of the division of responsibility between the master and the pilot may again assume some significance and the judgments given in the pre-1913 cases may well be used to assist the courts in apportioning blame.

**536.** It is proposed to examine these cases in detail, therefore, but before doing so there will be a brief examination of the general attitudes which masters and pilots have towards each other, with particular reference to their respective attitudes to the division of responsibility.

## General attitudes of masters and pilots

**537.** The atmosphere on a ship's bridge during the pilotage operation is usually one of cordial professionalism and mutual respect between master and pilot. Any personal views which the master might have about pilots in general, and vice versa,

---

1. Pilotage Act 1913 section 15(1), Pilotage Act 1983, section 35, and now Pilotage Act 1987, section 16.

are confined well below the surface and only very rarely manifest themselves in open mistrust or hostility. These attitudes are nevertheless of some importance, as they are generally symptomatic of a basic misunderstanding of the legal relationship between the master and the pilot—a misunderstanding caused by vaguely worded legislation and the fact that since 1913 the superior courts have seldom had occasion to give judgment on this particular aspect of the law. The respective views of the master and pilot are now considered.

### The master's view

**538.** From his earliest days at sea the master has seen the expression "proceeding to master's instructions and pilot's advice" written in the deck log on each occasion that a pilot has been on board, and he accepts this as documentary proof that he is personally responsible for all the acts and omissions of the pilot, a conviction which is frequently shared by his employers.

**539.** The amount of freedom which the master gives to the pilot varies considerably between masters. Generally speaking, the masters of smaller coasting vessels have a greater tendency to overrule or ignore a pilot's instructions than those in larger vessels. Masters of large foreign-going vessels are inclined to assume a more passive attitude, carefully observing but seldom interfering with the manoeuvring of the vessel. This difference in attitude is undoubtedly the result of the difference in background and training between the two types of master. The coasting master is called upon to perform his own pilotage duties in a number of ports with which he is familiar and therefore usually considers himself to be fairly skilled in basic ship handling. Also, by virtue of the type of trade in which he is engaged, the coasting master will frequently visit several ports in the course of a week. The master of a large vessel engaged on long international voyages, however, is seldom called upon to conduct his own vessel into or out of port, and the interval between such operations is usually much greater. It does not follow, however, that the foreign-going master has a greater faith in the ability of pilots than his coasting counterpart; he simply feels himself powerless to intervene through lack of local knowledge and lack of experience in practical ship handling.

**540.** In ports where pilotage is not compulsory, the coasting master's confidence in the ability of pilots will be reflected to a certain extent in his decision whether or not to employ them. The master of the larger foreign-going vessel, on the other hand, even if not compelled by law to take a pilot will usually feel compelled by expediency and, on occasions when casualties occur, will regard himself as the innocent victim of a system over which he has no control. Such masters are quite indifferent as to whether pilotage in a particular port is compulsory or not.

**541.** Irrespective of the legal position, masters are generally resigned to the fact that they will be held to blame by their owners for damage occasioned while under pilotage. The majority of incidents involving damage do not come before the courts, and in these cases blame is usually apportioned after an informal investigation by the owners. Disciplinary measures against the master can take several forms; he might be penalized financially by the forfeiture of his safe navigation bonus, although this is a practice which appears to be dying out; he might be demoted to first mate; and on some occasions might be dismissed from the company. Even in circumstances where no disciplinary action is taken, the master usually feels that damage sustained by any vessel under his command is a blot on his record, and it is often resented.

### The pilot's view

**542.** Pilots generally dislike interference in the conduct of the ship by the master. They interpret it as an imputation of incompetence by a person not fully qualified to judge and frequently attribute accidents to the master's unwarranted intrusion. They feel that whatever a person's sea-going experience, when he first becomes a pilot a minimum period of basic training is essential. Pilots believe, having undergone this extensive period of training in what they consider to be a highly specialized field, that in circumstances where there is no time for consultation and "instant" decisions are required the pilot is the person who is best qualified to appraise the situation. They consider that the master's duty is to advise the pilot of the handling characteristics of the vessel and to ensure that the crew carry out the pilot's instructions. The same view has been expressed by pilots with previous command experience.

**543.** The term "adviser", which is frequently applied to the pilot, is considered to be derogatory and contrary to the actual situation on board ship. They see it as a word which underrates their professional skill and casts the pilot in the role of a passive onlooker, watching the master navigate his ship into port and only offering opinions when they are asked for, or when they appear to be required. They also feel that the label "adviser" has been an impediment to them when conducting negotiations regarding their remuneration.

### Division of control under statute law

**544.** Although the Pilotage Acts 1913 and 1983 made no specific references to the duties of a pilot the general implication was that the pilot did not act simply as an adviser but was responsible for the navigation of the ship. When navigating in a compulsory pilotage area, for example, the master of a ship was obliged to "give the charge of piloting" to any licensed pilot for the district who offered his services. The courts generally took the view that the master was entitled to take control of the vessel if the considered the pilot to be incompetent, but that if an accident ensued he would have to justify his action. In the case of *The Tower Field*,[2] for example, Lord Norman said:

The master is not merely entitled but bound to point out to the compulsory pilot that he may

---

2. *Tower Field (Owners)* v. *Workington Harbour and Dock Board* (H.L.) (1950) 84 Ll.L.Rep. 233, at p. 259.

be mistaken in an opinion he has formed (*The Tactician*).[3] He is also entitled, in order to avoid immediate peril, to take the navigation out of the hands of the pilot, but if he does so he must be prepared to show justification (*The Prinses Juliana*).[4]

The court held in this case that of those on board the ship the pilot was solely to blame.

**545.** In *The Prinses Juliana* case cited above, Bucknill, J., said:

. . . if the master sees fit to take the navigation out of the hands of the pilot and counter-mands his orders, he must satisfy the court that he was justified in so doing, and that the action which he took was at all events more calculated to avoid a collision than the manoeuvre which he countermanded.[5]

**546.** In a collision case heard in 1952 the defendant was a master and part owner of a vessel which caused a collision in the entrance to Dover Harbour. The collision was caused by the pilot's admitted negligence in disregarding a local signal and the master sought to limit his liability as part owner on the ground that the accident occurred without his actual fault or privity. The plaintiffs contended that the master had contributed to the accident because, *inter alia*, he had failed to acquaint himself beforehand with the local regulations. Wilmer, J., however, granted a limitation decree and in giving his decision said:

It would be, in my judgment, putting too much upon a master, and would be asking him to exercise more than ordinary care, to regard him as being under a duty to know all the local signals when he has a pilot on board, or to expect him to be ready to query the pilot's actions in relation to such signals. In my judgment, on such matters of purely local knowledge, a master exercising ordinary and reasonable care is entitled to rely on the guidance which he obtains from the local pilot.[6]

**547.** In the case of *The Saltero* the pilot was instructed by the harbour master to arrive off the dock entrance at 10 minutes after high water. Because the only two available tugs had a previous commitment the pilot proceeded to navigate the vessel slowly up the approach channel in anticipation of the tugs meeting him at a certain distance along it. At approximately seven minutes after high water the pilot observed the two tugs engaged in towing a submarine, whereupon he stopped the engines. Three minutes later the vessel grounded and broke her back on the falling tide. It was held in this case that the grounding of the *Saltero* was due solely to the negligence of the pilot in that it was necessary to hold back; in that it was unseamanlike to lose steerage way while on the port side of the channel; and that through his own inobservance he failed to appreciate the danger of grounding.[7]

**548.** The Pilotage Act 1987 refers throughout to "piloting" and "pilotage" and section 31 states that the word "pilot" has the same meaning as in the Merchant Shipping Act 1894 and that "pilotage" shall be construed accordingly. As the definitions of "master" and "pilot" have not been changed it seems unlikely, there-

---

3. *The Tactician* [1907] P. 244; 10 Asp. M.L.C. 534.
4. *The Prinses Juliana* [1936] P. 139; 54 Ll.L.Rep. 234.
5. *The Prinses Juliana* [1936] 18 Asp. M.L.C. 614, at p. 619.
6. The *Hans Hoth* [1952] 2 Lloyd's Rep. 341, at p. 349.
7. *The Saltero* [1958] 2 Lloyd's Rep. 232.

fore, that the respective duties of the master and pilot have been affected by the change in legislation.

### The master's liability

**549.** The courts have never ruled as to whether the master is legally responsible for the pilot's mistakes but the weight of authoritative opinion seems to lie in favour of the view that the master is not responsible for damage incurred when the navigation of the vessel is in the hands of the pilot. MacLachlan, for example, says:

At common law the pilot, being appointed by the owners, or their servant the master, is their agent, and they are responsible for damage done by the ship while under his charge. How far the master, as having employed him, may be considered in the light of a principal, and answerable in that capacity for his acts, may be doubtful; but as master merely, notwithstanding the dictum of Mansfield, C.J., the better opinion seems to be that he is not responsible while the ship is in the hands of the pilot, if he takes care that the pilot's orders are promptly obeyed by the crew.[8]

**550.** The *dictum* of Mansfield, C.J., referred to by MacLachlan was given in the case of *Bowcher* v. *Noidstrom*. In this case the pilot of the defendant master's vessel ordered the crew to board the plaintiff's vessel to cut free the jib boom which had pierced the defendant's mainsail. An action for trespass was brought against the master who happened to be asleep at the time of the incident. With respect to the master's liability, Mansfield, C.J., was of the opinion that although there was a pilot on board, the pilot did not represent the ship, and the master was still answerable for every trespass.[9] In a later case, however, in which an action was brought against the owner of a ship for the negligence of a pilot employed by both himself and the master, it was held that the pilot was a competent witness for the defendant although he had not been released by the master "because the captain could not be responsible for the misconduct of the pilot".[10]

**551.** Marsden's opinion on this subject is as follows:

As regards the responsibility of the master when a pilot is on board, whether by compulsion of law or by the master's or owner's choice, it seems clear that for a collision caused by the fault of the pilot the master is not answerable, if the pilot has been placed in charge of the ship properly and in the ordinary course of navigation.[11]

**552.** Marsden cites Chancellor Kent as an authority who also doubts the judgment of Mansfield, C.J.

The pilot, while on board, has the exclusive control of the ship. He is considered as master *pro hac vice*, and if any loss or injury be sustained in the navigation of the vessel while under the charge of the pilot, he is answerable, as strictly as if he were a common carrier, for his default, negligence, or unskilfulness; and the owner would also be responsible to the party injured for the act of the pilot, as being the act of his agent. Though some doubt has been raised by the dictum of Ch.J.Mansfield in *Bowcher* v. *Noidstrom*, yet the weight of authority,

8. *MacLachlan's Treatise on the Law of Merchant Shipping*, 7th edn., London, 1932, p. 211.
9. *Bowcher* v. *Noidstrom* (1809) 127 E.R. 954.
10. *Aldrich* v. *Simmons* (1816) 171 E.R. 451.
11. Marsden: *The Law of Collisions at Sea. British Shipping Laws*, vol. 4, 11th edn., para. 69.

and the better reason is, that the master, in such a case, would not be responsible as master, though on board, provided the crew acted in regular obedience to the pilot.[12]

**553.** Marsden also cites the case of *Stort* v. *Clement*, but this case should be treated with some circumspection as on this occasion the pilot was also the ship's sailing master and a member of the ship's company. As such he would not come within the present definition of a pilot but rather within an earlier definition which did not preclude persons belonging to the ship. His position, however, was analogous with the modern pilot, for, by the terms of his commission, the sailing master was entrusted with the navigation of the ship under the command of his superior officer. In this case an action was brought against the pilot for running down a brig belonging to the plaintiff, and it was stated by Lord Kenyon that although the pilot might be obliged to act in obedience to the orders of the lieutenant, yet if in this case the accident had happened through the defendant's misconduct, he was answerable. It was proved, however, that the lieutenant had instructed him to conduct the ship in a particular manner, in consequence of which the accident occurred.[13]

**554.** In Canada the Royal Commission on pilotage gave the following opinion on the subject of the master's liability:

Whilst the master always retains his responsibility for the safety of the ship, his responsibility in the sense of liability is not absolute. Either civilly, criminally, or with respect to the safety of navigation, he is answerable only for his own acts, mistakes, negligence or omissions. At civil law he is merely a servant of the owner and he does not incur personally any civil responsibility for any damage caused by a pilot's error in which he did not participate or which he could not have prevented.[14]

**555.** It would seem from the authorities cited, therefore, that the master does not incur any personal liability for the actions of the pilot while the latter has the conduct of the ship. The pilot, however, does not supersede the master in his command of the ship, and if the master decides to overrule the pilot's directions the responsibility is transferred to him.

## The pilot's liability

**556.** Before the Pilotage Act 1987 came into force the pilot's personal liability was limited to £100, plus the amount of pilotage charges in respect of the voyage during which the liability arose. Under the new Act the figure of £100 has increased to £1,000.

**557.** Because of this strict limitation on personal liability actions against pilots have been rare. Nevertheless actions against pilots for personal negligence have occasionally taken place, although not in recent years. In *The Octavia Stella*, for example, a pilot was held solely to blame for damage caused by a vessel grounding

---

12. James Kent: *Commentaries on American Law*, vol. 3, 3rd edn., 1836, p. 176.
13. *Stort* v. *Clement* (1792) 170 E.R. 109.
14. CANADA. *Report of Royal Commission, &c., op. cit.*, Part 1, p. 27

on some oyster beds[15] and in the case of *Stort* v. *Clement, ante,* the judge made it clear that the pilot would have been answerable if the accident had been caused by his negligence. Again, in the case of *London School Board* v. *Lardner,* it was held that the pilot had given an incorrect helm order and he was ordered to pay damages of £75.[16]

**558.** A pilot whose negligence results in someone's death may be convicted of manslaughter. In the case of *R.* v. *Spence* it was alleged that a boat was run down and life was lost because a foreign helmsman had misunderstood the pilot's instructions and put the helm the wrong way. In giving his instructions to the jury Lord Denman, C.J., said:

The law is, that if the prisoner has produced the death by any conduct of his, he is guilty of manslaughter. It appears to me that he was the person guiding and directing the vessel, and that he is responsible for its management. It is extremely unfortunate that he did not, in the first instance, make the foreigners understand such simple directions as starboard and larboard. You will consider whether there was some negligence upon the part of the prisoner, in not making the foreigners understand thoroughly. I take your opinion whether he was guilty of negligence in this respect, and whether that negligence caused the death. If you think so, you will find him guilty.

The defendant was found not guilty on the facts.[17]

### Judicial attitude to "divided authority"

**559.** The attitude of the courts to the master-pilot relationship is based on precedents created more than a century ago, the guiding principle of which has been throughout that the paramount danger to a ship under pilotage is that created by a "divided authority". Attention was drawn to this danger on innumerable occasions, but was perhaps put most succinctly by Dr Lushington in the case of *The Peerless* in 1860:

There may be occasions on which the master of a ship is justified in interfering with the pilot in charge, but they are very rare. If we encourage such interfering, we should have a double authority on board, a *divisum imperium,* the parent of all confusion, from which many accidents and much mischief would probably ensue. If the pilot is intoxicated, or is steering a course to the certain destruction of the vessel, the master no doubt may interfere and ought to interfere, but it is only in urgent cases.[18]

**560.** It would appear, however, from what has been deduced so far, that the legal relationship between the master and the pilot is based on principles which are contradictory:

    (i) that division of authority is inimical to the safety of navigation;

    (ii) that the pilot, by definition, has the conduct of the ship;

15. *The Octavia Stella* (1887) 6 Asp. M.L.C. 182.
16. *London School Board* v. *Lardner. The Times,* 20 February 1884.
17. *R.* v. *Spence* (1846) 1 Cox C.C. 352.
18. *The Peerless* (1860) 167 E.R. 16, at p. 17.

    (iii)  that the master, by definition, has command or charge of the ship, a defi-
nition which specifically excludes the pilot.[19]

**561.**  In order to reconcile these apparent inconsistencies it becomes necessary to:

    (i)  differentiate between the expressions "to conduct a ship" and "to be in command of a ship"; and

    (ii)  draw up a code of procedure for vessels under pilotage based upon legal decisions, which defines the respective duties of the master and the pilot.

With regard to the first of these requirements it is evident that confusion as to the difference in meaning between these two terms is not confined to the layman. The words of Bargreave Deane, J., for example, in the case of *The Nord* would indicate that he considered the two expressions to be synonymous when he said: "I think the word 'conducted' means that the pilot is in charge . . . he is in command."[20]

**562.**  The Canadian Royal Commission, however, drew a very careful distinction between the two expressions thus:

"To conduct a ship" must not be confused with being "in command of a ship". The first expression refers to an action, to a personal service being performed; the second to a power. The question whether a pilot has control of navigation is a question of fact and not of law. The fact that a pilot has been given control of the ship for navigational purposes does not mean that the pilot has superseded the master. The master is, and remains, in command; he is the authority aboard. He may, and does, delegate part of his authority to subordinates and to outside assistants whom he employs to navigate his ship, i.e., pilots. A delegation of power is not an abandonment of authority, but one way of exercising authority.[21]

**563.**  With regard to the second requirement, having established that both the pilot and the master have active roles to play, it becomes essential that the duties of both should be clearly defined in order to minimize the dangers which are inherent in the "divided authority" situation. These respective duties are now considered.

### Division of control under case law

**564.**  What, then, are the respective duties of the master and pilot? The answer to this question lies mainly in the body of case law dating from the mid 19th century up to the effective date of the repeal of section 633 of the Merchant Shipping Act 1894, during which period it was possible for a shipowner to escape liability for damage when such damage was caused by a compulsory pilot. In order to rebut a defence of compulsory pilotage it was necessary to prove that there was contributory negligence on the part of the servants (i.e., the master and crew), and in many cases, therefore, it became necessary for the courts to distinguish between "pilot's duties" and "master's duties"; that is, to determine which components of the pilotage operation came within the master's jurisdiction and which came within that of the pilot. From a careful study of these cases it is possible to break down the pilotage operation into its constituent parts and to attribute responsibility for them

19. Merchant Shipping Act 1894, s. 742.
20. *The Nord* (1916) 13 Asp. M.L.C. 606, at p. 608.
21. CANADA. *Report of Royal Commission, &c., op. cit.*, Part 1, pp. 26–27.

either to the master or to the pilot. In studying these cases it is necessary to bear in mind that many of them took place more than a century ago and they should be considered in that light, and for this reason many of the cases which deal exclusively with the handling of sailing vessels have been omitted. On the other hand, despite the fact that the design of the power-driven vessel has changed considerably since its first appearance, the basic concept has remained unchanged, namely the provision of motive power by means of screw propulsion, and the provision of turning power by means of a rudder. Similarly, although sophisticated navigational aids have been produced, in recent years the basic technique of navigation in close waters is roughly the same—the direction-finding power of the compass has been improved by the gyroscope, the echo-sounder has replaced the hand lead but its function is precisely the same, and the look-out has been augmented, but not replaced by, the radar.

**565.** It should also be noted that nearly all the cases cited are concerned with compulsory pilotage, and it cannot be automatically assumed that the courts would assign the same degree of responsibility to the pilot if he was employed voluntarily. At the same time, in many of these cases it was a matter of considerable legal argument whether pilotage was compulsory for the ships concerned owing to the multifarious exemptions which were then available, and frequently the first task of the court was to rule upon this point before the defence of compulsory pilotage could be put forward. It would be difficult to see, therefore, how in practice a pilot's whole approach to the task of navigating a ship could vary depending on whether the particular ship concerned had employed him voluntarily or by compulsion, especially when this was, and still is, frequently in dispute.

### Master's duty to employ a pilot

**566.** A master is only legally bound to employ pilots in areas where pilotage is compulsory (assuming that neither he nor his first mate has a pilotage exemption certificate under section 8 of the Pilotage Act 1987). A master can, however, be held to blame for not employing a pilot, even when pilotage is not compulsory, if it can be shown that his failure to do so caused or contributed to an accident. This can be deduced from the judgment given in the case of a vessel which was exempt from compulsory pilotage and which caused a collision in the River Thames. It was held by the court that the vessel was negligent for proceeding without a pilot in that the absence of a pilot or similarly informed person was a dominant cause of the vessel's negligent navigation.[22]

**567.** In practice, given the choice, a ship's master might be motivated by a variety of factors when deciding whether or not to employ a pilot, with "local knowledge" not necessarily being on the top of his list of priorities. Masters of small coasting vessels are frequently under pressure from their owners to keep the employment of pilots to a minimum. Some owners allegedly pay their masters a

---

22. *The Alletta* [1965] 2 Lloyd's Rep. 479.

bonus for doing their own piloting, while others might require a written explanation if a master employs a pilot in a given port on more than a specified number of occasions. Some coasting masters take a pride in handling their own vessels and resent the imposition of compulsory pilotage upon them, while others seek every excuse to take pilots and see compulsory pilotage as a means of shifting their responsibilities. There is a feeling among some masters that if they do not employ pilots retaliatory action will be taken, and they will be kept waiting if they require pilots on subsequent occasions. Some also believe that ships carrying pilots are shown favourable treatment by port officials and they therefore take pilots on sufferance.

### General duties of master and pilot

**568.** Before dealing in detail with the various aspects of the pilotage operation, it is worth noting some general remarks which have been made by judges on the subject of the respective duties of master and pilot:

Per Baron Parke:

The duties of the master and the pilot in many respects are clearly defined. Although the pilot has charge of the ship, the owners are most clearly responsible to third persons for the sufficiencies of the ship and her equipments, the competency of the master and crew, and their obedience to the orders of the pilot in everything that concerns his duty, and under ordinary circumstances we think that his commands are to be implicitly obeyed. To him belongs the whole conduct of the navigation of the ship, to the safety of which it is important that the chief direction should be vested in one only.[23]

Per Brett, L.J.:

The duty of a pilot in England is too well known and too universally applied to require any enactment with regard to it at all. It is to regulate the navigation of the ship, and to conduct it so far as the course of the ship is concerned. He has no other power on board the ship; he has no power over the discipline of the ship, he has no power over the cargo on board; he has no power with regard to the various matters which are necessary to enable him to perform his duty; he cannot place a man on the look-out, or regulate the place at which the look-out man shall be on board the ship. He has nothing to do but to control the navigation.[24]

Per Lord Alverstone, C.J.:

I think the cardinal principle to be borne in mind in these cases . . . is that the pilot is in sole charge of the ship, and that all directions as to speed, course, stopping and reversing and everything of that kind are for the pilot . . . But side by side with that principle is the other principle that the pilot is entitled to the fullest assistance of a competent crew, of a competent look-out, and a well-found ship.[25]

Per Bargreave Deane, J.:

I have to . . . lay down what I think is the true principle as to the duty of ship's officers and crew towards the pilot, and . . . unless the man is incompetent in the sense of being ill

---

23. *The Christiana* (1850) 13 E.R. 841.
24. *The Guy Mannering* (1882) 4 Asp. M.L.C. 553, at p. 554.
25. *The Tactician* (1907) 10 Asp. M.L.C. 534, at p. 537.

or the worse for drink, or something of that sort which justifies force majeure, the officers of the vessel have no right to take control of the navigation out of the hands of the pilot, yet he is entitled to every assistance which can be rendered to him by those on board the ship.[26]

**569.** There is no absolute need for the master to be on the bridge throughout the entire period in which the pilot is on board. In the case of *The Umsinga*, for example, where a collision occurred when the master was momentarily below, Sir Samuel Evans said:

It is easy to conceive cases in which . . . a master must be on the bridge before it can be rightly said that all the assistance which the law requires to be given to the pilot by the master and the crew is given, and in which his absence might be evidence of negligence of default . . . But, in my opinion, it cannot be held as a matter of law, or as an inflexible rule of good navigation that the master must be there, or that his absence amounts to default for which his owners are liable, when he provides a competent officer, or where there are no special circumstances of difficulty, or no special matters within his knowledge of which he ought to be ready to inform the pilot . . .

It is beside the question to inquire whether the master, if on the bridge, might . . . have caused the pilot to avoid the collision. If he is not there, and is not bound by the law, or by the rules of good navigation to be there, the court cannot surmise what he would have done if he was there.[27]

## Legal meaning of "interference"

**570.** Many of the pre-1913 Act cases turned on the question of the master's right to interfere with the pilot's instructions. In these cases the master could be found to have contributed to the accident, thus destroying his owners' defence of compulsory pilotage, in one of two ways:

   (i) by interfering with the pilot when there was no just reason for doing so, or

   (ii) by failing to interfere with the pilot when the evidence showed that there was just reason for doing so.

**571.** Dr Lushington defined "interference" as follows:

I should never go to the length of saying that the mere suggesting to the pilot on the part of the master to take in this sail, or otherwise to keep as near the South Sand light, and vice versa, or to bring the ship up, was interfering, in the legal acceptation of the term, with the duties of the pilot; illegal interference is of a different description. If, for example, in this case the boatswain had called out to the men below to starboard the helm, or if the master had called out to port the helm, it would be interference; but it would not be interference to consult the pilot, or to suggest to him the measures pursued were not proper, or that other measures would in all probability be attended with greater success.[28]

**572.** Thus, in the case of *The Oakfield* where the pilot gave, at the suggestion of the master, an improper order which brought about a collision with a vessel at anchor, it was held that the master's intervention did not transfer the responsibility of the pilot to the master. The judge justified his decision as follows:

---

26. *The Ape* (1914) 12 Asp. M.L.C. 487, at p. 489.
27. *The Umsinga* (1912) 12 Asp. M.L.C. 174, at p. 176.
28. *The Lochlibo* (1850) 166 E.R. 978, at p. 985.

There is a conflict as to how this order to starboard came to be given, but the pilot admits that the words proceeded from his lips. To excuse himself he says he was merely carrying out the captain's order, and that it was not his order at all. I cannot accept that explanation. I feel convinced that the true solution of the case is, that when the *Duchess of Albany* was first seen there was no doubt as to whether she was or was not at anchor, that the captain very likely did strongly express an opinion that it would be safe and proper to starboard and go across her bows, that the pilot adopted that view and gave the order which brought about the collision.[29]

**573.** In another case where the master, for the benefit of the crew, merely repeated the pilot's instructions, it was held that the pilot was responsible for the manoeuvre carried out as a result even though the actual order proceeded from the master's lips.[30]

**574.** Interference by the master, therefore, must be of a positive nature either in the form of a direct order in the absence of any order being given by the pilot; or in the form of a direct revocation of an order given by the pilot, and the pilot who acts, contrary to his better judgment, on the mere advice or suggestion of the master may be held liable if an accident follows as a result.

**575.** In practice, interference comes in a variety of guises, of which "covert interference" is perhaps the most harmful. On board small vessels, for example, when entering or leaving port the master is often the only member of the ship's company on the bridge, and he not only steers the vessel but is responsible for engine movements as well. In the circumstances the pilot's instructions are frequently modified by the master. A request for "half astern" will often produce a movement of "full astern" and when altering course the master will frequently begin to steady the vessel before the pilot wishes to do so. This type of interference is more difficult to detect in vessels fitted with modern navigational aids such as bow-thrusts and variable pitch propellers, which are operated by the master with fingertip control, and in some cases the vessels concerned are fairly large. Here, a pilot who is unaware of what the master is doing, might attribute a sudden movement of the vessel caused by the surreptitious application of a bow thrust to the effect of wind or tide and take counteraction which is inappropriate. A further disadvantage of such vessels is that no written record is kept of movements so that in the event of an accident the facts would be difficult to prove.

**576.** When manoeuvring a vessel alongside a jetty or into a lock the dangers of a divided command are intensified, and it is in this critical part of the operation that damage is most likely to be incurred. Here, since split-second timing is essential, there is little opportunity for consultation or advice, and yet it is at this point that the master, if he is that way inclined, is most likely to interfere. It is here also that the contrast between coasting and foreign-going masters is most sharply defined, with the former sometimes attempting to take over the operation completely. In those smaller vessels where the master also doubles as helmsman, he suffers from the disadvantage of having his field of vision considerably reduced, and the master

---

29. *The Oakfield* (1886) 5 Asp. M.L.C. 575, *per* Sir James Hannen, at p. 577.
30. *The Admiral Boxer* (1857) 166 E.R. 1090.

who wishes to supervise the berthing operation himself has to spend his time oscillating between the bridge wing and the helm.

577.  On board foreign vessels, where the master is often the only member of the ship's company with a knowledge of English, the language barrier provides a useful smoke-screen for covert interference. Here, when a pilot gives an instruction the master, if he thinks a different movement is required, will give his own instructions in the vernacular, with the result that the pilot can never be sure that his orders are properly being carried out. In these cases, where the master not only interprets the pilot's instructions but censors them as well, the dangers of a divided authority are obviously exacerbated.

### Keeping a look-out

578.  It has been stated in general terms that it is the responsibility of the master and crew to keep a proper look-out and to pass on all relevant information to the pilot. This has been interpreted in the widest possible sense by the courts and includes the reporting of all circumstances and incidents which might influence the pilot's actions, and not merely the sighting of lights, buoys, beacons, etc. In the case of *The Batavier*, for example, a steamer which was proceeding up a river under the control of a pilot caused such a swell that a barge laden with coal was sunk. It was held that the steamer was to blame for failing to stop in time to avoid the accident. Although the pilot was to blame for failing to check the speed the owners were liable because it appeared in evidence that neither the swell nor the barge had been seen from the steamer, and that therefore there was not a good look-out.[31]

579.  Keeping a look-out also means the reporting of all material facts even if the pilot is in a position where he ought to be able to see things clearly for himself. In the case of *The Alexander Shukoff*, for example, a pilot was navigating a vessel at full speed in narrow waters among a large number of other vessels and the course taken was such that it must have been obvious to the master that a dangerous situation was developing. It was held in this case that it was the master's duty to call the pilot's attention to the risk, and that he was not justified in doing nothing. Lord Birkenhead, L.C., said;

In circumstances which called for the greatest care and fullest assistance he [the pilot] was left to his own observation. It is obvious from his own explanation that he was not fully aware of the position and intentions of both these vessels at the time of the collision. It may be (though I am not satisfied on this point) that he ought to have been aware, but a pilot's duty is that of controlling the navigation of the ship and his attention must at times be concentrated on some particular fact. He is entitled to have the assistance of a look-out and timely reports of material incidents.[32]

In the same case Lord Molton said:

The defendants say that the pilot ought to have found these things for himself and that, therefore, they are excused for having omitted to report them to him. Now it must be

31.  *The Batavier* (1854) 164 E.R. 218.
32.  *The Alexander Shukoff* (1920) 15 Asp. M.L.C. 122, at p. 125.

remembered that the pilot has many things to think of, especially where . . . he is leaving port in company with other vessels and new incidents may at any moment arise. He needs, therefore, to be in a position of feeling that he can give his whole attention to his duties of management secure that all relevant occurrences will be duly reported to him.[33]

**580.** If, however, it can be shown that the pilot was at all times fully aware of all the circumstances leading up to a collision, it would seem that the absence of an efficient look-out would not necessarily constitute evidence of contributory negligence on the part of the ship. In the case of *The Kamouraska*, for example, which ran down a torpedo-boat in the River Thames while under the control of a pilot, Viscount Finlay in the House of Lords said:

. . . He must have been, from his own observation, perfectly aware of the torpedo-boat and her movements at all material times. Under these circumstances it is not easy to see how, even if there had been an omission on the part of the lookout . . . to report the torpedo-boat, this omission could have contributed to the accident, as the pilot was throughout in full possession of all the facts himself.[34]

**581.** In practice, the quality of the look-out (in the broad sense of the term) varies from ship to ship and it is almost impossible to generalize on this point. There is an understandable reluctance on the part of the master to point out what is apparently obvious, and in good visibility the pilot is usually expected to observe things for himself. In thick weather, on the other hand, the pilot is usually given adequate assistance.

### The observance of Collision Regulations

**582.** As far as the question as to whether the master or the pilot is responsible for the observance of the Collision Regulations is concerned, it would appear that this would depend on the type of regulation involved, i.e., whether it concerns the exhibition of navigation lights, the use of sound signals, or the observance of the steering and sailing rules. In the case of *The Ripon*, for example, the vessel concerned was under tow and dropping stern foremost in the Humber with the tide, and was eventually brought athwart the tide to go into the dock. She was showing, in addition to the regulation masthead and sidelights, a white light showing astern, which had been placed there on the pilot's instructions. The exhibition of such a light was contrary to the Collision Regulations which were in force at that time. Another vessel coming down the Humber collided with the *Ripon* . Although the blame was admitted by the other vessel it was held that the *Ripon* was also to blame, as it was impossible to say that the improper exhibition of a stern light had not contributed to the collision. It was held that as the master had permitted an infringement of the regulations the defence of compulsory pilotage failed. Butt, J., justified his decision as follows:

It is clear that a master should not allow a light to be improperly carried as to cause an infringement of the regulations. Suppose for example a pilot for some reason chose to order

---

33. *Ibid.*, at p. 130.
34. *The Kamouraska* (1920) 2 Ll.L.Rep. 125, 299, at p. 300.

a green light to be carried on the port side, it would be impossible to say that this should be allowed by the master. The latter must consider for himself whether the law in respect to lights is being infringed, and if it is he must take steps to stop such infringement.[35]

## Sound signals

583. The law regarding the making of sound signals is unclear. In the case of *The Saint Paul* it was left open as to whether the master ought to call the attention of the pilot to the fact that sound signals (in this case fog signals) ought to be given, and also the point was left open as to whether the responsibility for giving such signals rests with the pilot or the master.[36] The first point, but not the second, seems to have been resolved in the case of *The Elysia*. In this case a vessel which was at anchor in the River Mersey and showing anchor lights was being attended by a tug which was stemming the tide but was not made fast to the vessel. The tug was showing the proper lights for a vessel under way and her green light was open to an upcoming steamship, under the control of a pilot, in such a position that the latter thought he was approaching a vessel under way showing a green light. It was held that although the pilot could not properly complain of being misled by the green light, the master had contributed to the accident because, *inter alia*, he knew what the pilot was doing and had failed to call his attention to the fact that no sound signal had been given. The President of the court, Sir Samual Evans, said:

> The master himself knew what the pilot was doing, and notwithstanding these three different orders to the helm, he did not call the attention of the pilot to the fact that he had not ordered any sound signals to be given. If sound signals had been given what would have happened? No answer would have been given . . . but some signal could be given . . . that the *Explorer* was not in a position to alter her course at all. In this way it would have been brought to the notice of those on the *Elysia* . . . that this vessel was at anchor. Then the collision might have been avoided at the last.[37]

## Private sound signals

584. The courts do not approve of the use of private sound signals between pilots in contravention of the Collision Regulations, but the position of the master in such a situation is unclear. In the case of *The Century* for example, Hewson, J., said:

> Whatever may be the understanding between pilots . . . in regard to the use of manoeuvring signals . . . these signals are signals which mean nothing more and nothing less than "I am directing my course to starboard" . . . and those signals mean nothing else. The danger of using such signals to convey any other meaning is this: though it may be understood between local people . . . to strangers using the port it can invite the greatest misunderstanding. The custom of a port does not override the regulations. The regulations are paramount and must be upheld.[38]

---

35. *The Ripon* (1885) 10 P.D. 65, at p. 69.
36. *The Saint Paul* (1908) 11 Asp. M.L.C. 169.
37. *The Elysia* (1912) 12 Asp. M.L.C. 198, at p. 202.
38. *The Century* [1963] 1 Lloyd's Rep. 99, at pp. 102–103.

**585.** With regard to the steering and sailing rules, it was held in the case of *The Argo* that although the pilot had taken a vessel on the port side of the fairway contrary to the Collision Regulations, the master was not responsible for failing to overrule the pilot. Dr Lushington justified his decision as follows:

I have said on many occasions . . . that a master has no right to interfere with the pilot, except in cases of the pilot's intoxication or manifest incapability, or in cases of danger which the pilot does not foresee, or in cases of great necessity. The master of the *Argo* says "It is not my province to take notice of the ship, or on what shore she is navigating. She may be taken here or there, while she is in charge of the pilot, without my knowing the cause; there may be reason under water why the pilot does it. All my duty is, to take care that all the pilot's orders are promptly and properly obeyed"; and I think he says so rightly.[39]

**586.** Here again, however, pilots will be censured by the courts if they contravene the regulations simply to honour some private arrangements with their colleagues. In the case of *The Hjortholm*, for example, where it was revealed that there was a private practice among Swansea pilots to pass starboard to starboard in the entrance channel under certain circumstances, Langton, J., said:

It has been said times without number that as to practices among pilots—understandings or customs of this kind—which are not enshrined in rules and by-laws, and which are in contravention of rules and by-laws, that they are not matters of which this Court can take the slightest notice.[40]

And in a similar case involving Liverpool pilots, Willmer, L.J., said:

What I would say about it is this, that if any such practice does exist among pilots in the River Mersey the sooner it is discontinued the better . . . the duty of a down coming vessel . . . is to obey Rule 25 of the Collision Regulations . . . and to keep to her own starboard side.[41]

### Criminal liability for infringement of Collision Regulations

**587.** So far as criminal liability for infringement of the Collision Regulations is concerned, until recently it appeared from the terms of section 419(2) of the Merchant Shipping Act 1894 that the pilot could not be guilty of an offence under this provision and that the master would only be guilty of a criminal offence if the infringement was caused by his wilful default. See also the case of *Henry Broadshaw* v. *Alan Ewat James* (*The Tiger*) in which it was held that for the master to be guilty of an offence under section 419(2) there must be *mens rea* on his part.[42] However, the Merchant Shipping (Distress Signals and Prevention of Collisions) Regulations 1983, made under sections 21 and 22 of the Merchant Shipping Act 1979, which came into force on 1 June 1983, repealed (*inter alia*) section 419 of the Merchant Shipping Act 1894 and provided in regulation 5(1) that "where any of these Regulations is contravened, the owner of the vessel, the master and any

---

39. *The Argo* (1859) 166 E.R. 1217, at p. 1218.
40. *The Hjortholm* (1935) 52 Ll.L.Rep. 223, at p. 228.
41. *The Santander* [1966] 2 Lloyd's Rep. 77, at p. 83.
42. *The Tiger* [1983] 1 All E.R. 12.

person for the time being responsible for the conduct of the vessel shall each be guilty of an offence . . . ". It appears, therefore, that a pilot may now be criminally liable for an infringement of the Collision Regulations. Regulation 5(2) provides that is shall be a defence for any person charged with an infringement of the Collision Regulations that he took all reasonable precautions to avoid the commission of the offence.

## Whether to proceed

**588.** It would appear that the courts, in most cases, take the view that the pilot should decide whether or not it is prudent to proceed in bad weather conditions. Thus in a case where the court had to decide upon the wisdom of taking a vessel through the Downs in bad weather, the judge said:

It was contended at the bar that in this case the impropriety of sailing through the Downs was so manifest that the captain ought to have refused, in spite of the pilot's opinion, to permit the ship to proceed. But we cannot assent to this. It would be very dangerous to hold that there can be any divided authority in the ship with reference to the same subject, and whether the ship was to anchor or to proceed was a matter which we think belonged exclusively to the pilot to decide.[43]

**589.** Similarly, in the case of *The Oakfield*, which was involved in a collision with a vessel at anchor in the River Mersey in poor visibility, Sir James Hannen said:

I think if there was such a state of obscurity owing to fog as would give rise to a plain prospect of danger, the master could in those circumstances throw the whole responsibility on the pilot if he ordered the vessel to get under way. But in this case it is said that the circumstances did not give rise to such a plain prospect of danger, for although the weather was admittedly foggy, yet vessels might be seen at a very considerable distance; the evidence is, from 300 yards to half a mile. If vessels can be seen at such a distance as that, then it is a question for the pilot to determine whether it was wise to weigh anchor, and the master would be relieved from responsibility. The pilot knows all the local dangers and knows as it were by instinct where he may go and where he may not go. It is therefore obvious that the master would leave it to the pilot to judge whether it would be safe to proceed in such a state of weather.[44]

**590.** In practice, where the possibility of causing serious damage through attempting to dock or sail a vessel in strong winds arises, the master usually accepts the decision of the pilot. In borderline cases, particularly involving large vessels, he prefers to err on the side of caution and will often cancel the operation without consulting the pilot. It is very rare, in these circumstances, for a master to insist on proceeding when it is contrary to the pilot's view that it would be imprudent to do so. In fog also, the master almost invariably accepts the judgment of the pilot, but again he usually prefers to err on the side of caution.

**591.** The question also arises in tidal ports where the danger of having insufficient water presents itself, particularly on a falling tide. Here again the master is usually willing to accept the decision of the pilot, although pilots have occasionally

---

43. *Pollock* v. *M'Alpin* (1851) 13 E.R. 945, *per* Lord Kingsdown, at p. 946.
44. *The Oakfield* (1886) 5 Asp. M.L.C. 575, at p. 576.

been known to have been persuaded against their better judgment by over-zealous masters anxious to "catch the tide".

## Anchoring

**592.** This is generally within the purview of the pilot. In *The Octavia Stella* a vessel under the control of a compulsory pilot was brought to anchor at high water in a position which was not usually used by a vessel of her size and draught. At low water the vessel grounded and damaged some oyster beds, the existence of which were known to the pilot. In an action brought by the lessee of the oyster beds against the pilot and master it was held that the pilot alone was liable for anchoring the vessel in that position.[45] Similarly, in the case of *The George*, where a vessel approaching an anchorage in the dark ran down a vessel at anchor, it was held that the position in which a vessel brought up was entirely within the province of the pilot. It was also held in this case that the time of letting go was to be decided by the pilot.[46] In the case of *The Agricola* it was held that when a vessel is taking up her berth in a dock the time and the manner of dropping the anchor is exclusively within the pilot's province.[47]

**593.** In the case of *The Rigborgs Minde*, a schooner proceeding through the Humber Dock, Hull, collided with a flyboat, and the latter was damaged by the fluke of her anchor, which had been placed in a certain position prior to letting go. It was held that the damage was caused by the fault of the pilot alone. Brett, M.R., summed up as follows:

It is next said that the *Rigborgs Minde* did not manage her sternrope properly, that she came up the dock fast and should have had a check rope to the dolphins, and that her anchor was wrongly and improperly slung, and that when the final order to let go was given, that it was done in an unseamanlike manner. But all these matters, with the exception of the last, are connected with the navigation of the ship by way of steering her course, and attention to them is within the pilot's duty . . . Assuming that anything done wrongly up to the moment of letting go the anchor was the fault of the pilot alone, anything done after that moment would be, no doubt, the fault of the crew.[48]

**594.** Similarly, it was held in the case of *The Monte Rosa* that if damage is caused by the anchor, so placed by the pilot's authority, then the fault lies with him, notwithstanding the fact that the position of the anchor is in breach of a port rule.[49]

**595.** It frequently occurs that a vessel approaching or leaving a port is delayed through tidal conditions, weather conditions, or other similar causes, and is obliged to anchor for a period of time. It has been held by the courts that on such occasions vessels in a compulsory pilotage district are still under the directions of the pilot while at anchor. In the case of *The City of Cambridge*, for example, where a vessel parted her cable in the River Mersey and subsequently collided with another

---

45. *The Octavia Stella* (1887) 6 Asp. M.L.C. 182.
46. *The George* (1845) 166 E.R. 800.
47. *The Agricola* (1843) 2 Wm. Rob. 10.
48. *The Rigborgs Minde* (1883) 8 P.D. 132, at pp. 135–136.
49. *The Monte Rosa* (1892) 7 Asp. M.L.C. 326.

vessel, it was held to be the duty of the pilot to decide upon the length of cable at which the vessel rides, and when the vessel swings to the tide to superintend that manoeuvre and to give any helm orders that may be necessary. It was also held that the pilot should not leave the bridge before the vessel is fully swung and if the vessel sheers and parts her cable as a result of insufficient length, or as a result of failure to regulate the helm, the pilot is solely responsible provided that the watch on the bridge takes the right manoeuvre to counteract the sheer. Also under these circumstances the necessity for letting go a second anchor is within the discretion of the pilot and that manoeuvre should also be superintended by him. If the pilot is below at the time, the officer of the watch is justified in calling the pilot before giving any orders to bring up the vessel provided she is not in imminent danger.[50]

**596.** In the case of *The Princeton*, where the vessel concerned dragged her anchor and collided with another vessel, it was held that the pilot ought to have let go a second anchor and should also have realized the state of affairs for himself despite an alleged bad look-out.[51] Again, in the case of *The Northampton*, the vessel concerned also dragged her anchor and collided with another vessel. It was held that this collision also could have been avoided by dropping a second anchor and for failing to do this the pilot was solely to blame.[52] In the case of *The Massachusetts*, on the other hand, which collided in similar circumstances to the two preceding incidents, it was held that the owners had contributed to the accident because it was shown that the anchor was too light to hold the ship.[53]

**597.** If, however, a vessel is not anchored temporarily to await weather or tide, but is anchored in her final position in the port, then the pilot is not to blame for accidents which occur some considerable time after he has left the ship. In the case of *The Woburn Abbey*, for example, a pilot anchored the vessel in her berth, and several days later she swung and hit the *British Trident* which had anchored before her. It was held that at the time of the collision the pilot was no longer in compulsory charge of the vessel and it was for those on board to make themselves aware of any impending danger.[54]

## Speed

**598.** It would appear from reported cases that the speed at which a vessel should proceed is within the province of the pilot. In *The Maria*, for example, Dr Lushington said:

... it would be a most dangerous doctrine to hold, except under most extraordinary circumstances, that the master could be justified in interfering with the pilot in his proper

---

50. *The City of Cambridge* (1874) 2 Asp. M.L.C. 193, 239.
51. *The Princeton* (1878) 3 Asp. M.L.C. 562.
52. *The Northampton* (1853) 164 E.R. 88.
53. *The Massachusetts* (1842) 166 E.R. 612.
54. *The Woburn Abbey* (1869) 20 L.T. 621.

vocation . . . If no order was given to ease the steamer, the fault was in the pilot, not in the master.[55]

**599.** Similarly, in the case of *The Batavier*, Dr Lushington said that with regard to the speed at which the vessel was going, it appeared to him that the pilot was solely to blame,[56] and in the case of *The Calabar*, Sir James W. Colville said that it was within the province of the pilot in giving directions for the navigation of a steam vessel to determine the rate of speed at which she should proceed.[57]

**600.** In practice, if the master has any criticism to make of the vessel's speed, it is usually in circumstances when it appears to him that she is approaching a lock or a jetty too quickly. Sometimes, of course, such criticism is shown by subsequent events to be justified, but it is more often made through lack of knowledge of the local tides and currents, under the effects of which a vessel might be in more danger through approaching too slowly. Some masters adopt a more subtle approach and attempt to induce the pilot to proceed with less speed by over-emphasizing the weakness of his vessel's engines when moving astern.

### Navigating with radar

**601.** It would appear from the judgment given in the case of *The Fina Canada* that provided a radar watch is being kept by an efficient officer who passes on all "relevant" information to the pilot, the latter is not bound to keep a radar watch himself. In this case Hewson, J., said:

As the *Fina Canada* progressed towards the Medway buoy, the pilot was in charge of the navigation, and on the bridge with him were the master, the senior chief officer (who kept the radar watch), and the second and third officers, who were on the starboard and port wings respectively. There were no other officers and seamen on the forecastle head. At no time did the pilot look in the radar. The radar watch was kept exclusively by the chief officer. It was kept continuously by him, except for two brief visits to the chartroom to consult the chart. This officer, who struck me as being efficient and responsible, reported what he observed to the pilot and master. In such conditions as we are considering in this case, when reliance is placed upon radar, it cannot be too strongly emphasized that a continuous radar watch should be kept by one person experienced in its use, as this officer was, and further, that such a person should keep those in charge of the navigation informed of all matters relevant to the safe handling of the ship.[58]

**602.** In the same case in the Court of Appeal, Willmer, L.J., concurred with this view.[59] It should be noted, however, that radar was being used in this case primarily for the purpose of collision avoidance. If the radar was being used mainly for navigational purposes in (say) a narrow river it would be difficult to see how a ship's officer, who possessed no local knowledge, could accurately distinguish between "relevant" and "irrelevant" information. It might be appropriate at this

---

55. *The Maria* (1839) 166 E.R. 508, at p. 514.
56. *The Batavier* (1854) 164 E.R. 218, at p. 221.
57. *The Calabar* (1868) L.R. 2 P.C. 238, at p. 241.
58. *The Fina Canada* [1962] 2 Lloyd's Rep. 113, at p. 117.
59. *Ibid.* [1962] 2 Lloyd's Rep. 445, at p. 450.

point to note the views of the Canadian Royal Commission on the subject of the use of radar by pilots:

With the aid of various electronic instruments, the pilot is now provided with means which are constantly being improved to "see" when visual means fail but this electronic "sight" has its limitations, and the images and information provided differ from what is seen by the naked eye. Therefore, to take advantage of these technical developments, pilots must acquire the necessary knowledge and skill to understand and use these instruments. The strange images that appear on the radar screen should be as familiar to the pilot as the land features in time of clear visibility and such local knowledge must form part of the qualifications of pilots today.[60]

**603.** The practical situation in these circumstances varies from ship to ship. When navigating in fog some masters will commandeer the radar set completely and simply pass on any information they think the pilot might require, while others will leave it almost entirely to the pilot. A properly recognized procedure is the exception rather than the rule in these cases.

### Division of control in other countries

**604.** Section 15(1) of the Pilotage Act 1913 (the substance of which is now contained in section 16 of the Pilotage Act 1987) was enacted in order to give effect to an international Convention, the purpose of which was, *inter alia*, to abolish the shipowner's immunity from damages in cases where a collision was caused by the fault of a pilot who was "carried by compulsion of law". This was effected by the countries which subscribed to that Convention usually in one of two ways, i.e., either, as in the United Kingdom, by a specific enactment to the effect that the shipowner was in all circumstances vicariously reponsible for the torts of the pilot, or by demoting the pilot to the role of adviser and thus making the master solely responsible for the safe navigation of the ship. What, then, is the nature of the master-pilot relationship when the latter is engaged merely as an adviser? In practice the situation on the ship's bridge when entering or leaving a foreign port is not much different from that in the United Kingdom. The way in which this relationship has been spelled out in legislative terms, however, does vary and it is to say the least questionable whether they all have precisely the same meaning. In Denmark, for example, the pilotage legislation states that:

. . . the pilot has no right to command the ship's crew but if the person in command does not carry out with necessary speed the pilot's demands in regard to navigation or manoeuvring the pilot is without responsibility.[61]

In South Australia section 114(1) of the Harbours Act 1936 describes the pilot's function as follows:

The duty of a pilot shall be to pilot the ship subject to the authority of the master, but the master shall not be relieved, by reason of the ship being under pilotage, from responsibility of the conduct and navigation of the ship.

60. Canada, *Report of Royal Commission, &c., op. cit.*, Part 1, p. 44.
61. As quoted in: Canada, *Report of Royal Commission, &c., op.cit.*, Part 1, p. 31.

A similar provision is contained in the Greek Pilotage Act which states:

The presence of a pilot aboard shall not relieve the master of the ship of his responsibility nor is he prevented by the presence of the pilot from navigating or manoeuvring the vessel as he thinks best.[62]

And in the Corinth Canal, which is under Greek jurisdiction, the pilotage regulations state:

Pilots place at the disposal of captains their experience and knowledge of the Canal, but as they cannot know the defects and difficulties of manoeuvring, stopping, starting, etc., which differ for every ship, according to her engines and conformation, the whole responsibility of the ship's movement rests with the captain.[63]

The pilot in the Suez Canal is assigned the role of adviser but the Rules of Navigation tacitly admit that this is an artificial concept. They state:

Pilots only give advice on manoeuvring the vessel. They place at the disposal of the masters their experience and practical knowledge of the Canal, but as they cannot be acquainted with the defects and difficulties in manoeuvring, stopping, starting, etc., peculiar to each vessel, the responsibility of handling the vessel devolves solely upon the master. It is therefore for the master, taking into account the indications given by the pilot, to give the necessary orders to the helm, to the engines, and to the tugs. If in the interest of rapid manoeuvring the master thinks it preferable to allow the pilot to give orders direct, manoeuvres carried out in these circumstances shall be considered as having been carried out on the orders of the master and engage his sole responsibility.

Masters are held solely responsible for all damage or accidents of whatever kind resulting from the navigating or handling of their ships by day or night.[64]

**605.** By way of contrast it is perhaps worth noting that in the Panama Canal the regulations state that the pilot is to have full control of the navigation and movements of the vessel. In recognition of this the Panama Canal Company undertakes to pay immediate compensation for all damage or injuries incurred during transit.

---

62. As quoted in: Canada, *Report of Royal Commission, &c., op. cit.*, Part 1, p. 32.
63. As quoted in: Derek H. Hene: *The Law of Sea and Air Traffic*, p. 153.
64. As quoted in: Marsden, *op. cit.*, para. 295.

## CHAPTER 14

# DIVISION OF CONTROL BETWEEN
# SHIP AND TUGS

**606.** In a port which is regularly used by medium and large sized vessels, and particularly in a port which contains an enclosed docks system, there is usually a permanently based fleet of tugs available to assist in the berthing and manoeuvring of these vessels. Through being closely involved with each other over a period of time, a working relationship is usually built up between the port's pilots and tug masters which is based on mutual understanding and trust. The tug master who "knows his pilot" will, by intelligent anticipation, position his tug so as always to be ready to give instant assistance. From similar experience, the pilot will know which tugs are more powerful or manoeuvrable than the others, and will therefore be in a position to deploy them in his best advantage.

**607.** Unfortunately, however, accidents involving vessels under tow do sometimes occur, and are usually caused either by a collision between the tug and tow; or between the tug or tow and another vessel or a stationary object such as a pier or dock wall. This chapter examines the courts' decisions relating to such incidents, and, in the same manner as in the previous chapter, attempts to break down the towing operation into its constituent parts with a view to apportioning responsibility between the ship and the tugs.

### Responsibility for hiring tugs

**608.** In 1860 Dr Lushington held that in "ordinary circumstances" the responsibility for engaging a tug rested with the master and not with the pilot. He qualified his judgment, however, as follows:

I am speaking of the ordinary case where a tug is employed for accelerating speed and for completing the voyage in a short time for the benefit of the owners . . . It may be different in cases where a ship is in distress, and if it is a critical question whether to employ a tug or not. Those are cases in which the master ought to attend to the pilot's voice.[1]

**609.** In modern times tugs are rarely, if ever, employed simply to expedite a ship's passage, and Dr Lushington's proposition clearly belongs to the days of sail. Today, tugs are mainly employed to manoeuvre large vessels into confined spaces where their absence, particularly in adverse weather conditions, would give rise to

---

1. *The Julia* (1860) 15 E.R. 284, at p. 288.

the danger of colliding with piers or other vessels, or to the danger of grounding. In more exceptional circumstances tugs are employed when vessels are suffering from some mechanical deficiency such as the breakdown of engines or steering gear.

610. In practice, the decision to employ tugs is normally taken by the master or agent who sometimes, if in doubt, will consult the pilot beforehand. On occasions where their advice has not been sought pilots are frequently critical of these decisions and claim that they are often hampered by tugs when they are unnecessary and are often obliged to perform difficult manoeuvres without tugs when their assistance would be useful.

### Division of control—A general rule

611. The following general proposition was laid down by Dr Lushington in the case of *The Gipsey King* in 1847:

. . . a vessel in charge of a licensed pilot, whilst in tow of a steam tug is, under ordinary circumstances, to be considered as navigated by the pilot in charge. That if the course pursued by the steam tug is in conformity with his directions, and a collision takes place, the pilot is responsible, and not the owners of the vessel or of the steam tug. If on the contrary, the steamer disregarded the directions of the pilot, and the collision was occasioned by her misconduct, the owner of the ship would, in that case be responsible.[2]

612. In a later case, however, Dr Lushington made one exception to this rule, that exception being the case of a ship being shifted from one dock to another, at night and in thick weather, the ship herself being without motive power. He said in this case:

As regards the *Borussia* it will be a question whether it was expedient to move such a vessel, by means of a steam-tug, in anything like thick weather? She was in charge of a pilot; but it is not pretended that his presence can excuse the master from his responsibility; the circumstances are quite different from those of a vessel in tow of a steam-tug in broad daylight, where the tug ought to obey the orders of the pilot.[3]

### Tug master's right to interfere

613. The master of a tug is in the same position as any other ship's master when confronted with a case of manifest incompetence on the part of the pilot. In the case of *The Duke of Manchester* Dr Lushington said:

It is, I conceive, the duty of the master to observe the conduct of the pilot, and in the case of palpable incompetency, whether arising from intoxication or ignorance or any other cause, to interpose his authority for the preservation of the property of his employers . . . So in the case of a steamer which has a vessel in tow with a licensed pilot on board, if the master of the steamer sees the pilot is incompetent to direct the course of the vessel, is he

---

2. *The Gipsey King* (1847) 166 E.R. 858.
3. *The Borussia* (1856) 166 E.R. 1037, at p. 1038.

blindly to follow his orders and allow a valuable property, and still more valuable lives, to be imperilled? I never laid down such a proposition.[4]

## Making fast

**614.** When making fast while under way, it would appear to be the duty of the tug to keep clear and avoid collision. In the case of *Contest* v. *Age* a collision with the tow occurred shortly after the tug had taken a hawser from the forecastle and made it fast to the towing hook. Hill, J., in finding that there had been no negligence on the part of the tow said:

Tugs which are making fast to a ship necessarily take upon themselves the main burden of keeping clear; and there are many ways in which careless handling of the tugs may, in the very close quarters in which they have to work, bring themselves into contact with the ship.[5]

**615.** In a similar case, in which a tug was rammed while making fast to a ship and subsequently sank, it was claimed by the owners of the tug that the accident had been caused by the ship deviating from her course shortly before the collision occurred. Here, again, however, Hill, J., found that there was no negligence on the part of the tow. In this case he said that "if there was a slight deflection involved in keeping course that was a thing which the tug must expect and be prompt to follow".[6]

**616.** This does not mean, however, that those on board the tow can completely ignore the presence of the tug when she is making fast. In the case of *Harmony* v. *Northborough* the tug, which was already fast on the *Northborough's* port bow, was ordered by the pilot to transfer to the starboard quarter. She cast off and was attempting to re-secure on the starboard quarter, as directed, when the pilot put the ship's engines ahead. The propeller then struck the tug which sank shortly afterwards. In this case the pilot was held to be negligent for using the engines before ensuring that the tug was out of danger. In giving judgment, the President of the court said:

The pilot seemed to me to put on the *Harmony* the absolute duty, under the circumstances of her relation with the *Northborough*, to look out for her own safety. There is no unilateral duty of that kind in the relations of tug and tow. Each of them has to exercise proper care.[7]

## Extent of pilot's authority in directing course of tug

**617.** The precise extent to which a pilot should go in giving instructions to the tug is not clear. In the case of *The Energy* a barque with a pilot on board was being towed by a steam tug which ported her helm and passed across the bows of a brig under way, causing a collision between the brig and the barque. It was revealed in

4. *The Duke of Manchester* (1846) 166 E.R. 833, at p. 837.
5. *Contest* v. *Age* (1923) 17 Ll.L.Rep. 172, at pp. 173–174.
6. *Assistance and Others* v. *Lagarto* (1923) 17 Ll.L.Rep. 264.
7. *The Harmony* v. *The Northborough* (1923) 15 Ll.L.Rep. 119, *per* Sir Henry Duke, at p. 120.

evidence that the pilot gave no orders to the tug either before or after she ported her helm. It was held by the court that the tug was to blame for attempting to tow the barque across the bows of the brig, but that the pilot had contributed to the accident by failing to give proper instructions to the tug.[8] In the case of *The Sinquasi*, on the other hand, a collision was caused by a tug executing a wrong manoeuvre, and it was held by the court that the fact that the pilot had not given instructions to the tug prior to the collision did not relieve the owners of the ship from liability. In this case the judge said that it was not necessary that the pilot "should be giving orders perpetually for every movement of the helm of the tug".[9] Again, in the case of *Smith etc.* v. *The St. Lawrence Tow Boat Company* it was decided that a tug towing a sailing vessel is responsible for the course of both vessels, so long as no orders are given by the person in charge of the tow. The court stated that although the tug is the motive power, she is under the control of the person in charge of the vessel being towed.[10]

### Extent of pilot's control over engine movements of tug

**618.** In the case of a vessel proceeding up the Manchester Ship Canal the stern tug collided with a barge which was going in the opposite direction. After the collision the port propeller of the tug was improperly kept turning with the result that it struck the barge several times until she finally sank. It was held by Willmer, J., that the pilot was not at fault for failing to instruct the tug to stop her engines. He gave his reasons as follows:

No pilot can possibly be expected to control the individual engine manoeuvres of his two tugs. The evidence shows that in practice the detailed manoeuvres of the tug are, and must be, left to the discretion of the tug master, the duty of the pilot being confined to giving general directions, such as to start or stop towing, or to tow in this or that direction. I do not see how a pilot on the bridge of a large ship can possibly be expected to direct the engine movements of a stern tug, operating some three or four hundred feet behind him, and mostly out of sight, or even to know how the engines of the tug are working at any particular moment.[11]

### Swinging

**619.** When a ship is swinging with the assistance of tugs it is the duty of the stern tug to keep herself off the ship's propeller and to have her tow rope properly secured. In the case of a ship which was attempting to swing to starboard with the aid of tugs, it was revealed that at the start of the operation the stern tug was made fast on the ship's starboard quarter with her tow rope secured to the forward bitts instead of the main hook. When instructed to tow on the port quarter she moved

---

8. *The Energy* (1870) L.R. 3 A. & E. 48.
9. *The Sinquasi* (1880) 4 Asp. M.L.C. 383, *per* Sir Robert Phillimore, at p. 384.
10. *Smith and Others* v. *The St. Lawrence Tow Boat Company* (1873) 2 Asp. M.L.C. 41.
11. *Trishna (Owners, master and crew)* v. *M.S.C. Panther and Ericbank (Owners)* [1957] P. 143, at p. 147.

under the stern of the ship and at that moment the pilot put the ship's engines astern with the result that she struck the tug. It was held by Hill, J., that the tug should have shifted her rope to the main hook before passing under the ship's stern, in which event the collision would have been avoided. He summed up as follows:

In general, when a tug is acting as this tug was doing as the stern tug of the ship, it must be the business of the tug to keep herself clear of the ship. The tug knows that the steamer is turning. She knows that in doing that the steamer will very likely move her engines ahead and astern as required, and in this the tug master knew that the steamer was moving her engines ahead and astern. I am advised that the proper handling of this tug, in order to carry out the manoeuvre of assisting the turning of the steamer, required that the tug should not continue to hang on to the ship by the rope to the forward bitts, but that it should be placed on the towing hook in proper time to carry out the manoeuvre.[12]

### Where tow is in imminent danger

**620.** In a situation of impending peril to the ship, a tug is bound to endeavour to save her, especially when instructed to do so by the pilot. Thus, in the case where a ship was entering a dock with a tug lashed alongside, and was forced by the tide into close proximity to a landing stage with the tug nearest the stage, it was held that it was the tug's duty to hold on and go ahead as the pilot had instructed. In this case the tug struck the landing stage and was damaged, and it was held by the court that the tug was entitled to full compensation for damage and a salvage award.[13]

### When navigating in fog

**621.** In a case where a vessel, with a pilot on board, was being towed by a tug in a river where, due to dense fog, neither bank of the river could be seen, it was held that it was negligent on the part of both vessels to proceed under such circumstances. It was also held that it was the duty of the pilot to order the tug to stop in order that the vessel under tow could come to anchor.[14]

---

12. *The Alexandra (Newport and South Wales) Docks and Railway Company* v. *Cape Colony* (1920) 4 Ll.L.Rep. 116, at p. 118.
13. *The Saratoga* (1861) 167 E.R. 140.
14. *Smith and Others* v. *The St. Lawrence Tow Boat Company* (1873) 2 Asp. M.L.C. 41.

# CHAPTER 15

# DIVISION OF CONTROL BETWEEN SHIP AND HARBOUR MASTER

**622.** When a ship is navigating within the limits of a harbour authority she is subject to a certain degree of control by the harbour master or his assistants. Disputes occasionally arise as to the wisdom or practicability of instructions given by harbour officials and on such occasions the pilot invariably plays a prominent part. The question therefore arises as to what extent the harbour master is entitled to interfere in the navigation of a vessel when she is within his jurisdiction and this chapter examines the harbour master's powers under the present law.

## Harbour master's statutory powers

**623.** As indicated in Chapter 6 *ante*, a harbour master derives his power to control the movement of shipping chiefly from the provisions contained in, or incorporated by, the local Acts and statutory orders of his authority. Until fairly recently the provisions in question were usually those of sections 52 and 53 of the Harbours, Docks and Piers Clauses Act 1847 which were incorporated with the special legislation of nearly all harbour authorities (and still frequently are). Under the first of these sections the harbour master is entitled to give directions for, *inter alia*:

regulating the time in which and manner in which any vessel shall enter into, go out of, or lie at the harbour, dock, or pier, and within the prescribed limits, if any, and its position, mooring or unmooring, placing and removing, whilst therein;

and under section 53:

. . . any master of a vessel who, after notice of any such direction by the harbour master served upon him, shall not forthwith regulate such vessel according to such direction shall be liable to a penalty not exceeding (now in most cases level 3 on the standard scale).

**624.** At most major ports, these provisions of the Harbours, Docks and Piers Clauses Act have now been superseded by more flexible and sophisticated powers to regulate the movement, etc., of vessels (for example, sections 111 and 112 of the Port of London Act 1968). However, except that the harbour master's power to give directions is in somewhat wider terms, and is geared to some extent to the implementation of "general directions" given by the harbour authority, the principles as respects the division of control between ship and harbour master appear to be essentially the same as where sections 52 and 53 of the 1847 Act apply.

## Judicial decisions

**625.** In most court cases dealing with the harbour master's powers it has been decided that, unless there was manifest evidence that obedience to a harbour master's instructions would lead to an accident, those instructions had to be obeyed. In *Reney* v. *Magistrates of Kirkcudbright,* for example, where a vessel ran on to a sandbank in consequence of a mistake as to the state of the tide by the harbour master, Halsbury, L.C., said:

to say that the harbour master's authority is limited, or that a person is at liberty to disregard the orders of the harbour master, who has by law power to give orders . . . would be, to my mind, a most dangerous principle to establish. A double authority would be in many cases fatal. Those who have the power to give orders have the right to consider that they will be obeyed.[1]

**626.** It was held in the above case that the accident was caused by the negligence of the harbour master, but it should be noted that the vessel was not at the time under the control of a licensed pilot but was being navigated by the master with the assistance of two local fishermen who were employed as "advisers". It would be reasonable to assume that, if there had been a licensed pilot on board to whose certain knowledge the grounding was inevitable, the court might have held that he was entitled to disregard the harbour master's instructions, as the judgment in the following cases might indicate.

**627.** In the case of *Taylor* v. *Burger,* where an accident was caused, *inter alia,* by a steamer disobeying an order from the harbour master to go astern, Halsbury, L.C., modified his view on the subject, while adhering to the principle that there should be no divided authority with reference to the same subject:

. . . a man is not blindly to run into danger or encounter wilfully what would result in a collision if he could see that it must take place. I suppose that no one would contend that obedience to an order should be carried to the extent of leading to an inevitable disaster. The broad proposition must be admitted that you must not knowingly run into danger by the order of a harbour master or any one else. That assumes the fact that a disaster must happen. I adhere to what I said in *Reney* v. *Magistrates of Kirkcudbright* that if it was once supposed that a person acting under the orders of a harbour master is to exercise his own judgment whether or not the harbour master's orders are most consistent with prudence, and then refuse to obey the order given, that would lead to very serious consequences indeed.[2]

**628.** In 1936, in the case of *The Framlington Court,* the ship involved was attempting to move stern first out of the Greenland Dock entrance, in the River Thames. The dock master was supervising the manoeuvre by virtue of his powers

---

1. *Reney* v. *Magistrates of Kirkcudbright* (1892) 7 Asp. M.L.C. 221, at p. 222.
2. *Taylor* v. *Burger and Another* (1898) 8 Asp. M.L.C. 364, at p. 365.

under section 160 of the Port of London (Consolidation) Act 1920 (now repealed and replaced by section 113 of the Port of London Act 1968) which stated that every master should navigate his vessel in accordance with the dock master's instructions, and was liable to a fine of £20 (now level 2 on the standard scale) if he failed to do so. On this occasion the dock master instructed the ship to leave the dock, despite the fact that the entrance was obstructed by a flotilla of barges, and the pilot responded to the order by putting the engines astern. When the dock master realized that a collision was likely to occur he first signalled the ship to stop her engines, and then to put them ahead in order to reduce her sternway. When, however, one of the barges drifted close to the stern of the ship he signalled to the pilot to stop the engines. This instruction was not carried out immediately and the ship's propeller struck the barge, causing damage to three of its blades. The owners of the ship brought an action against the Port of London Authority on the ground that the dock master was negligent in (a) failing to remove the barges, which was within his powers, and (b) ordering the vessel to leave the dock when the entrance was obstructed. The defendants claimed, *inter alia*, that having instructed the vessel to leave, the dock master was under no obligation to give any further instructions and that those that he did give were only in the nature of voluntary advice.

629. The court held that although the dock master had been negligent in ordering the vessel to leave the dock, those on board the ship had contributed to the accident by failing to stop the engines in sufficient time. Referring to the subject of divided authority, Langton, J., said:

As far as this court is concerned there is only one control about the safety of a ship; I have laid it down again and again. When ships are coming out of dock, the dock master gives the orders and the pilot is bound to obey them, but he is not bound to obey an order which will take his ship into danger. It is for him to decide whether he is taking his ship into danger or not. That is as I have understood the law ever since I have practised it. It will take a good deal to shift me from that conviction. There is no dual control at all. That does not preclude all these other points. You may get a case . . . in which a dock master gives an order and the range is so short that there is no negligence on the part of the pilot in not taking some other step. We have not finished with this matter when we have finished with dual control. It does not mean that a dock master has only to give an order, and if anything goes wrong it is the pilot's fault . . . A pilot must have a reasonable chance.[3]

630. In referring to the contention that the dock master was not under a continuing obligation to supervise the manoeuvre once he had given the ship permission to leave, he said:

For my part I cannot accept the contention that the dock master who continues in these circumstances to give orders to the ship within the prescribed limits can divest himself either of authority or of responsibility. He may not be under an obligation to direct the ship's movements when leaving his dock, but if he elects to give orders these orders must be

---

3. *United British Steamship Co. Ltd.* v. *Port of London Authority (The Framlington Court)* (1936) 56 Ll.L.Rep. 200, at p. 203.

obeyed and the dock authority must shoulder the responsibility if these orders given within the scope of his authority are negligent and improper.[4]

**631.** It should be noted that section 53 of the Harbours, Docks, and Piers Clauses Act specifically states that the master is personally liable to a fine for any infringement of the provisions contained in section 52, and to that extent he must also be responsible for the actions of the pilot. The by-laws of most former pilot-age authorities contained a provision that the master is to comply with the directions of the harbour master in connection with the docking or undocking of any ship, though in the light of the decision given in the case above this would appear to be superfluous. In practice, the extent to which the harbour master chooses to exercise his powers varies considerably. In some ports he simply gives ships permission to enter or leave the dock, while in others he directs all movements of the ship.

4. *The Framlington Court, ante,* at p. 208.

# APPENDIX A

# PORT AUTHORITY CONSTITUTION ORDER

**700**    THE PORT OF TYNE AUTHORITY
(CONSTITUTION) REVISION ORDER 1974

| | |
|---|---|
| *Made* | 8th February 1974 |
| *Laid before Parliament* | 26th March 1974 |
| *Coming into Operation* | 21st May 1974 |

The Secretary of State for the Environment,* in exercise of the powers conferred by section 15 of the Harbours Act 1964 and now vested in him and of all other powers enabling him in that behalf, and on a representation made to him by the National Ports Council, hereby makes the following order:—

PART I. PRELIMINARY

**Citation and commencement**

1. This Order may be cited as the Port of Tyne Authority (Constitution) Revision Order 1974 and shall come into operation on the date fixed in accordance with the Statutory Orders (Special Procedure) Acts 1945 and 1965.

**Interpretation**

2.—(1) In this Order, unless the context otherwise requires, the following expressions have the respective meanings hereby assigned to them:—
  "the Authority" means the Port of Tyne Authority;
  "the new constitution date" means the first day of the third month after the expiry of the month current at the commencement of this order;
  "the Port" has the same meaning as in the Port of Tyne Reorganisation Scheme 1967.
  (2) The Interpretation Act 1889 shall apply for the interpretation of this order as it applies for the interpretation of an Act of Parliament.

---

* When this order was made the powers originally conferred by the Harbours Act 1964 on "the Minster of Transport" and now vested in the Secretary of State for Transport were vested in the Secretary of State for the Environment.

175

PART II. CONSTITUTION OF THE AUTHORITY

**The new constitution**

3.—(1) On and after the new constitution date the Authority shall consist of :—
  (a) a chairman and not less than six and not more than seven other members appointed by the Secretary of State,
  (b) the general manager of the Authority for the time being, and
  (c) (as from the time when officers of the Authority are appointed to serve as members thereof in accordance with paragraph 2 of the Schedule to this order) not less than two and not more than three other full-time officers of the Authority appointed on the occasion of the first appointment of such officers under the said paragraph 2 by the members referred to in sub-paragraphs (a) and (b) above on subsequent occasions by the Authority.

(2) The Secretary of State shall consult the Council* on the appointments to be made under paragraph (1)(a) above and shall also consult the chairman on such appointments other than that of the chairman. The Council, in considering the appointments which are the subject of such consultation, shall themselves consult with such bodies, being bodies which, in the Council's opinion, are likely to be substantially affected by the way in which the functions of the Authority are discharged or which appear to the Council to be representative of interests likely to be so affected, as the Council consider appropriate. Before making the first appointments under the said paragraph (1)(a) (including that of chairman) the Secretary of State shall also consult the person then holding office as chairman of the Authority.

(3) In selecting persons for appointment as members of the Authority the Secretary of State shall—
  (a) select persons who appear to him to have wide experience of, and to have shown capacity in, one or more of the matters mentioned in paragraph (4) below or to have in some other respect knowledge or experience that would be of value to the Authority in the discharge of their functions, and
  (b) have regard to the desirability of having members who are familiar with the area served by the port.

(4) The matters referred to in paragraph (3)(a) above are—
  (a) the management of harbours;
  (b) shipping or other forms of transport;
  (c) industrial, commercial or financial matters;
  (d) administration;
  (e) the organisation of workers; and
  (f) environmental matters affecting the area of the Port.

**Appointment and terms of office of members appointed by Secretary of State**

4.—(1) The Secretary of State shall appoint the first members to be appointed by him under article 3(1)(a) above before the new constitution date and each member so appointed shall come into office on that date and, subject to the provisions of Schedule 1 to the Port of Tyne Reorganisation Scheme 1967, shall continue in office until either the end of June

* The National Ports Council which was abolished by the Transport Act 1981. That Act also provided that any statutory requirement to consult the NPC should cease to have effect.

1976 or the end of June 1977 as the Secretary of State may specify when he makes the appointment. The members of the Authority holding office immediately before the new constitution date shall go out of office on that date.

(2) A member subsequently appointed by the Secretary of State under the said article 3(1)(a) shall, unless appointed to fill a casual vacancy, come into office on the 1st July following his appointment and, subject to the provisions of Schedule 1 to the Port of Tyne Reorganisation Scheme 1967, shall continue in office until the end of June in either the second or third year thereafter as the Secretary of State may specify when he makes the appointment. A member appointed by the Secretary of State may specify when he makes the appointment and, subject as aforesaid, shall continue in office until the end of June occurring within four years after that date which the Secretary of State may specify when he makes the appointment.

### Incidental provisions relating to Authority

**5.** On and after the new constitution date the provisions of the Schedule to this Order shall have effect with respect to the members and proceedings of the Authority (in addition to the provisions of Schedule 1 to the Port of Tyne Reorganisation Scheme 1967 which are not repealed by this Order).

### Repeal of certain provisions relating to existing constitution etc.

**6.** On the new constitution date articles 5 and 6 of, and paragraphs 1 to 5, the words "Except in the case of the first appointments made under this Scheme" in paragraph 9 and paragraph 14 of Schedule 1 to, the Port of Tyne Reorganisation Scheme 1967 shall be repealed and paragraph 7 of the said Schedule 1 shall have effect as if for the words "31st December" there were substituted the words "30th June".

Signed by authority of the Secretary of State
8th February 1974.

John Peyton,
Minister for Transport Industries,
Department of the Environment.

SCHEDULE. INCIDENTAL PROVISIONS WITH RESPECT TO THE AUTHORITY

1. The first meeting of the Authority after the new constitution date shall be convened by the chairman of the Authority for such date and at such place as he may fix and the chairman shall make arrangements for notice of that meeting to be sent by post to each of the other members of the Authority appointed by the Secretary of State and to the general manager of the Authority.

2. At the first meeting of the Authority after the new constitution date the members appointed by the Secretary of State and the general manager of the Authority (or as many of them as are present) shall, as the first item of business, appoint not less than two and not more than three other full-time officers of the Authority to serve as members thereof.

3. The Authority shall at their first meeting after the new constitution date and subsequently at their first meeting after 30th June in each year appoint one of their number (being a member appointed by the Secretary of State) to be deputy chairman and the deputy

chairman shall, unless he resigns his office or ceases to be a member of the Authority, continue in office until the next annual appointment of a deputy chairman.

4. On a casual vacancy occurring in the office of deputy chairman of the Authority the vacancy shall be filled by the appointment by the Authority of one of their number (being a member appointed by the Secretary of State) at a meeting held as soon as practicable after the vacancy occurs and the person so appointed shall hold office until the date on which the person in whose place he is appointed would ordinarily have retired and shall then retire.

5. A full-time officer of the Authority other than the general manager who is appointed to serve as a member thereof under paragraph 2 of this Schedule or subsequently by the Authority shall hold and vacate his office as a member at the discretion of the Authority but may at any time resign his membership by notice in writing given to the chairman of the Authority. If such a member shall cease to be a full-time officer of the Authority he shall thereupon cease to be a member of the Authority but the termination by the Authority of the appointment as a member thereof of a full-time officer other than the general manager shall be without prejudice to his appointment as an officer of the Authority.

6. At meetings of the Authority the quorum shall be five.

7. Subject to the provisions of this Schedule and of Schedule 1 to the Port of Tyne Reorganisation Scheme 1967 the Authority shall have power to regulate their own procedure.

701

# GENERAL DUTIES AND POWERS

## I. SECTION 9 OF TRANSPORT ACT 1981

**General duties of Associated British Ports**

9.—(1) It is the duty of Associated British Ports to provide port facilities at its harbours to such extent as it may think expedient.

(2) Associated British Ports shall have due regard to efficiency, economy and safety of operation as respects the services and facilities provided by it and its subsidiaries.

(3) In the performance of its functions Associated British Ports shall have regard to the interests in general of its employees and the employees of its subsidiaries.

(4) This section does not impose any form of duty or liability enforceable, either directly or indirectly, by proceedings before any court.

## II. SECTION 5 OF PORT OF LONDON ACT 1968

**General duties and powers**

5.—(1) It shall be the duty of the Port Authority—
  (a) to provide, maintain, operate and improve such port and harbour services and facilities in, or in the vicinity of, the Thames as they consider necessary or desirable and to take such action as they consider incidental to the provision of such services and facilities;
  (b) to take such action as they consider necessary or desirable for or incidental to the improvement and conservancy of the Thames.

(2) The Port Authority shall have power either themselves or by arrangement between themselves and another person to take such action as the Port Authority consider necessary or desirable whether or not in, or in the vicinity of, the Thames—
  (a) for the purpose of discharging or facilitating the discharge of any of their duties, including the proper development or operation of the undertaking;
  (b) for the provision, maintenance and operation of—
    (i) warehousing services and facilities;

    (ii) services and facilities for the consignment of goods on routes which include the port premises;

   (c) for the purpose of turning their resources to account so far as not required for the purposes of the undertaking.

(3) Particular powers conferred or particular duties laid upon the Port Authority by this Act shall not be construed as derogating from each other or from the generality of subsection (1) and (2) of this section.

# APPENDIX C

# LICENSING OF WORKS

702    SECTIONS 37–41 OF MEDWAY PORTS
AUTHORITY ACT 1973

**Licensing of works**

37.—(1) The Authority may upon such terms and conditions as they think fit grant to any person a licence to construct, alter, renew, extend or maintain any works on, under or over tidal waters or tidal lands below the level of high water in the port notwithstanding interference with public rights of navigation and other public rights by such works as constructed, altered, renewed, extended or maintained.

(2) Application for a works licence shall be made in writing to the Authority and shall be accompanied by plans, sections and particulars of the works to which the application relates and shall specify whether the applicant holds such rights in, under or over land as are necessary to enable him to enjoy the benefit of the licence and, if not, the action taken to enable him to obtain such rights if the licence is granted, and in granting any such licence the Authority may require modifications in the plans, sections and particulars so submitted.

(3) If within three months from the date of the making of an application under subsection (2) of this section the Authority do not grant a works licence in accordance with the application, they shall be deemed to have refused the application.

(4) For the purposes of section 7 of the Telegraph Act, 1878, any work proposed to be done under a works licence shall be deemed to be work proposed to be done in the execution of an undertaking authorized by an Act of Parliament.

(5) In the exercise of the powers conferred by a works licence, the holder of the licence shall not damage or injuriously affect any electrical work, gas work or sewerage work or, without the consent of the electricity undertakers, the gas undertakers or the sewerage board, as the case may be, interfere with or adversely affect the operation of any such work.

**Licence to dredge**

38.—(1) The Authority may upon such terms and conditions as they think fit grant to any person a licence to dredge in any part of the bed and foreshore of the waters of the port.

(2) Application for a dredging licence shall be made in writing to the Authority and shall be accompanied by plans, sections and particulars defining the nature, extent and manner of the operations to be carried out in the exercise of the powers granted by the licence and in granting any such licence the Authority may require modifications in the plans, sections and particulars so submitted.

(3) If within three months from the date of the making of an application under subsec-

tion (2) of this section the Authority do not grant a dredging licence in accordance with the application, they shall be deemed to have refused the application.

(4) The issue of a licence under this section shall not confer statutory authority for the carrying out of the work covered by the licence.

(5) Any materials taken up or collected by means of dredging in pursuance of a dredging licence shall be the property of the holder of the licence and he may use, sell or otherwise dispose of or remove or deposit the same as he thinks fit:

Provided that—

(a) no such materials shall be laid down or deposited in any place below the level of high water except in such position as may be approved by the Authority and subject to such conditions or restrictions as may be imposed by the Authority;

(b) if it appears to the holder of a dredging licence that the Authority have unreasonably withheld their approval under paragraph (a) of this proviso or that any restriction or regulation imposed by the Authority under that paragraph is unreasonable, he may appeal to the Secretary of State whose decision shall be binding upon the parties;

(c) no such materials shall be laid down or deposited in any place or manner so as to cover any subaqueous cable belonging to or used by the Post Office or to impede in any way the inspection, maintenance, removal or renewal of any such cable.

(6) In the exercise of the powers conferred by a dredging licence the holder of the licence shall not interfere with, damage, injuriously affect or adversely affect the operation of—

(a) any electricity work without the consent of the electricity undertakers;

(b) any gas work without the consent of the gas undertakers; or

(c) any sewerage work without the consent of the sewerage board.

(7) Not less than twenty-eight days before the exercise of any powers under a dredging licence within a distance of 50 yards of any subaqueous cable belonging to or used by the Post Office, the holder of the licence shall give notice in writing to the Post Office of such intended exercise.

### Appeals in respect of works licence or dredging licence

39.—(1) Any applicant for a works licence or a dredging licence who is aggrieved by—

(a) the refusal of the Authority to grant the licence;

(b) any terms or conditions upon which the licence is granted;

(c) any modifications required by the Authority in the plans, sections and particulars submitted by the applicant;

may, within twenty-eight days from the date upon which the Authority notify the applicant of their decision or the date on which the Authority are under subsection (3) of section 37 (Licensing of works) of this Act or subsection (3) of section 38 (Licence to dredge) of this Act deemed to have refused the application, appeal to the appropriate Minister whose decision shall be binding upon the parties.

(2) A person who appeals to the appropriate Minister under this section shall give to the Authority notice of his appeal accompanied by a copy of his statement of appeal and the Authority shall within twenty-eight days from the receipt of such notice be entitled to furnish the appropriate Minister with their observations on the appeal.

(3)(a) On an appeal under this section the appropriate Minister may—

(i) dismiss the appeal; or

(ii) require the Authority to grant the licence upon such terms and conditions as the appropriate Minister may determine; or

(iii) require the Authority to approve the plans, sections and particulars without modification or subject to such modifications as the appropriate Minister may determine.

(b) The Authority shall give effect to any requirement made by the appropriate Minister under paragraph (a) of this subsection.

(4) In this section "the appropriate Minister" means—

(a) in the case of an appeal by the applicant for a works licence, the Secretary of State;

(b) in the case of an appeal by the applicant for a dredging licence, the Secretary of State for the Environment.

## Restriction on construction of works and dredging

40.—(1) No person shall—

(a) construct, alter, renew or extend any works on, under or over tidal waters or tidal lands below the level of high water in the port unless he is licensed so to do by a works licence and except upon the terms and conditions (if any) upon which the licence is granted and in accordance with the plans, sections and particulars approved in pursuance of section 37 (Licensing of works) or section 39 (Appeals in respect of works licence or dredging licence) of this Act;

(b) dredge, dig or raise any gravel, sand, clay or other substance in the bed and foreshore of the waters of the port unless he is licensed so to do by a dredging licence and except upon the terms and conditions (if any) upon which the licence is granted and in accordance with the plans, sections and particulars approved in pursuance of section 38 (Licence to dredge) or section 39 (Appeals in respect of works licence or dredging licence) of this Act:

Provided that this subsection shall not apply to the construction, alteration, renewal or extension of any works or any dredging specifically authorized by any enactment.

(2) Any person offending against the provisions of this section or who contravenes or who fails to comply with any term or condition upon which a works licence or a dredging licence, as the case may be, is granted by the Authority shall be liable on summary conviction to a fine not exceeding the prescribed sum and on conviction on indictment to a fine.

(3) A works licence shall not be required for the carrying out, construction, placing, alteration, renewal, maintenance or retention of any work by the river authority or any drainage authority in the exercise of their functions under any enactment and a dredging licence shall not be required by the river authority or any drainage authority in the exercise of their functions under any enactment.

(4) Nothing in this section shall affect the powers of the Post Office under the Telegraph Acts, 1983 to 1916.

## Crown property

41. Without prejudice to the provisions of section 86 (Crown rights) of this Act, a person licensed by the Authority under section 37 (Licensing of works) or section 38 (Licence to

dredge) of this Act to carry out any work or to dredge in, upon or from any part of the bed of the port belonging to Her Majesty shall, in addition to the licence of the Authority, require the consent of the Crown Estate Commissioners on behalf of Her Majesty to carry out the work or to dredge.

# APPENDIX D

# NAVIGATION

SECTIONS 42–45 OF MEDWAY
PORTS AUTHORITY ACT 1973

**Provision against danger to navigation**

42.—(1) In case of injury to or destruction or decay of a tidal work or any part thereof the Authority shall forthwith notify Trinity House and shall lay down such buoys, exhibit such lights and take such other steps for preventing danger to navigation as Trinity House shall from time to time direct.

(2) If the Authority fail to notify Trinity House as required by this section or to comply in any respect with a direction given under this section they shall be liable on summary conviction to a fine not exceeding the prescribed sum and on conviction on indictment to a fine.

**Abatement of works abandoned or decayed**

43.—(1) Where a tidal work is abandoned, or suffered to fall into decay, the Secretary of State may by notice in writing require the Authority at their own expense either to repair and restore the work or any part thereof, or to remove the work and restore the site thereof to its former condition, to such an extent and within such limits as the Secretary of State thinks proper.

(2) Where a work consisting partly of a tidal work and partly of works of the Authority on or over land above the level of high water is abandoned or suffered to fall into decay and that part of the work on or over land above the level of high water is in such condition as to interfere or to cause reasonable apprehension that it may interfere with the right of navigation or other public rights over the foreshore, the Secretary of State may include that part of the work, or any portion thereof, in any notice under this section.

(3) If, on the expiration of thirty days from the date when a notice under this section is served upon the Authority, they have failed to comply with the requirements of the notice, the Secretary of State may execute the works specified in the notice and any expenditure incurred by him in so doing shall be recoverable from the Authority as a simple contract debt.

**Survey of tidal works**

44. The Secretary of State may at any time if he deems it expedient order a survey and examination of a tidal work or of the site upon which the Authority propose to construct a

tidal work, and any expenditure incurred by the Secretary of State in any such survey and examination shall be recoverable from the Authority as a simple contract debt.

### Permanent lights on tidal works

45.—(1) The Authority shall exhibit on each tidal work every night from sunset to sunrise such lights, if any, and take such other steps for the prevention of danger to navigation as Trinity House shall from time to time direct.

(2) If the Authority fail to comply in any respect with a direction given under this section they shall be liable on summary conviction to a fine not exceeding the prescribed sum and on conviction on indictment to a fine.

# APPENDIX E

# WRECKS

704    I. SECTIONS 530 AND 532 OF
       MERCHANT SHIPPING ACT 1894

### Removal of wreck by harbour or conservancy authority

530. Where any vessel is sunk, stranded, or abandoned in any harbour or tidal water under the control of a harbour or conservancy authority, or in or near any approach thereto, in such manner as in the opinion of the authority to be, or be likely to become, an obstruction or danger to navigation or to lifeboats engaged in lifeboat service in that harbour or water or in any approach thereto, that authority may—

(a) take possession of, and raise, remove, or destroy the whole or any part of the vessel; and

(b) light or buoy any such vessel or part until the raising, removal, or destruction thereof; and

(c) sell, in such manner as they think fit, any vessel or part so raised or removed, and also any other property recovered in the exercise of their powers under this section, and out of the proceeds of the sale reimburse themselves for the expenses incurred by them in relation thereto under this section, and the authority shall hold the surplus, if any, of the proceeds in trust for the persons entitled thereto.

Provided as follows:

(1) A sale shall not (except in the case of property which is of a perishable nature, or which would deteriorate in value by delay) be made under this section until at least seven clear days' notice of the intended sale has been given by advertisement in some local newspaper circulating in or near the district over which the authority have control; and

(2) At any time before any property is sold under this section, the owner thereof shall be entitled to have the same delivered to him on payment to the authority of the fair market value thereof, to be ascertained by agreement between the authority and the owner, or failing agreement by some person to be named for the purpose by the Minister of Transport,* and the sum paid to the authority as the value of any property under this provision shall, for the purposes of this section, be deemed to be the proceeds of sale of that property.

---

* Now the Secretary of State.

**Powers of removal to extend to tackle, cargo, etc.**

**532.** The provisions of this Part of this Act relating to removal of wrecks shall apply to every article or thing or collection of things being or forming part of the tackle, equipments, cargo, stores, or ballast of a vessel in the same manner as if it were included in the term "vessel", and for the purposes of these provisions any proceeds of sale arising from a vessel and from the cargo thereof, or any other property recovered therefrom, shall be regarded as a common fund.

705       # II. SECTIONS 46 AND 47 OF MEDWAY PORTS AUTHORITY ACT 1973

**Powers with respect to disposal of wrecks**

**46.**—(1) In their application to the Authority, sections 530 and 532 of the Merchant Shipping Act, 1894, shall have effect—

    (a) subject to the provisions of section 47 (Protection of Crown interests in wrecks) of this Act; and

    (b) in relation to a vessel sunk, stranded or abandoned before as well as after the passing of this Act.

(2) Subject to subsection (3) of this section, and to any enactment for the time being in force limiting his liability, the Authority may recover as a simple contract debt from the owner of any vessel in relation to which they have exercised their powers under the said section 530 or the said section 532 any expenses reasonably incurred by them under those sections in relation to that vessel which are not reimbursed out of the proceeds of sale (if any) within the meaning of those sections.

(3) Except in a case which is, in the opinion of the Authority, a case of emergency, subsection (2) of this section shall not apply in relation to any vessel unless, before exercising in relation to that vessel any of the powers conferred on them by the said section 530, other than the power of lighting and buoying, the Authority have given to the owner of the vessel not less than forty-eight hour's notice of their intention to do so; and if before the notice expires they receive from the owner counter-notice in writing that he desires to dispose of the vessel himself, and no direction is served in respect of the vessel under paragraph (b) of subsection (2) of the said section 47 he shall be at liberty to do so, and the Authority shall not exercise the powers aforesaid in relation to that vessel until the expiration of seven days from the receipt of the counter-notice and of any further continuous period thereafter during which the owner of the vessel proceeds with the disposal thereof with all reasonable diligence and in compliance with any directions for the prevention of interference with navigation which may be given to him by the Authority.

(4) Notice under subsection (3) of this section to the owner of any vessel may be served by the Authority either by delivering it to him or by sending it to him by registered post or the recorded delivery service addressed to him at his last known place of business or abode in the United Kingdom, or, if the owner or any such place of business or abode is not known to the Authority or is not in the United Kingdom, by displaying the notice at the principal office of the Authority for the period of its duration.

(5) Except in the case which is, in the opinion of the Authority, a case of emergency, the Authority shall, before raising, removing or destroying under the powers conferred upon them by the said section 530 any vessel sunk, stranded or abandoned in the port or in or

near any approach thereto and within a distance of 200 yards of any subaqueous cable belonging to or used by the Post Office, give to the Post Office in writing as long notice as is practicable of their intention to do so.

(6) In this section the expression "owner" in relation to any vessel means the person who was the owner of the vessel at the time of the sinking, stranding or abandonment thereof.

## Protection of Crown interests in wrecks

47.—(1) Without prejudice to section 741 of the Merchant Shipping Act, 1894, the powers conferred on the Authority by sections 530 and 532 of the said Act of 1894 shall not be exercisable—

  (a) in relation to any vessel sunk, stranded or abandoned by design by or under the orders of a person acting on behalf of Her Majesty or an officer or servant of the Crown acting in the course of his duty as such;

  (b) except with the consent of the Secretary of State for Defence, which may be given with or without such a direction as is referred to in paragraph (b) of subsection (2) of this section, in relation to any vessel which is not excluded from the exercise of those powers by virtue of being a vessel belonging to Her Majesty but which, at the time when the vessel was sunk, stranded or abandoned—

    (i) had been required to be placed at the disposal of Her Majesty or of a government department; and

    (ii) was appropriated to the service, under the direction and control of the Secretary of State for Defence, of Her Majesty's ships of war.

(2) The Authority shall give notice in writing to the Secretary of State for Defence and to the Secretary of State for Trade and Industry* of any decision of the Authority to exercise in relation to any vessel referred to in paragraph (b) of subsection (1) of this section any of the powers aforesaid other than the power of lighting and buoying and, except in a case which is in the opinion of the Authority a case of emergency, shall not proceed with the exercise thereof—

  (a) except with the consent of the Secretary of State for Defence and the Secretary of State for Trade and Industry* before the expiration of a period of fourteen days from the giving of the notice; or

  (b) if before the expiration of the said period there is served on the Authority a direction by the Secretary of State for Defence or the Secretary of State for Trade and Industry* that those powers shall not be exercised in relation to that vessel except in such a case as aforesaid;

and where, in any such case as aforesaid, the Authority proceed to exercise those powers without the consent and before the expiration of the period mentioned in paragraph (a) of this subsection or after a direction has been served on them as aforesaid, they shall not in the exercise of those powers use any explosives and, if, before the expiration of the period aforesaid, such a direction as aforesaid is served on them, shall not be entitled to exercise the power of sale conferred by the said section 530 or the power conferred by subsection (2) of section 46 (Powers with respect to disposal of wrecks) of this Act:

Provided that—

    (i) the Authority shall not be required to give notice under this subsection in respect of any vessel in respect of which they have received a consent under paragraph (b)

* Now the Secretary of State for Transport.

189

of subsection (1) of this section, but any direction such as is referred to in paragraph (b) of this subsection accompanying that consent shall be deemed for the purposes of this subsection and of subsection (3) of the said section 46 to have been duly served under paragraph (b) of this subsection;

(ii) the prohibition on the use of explosives imposed by this subsection shall not apply to the use for cutting away the superstructure of a vessel of such small explosive charges as may for the time being be approved by the Secretary of State for the purposes of this proviso.

(3) Without prejudice to the powers of sale conferred on the Authority by the said section 530, the Authority shall hold and dispose of any wreck within the meaning of Part IX of the said Act of 1894 raised, removed or recovered under that section, and any surplus proceeds of sale within the meaning of that section, in accordance with such directions (if any) as may be given to them by the receiver of wreck; and on exercising the said power of sale in the case of any property the Authority shall discharge any sums payable in respect of that property by way of duties of customs or excise and any sums so discharged shall be deemed to be expenses incurred by the Authority under that section.

(4) Any limitation on the powers of the Authority in relation to any vessel arising by virtue of subsection (1) or subsection (2) of this section shall not operate to authorise the exercise in relation to that vessel of the powers conferred on Trinity House by section 531 of the said Act of 1894.*

## 706     III. SECTION 56 OF HARBOURS, DOCKS AND PIERS CLAUSES ACT 1847

**Harbour masters may remove wrecks, etc.**

56.—The harbour master may remove any wreck or other obstruction to the harbour, dock, pier, or the approaches to the same, and also any floating timber which impedes the navigation thereof, and the expense of removing any such wreck, obstruction, or floating timber shall be repaid by the owner of the same; and the harbour master may detain such wreck or floating timber for securing the expenses, and on non-payment of such expenses, on demand, may sell such wreck or floating timber, and out of the proceeds of such sale pay such expenses, rendering the overplus, if any, to the owner on demand.

## 707     IV. SECTIONS 121 AND 122 OF PORT OF LONDON AUTHORITY ACT 1968

**Removal of obstructions other than vessels**

121.—(1)  The Port Authority may remove—

(a) anything, other than a vessel, causing or likely to become an obstruction or impediment in any part of the Thames or in a dock;

---

* This section confers powers to raise wrecks etc. on Trinity House in cases where there is no harbour authority with powers for the purpose.

(b) anything, other than a vehicle, causing or likely to become an obstruction or impediment to the proper use of a towpath on the Thames.

(2) (a) If anything removed by the Port Authority under subsection (1) of this section is so marked as to be readily identifiable as the property of any person, the Port Authority shall within one month of its coming into their custody give notice, as required by subsection (5) of this section, to that person and if possession of the thing is not retaken within the period specified in, and in accordance with the terms of, the notice it shall at the end of that period vest in the Port Authority.

(b) If anything removed by the Port Authority under subsection (1) of this section which is not so marked is not within three months of its coming into the custody of the Port Authority proved to the reasonable satisfaction of the Port Authority to belong to any person, it shall thereupon vest in the Port Authority.

(3) The Port Authority may at such time and in such manner as they think fit dispose of anything referred to in paragraph (b) of subsection (2) of this section which is of a perishable nature or the custody of which involves unreasonable expense or inconvenience notwithstanding that it has not vested in the Port Authority under this section, and if it is sold the proceeds of sale shall be applied by the Port Authority in payment of the expenses incurred by them under this section in relation to the thing, and any balance—

(a) shall be paid to any person who within three months from the time when the thing came into the custody of the Port Authority proves to the reasonable satisfaction of the Port Authority that he was the owner thereof at that time; or

(b) if within the said period no person proves his ownership at the said time, shall vest in the Port Authority.

(4) If anything removed under this section—

(a) is sold by the Port Authority and the proceeds of sale are insufficient to reimburse the Port Authority for the amount of the expenses incurred by them in the exercise of their powers of removal; or

(b) is unsaleable;

the Port Authority may recover as a debt in any court of competent jurisdiction the deficiency or the whole of the expenses, as the case may be, from the person who was the owner at the time when the thing removed came into the custody of the Port Authority or who was the owner at the time of its abandonment or loss.

(5) A notice given under paragraph (a) of subsection (2) of this section shall specify the thing removed and state that upon proof of ownership to the reasonable satisfaction of the Port Authority possession may be retaken at a place named in the notice within the time specified in the notice, being not less than fourteen days after the date when the notice is served.

(6) The Port Authority shall not under the powers of this section remove anything placed or constructed by a local authority or statutory undertakers under the provisions of a statute or of a consent or licence given or issued by the Port Authority thereunder.

(7) In subsection (6) of this section—

"local authority" means the Greater London Council, the Common Council of the City of London and the council of any county, county borough, London borough or county district;

"statutory undertaker" means a person authorised by statute to carry on any undertaking for the supply of electricity, gas or water.

## Removal of projections

122.—(1)  In this section—

"projection" means anything which projects over the Thames and includes stairs and any tree, bush or other plant but does not include any such thing authorised by or under statute or by a works licence to be placed or constructed.

(2) (a)  If any projection is a danger to the navigation of the Thames, the Port Authority may remove it and recover the expenses of removal from the owner or occupier of the land on which the projection was situated as a debt in any court of competent jurisdiction.

(b)  Before exercising their powers under this subsection the Port Authority shall, if it is reasonably practicable to do so, give notice of their intention to the owner and occupier of the land on which the projection is situated.

(c)  In proceedings to recover expenses under paragraph (a) of this subsection the court may inquire whether the Port Authority might reasonably have proceeded instead under subsection (3) of this section, and, if the court determines that the Port Authority might reasonably have proceeded instead under the said subsection (3), the Port Authority shall not recover the expenses.

(3) (a)  If any projection is an obstruction or inconvenience to the navigation of the Thames but not a danger thereto, the Port Authority may by notice in writing require the owner or occupier of the land on which the projection is situated to remove the projection within such time, not being less than seven days, as may be specified in the notice.

(b)  If a person to whom notice is given under paragraph (a) of this subsection fails to comply with the notice within the time stated in the notice, or, if he appeals and the appeal is not allowed, within the time stated in the notice or such other time as the court may substitute therefor, the Port Authority may themselves remove the projection and recover the expenses of removal from the person on whom the notice was served as a debt in any court of competent jurisdiction.

(4)  A notice under paragraph (a) of subsection (3) of this section shall have annexed to it a copy of this section.

(5)  A person aggrieved by a notice served by the Port Authority under subsection (3) of this section may appeal to a magistrates' court.

(6)  This section is subject to section 84 (Replacement of marked landing places) of this Act.

# APPENDIX F

# DIRECTIONS TO VESSELS

**708**     SECTIONS 20–27 OF MEDWAY PORTS
AUTHORITY ACT 1973

### General directions to vessels in the port and the Medway approach area

20.—(1) The Authority may, after consultation in each case with the pilotage authority and the Chamber of Shipping of the United Kingdom*, give directions for the purpose of promoting or securing conditions conducive to the ease, convenience or safety of navigation in the port and the Medway approach area and, without prejudice to the generality of the foregoing, for any of the following purposes:—

(a) for designating areas, routes or channels in the port or the Medway approach area which vessels are to use or refrain from using for movement or mooring;

(b) for securing that vessels move only at certain times or during certain periods;

(c) for prohibiting—

(i) entry into or movement in the port or the Medway approach area by vessels at times of poor visibility due to the weather or to the presence of dust or smoke; and

(ii) entry into the port or the Medway approach area by a vessel which for any reason would be, or be likely to become, a danger to other vessels in the port or the Medway approach area;

(d) requiring the master of a vessel to give to the harbour master information relating to the vessel reasonably required by the harbour master in order to effect the objects of this subsection.

(2) Directions given under subsection (1) of this section may apply—

(a) to all vessels or to a class of vessels designated, or the designation of which is provided for, in the direction;

(b) to the whole of the port of the Medway approach area or to a part designated, or the designation of which is provided for, in the direction; and

(c) at all times or at times designated, or the designation of which is provided for, in the direction;

and every direction made under this section shall specify the extent of its application in relation to the matters referred to in paragraphs (a), (b) and (c) of this subsection.

(3) The Authority may, after consultation with the pilotage authority and the Chamber of Shipping of the United Kingdom,* revoke or amend directions given under this section.

---

\* Now the General Council of British Shipping.

193

## Special directions to vessels in the port and the Medway approach area

**21.**—(1) A direction under this section may be given for any of the purposes set out in subsection (2) of this section by the harbour master to a vessel anywhere in the port or the Medway approach area and to a vessel prior to its entering the port from a dock.

(2) A direction under this section may be given for any of the following purposes:—

    (a) requiring a vessel to comply with a requirement made in or under a general direction;

    (b) regulating or requiring for the ease, convenience or safety of navigation the movement, mooring or unmooring of a vessel;

    (c) regulating for the safety of navigation the manner in which a vessel takes in or discharges cargo, fuel, water or ship's stores.

## Directions to vessels at the docks

**22.**—(1) The Authority may give directions applicable to all vessels, or to a specified class of vessels, at the docks, for the purpose of ensuring the safety of vessels at the docks, preventing injury to persons at, or to property at, or forming part of, the docks or of securing the efficient conduct of the business carried on at the docks and, without prejudice to the generality of the foregoing, such directions may relate to—

    (a) the movement, berthing or mooring of a vessel;

    (b) the dispatch of its business at the dock;

    (c) the disposition or use of its appurtenances or equipment;

    (d) the use of its motive power;

    (e) the embarking or landing of passengers;

    (f) the loading or discharging of cargo, fuel, water or ship's stores;

    (g) the use of ballast.

(2) The harbour master may give a direction requiring the removal from a dock of a vessel if—

    (a) it is on fire;

    (b) it is in a condition where it is liable to become immobilised or waterlogged, or to sink;

    (c) it is making an unlawful or improper use of the dock;

    (d) it is interfering with the use of the dock by other vessels, or is otherwise interfering with the proper use of the dock or the dispatch of business therein;

    (e) the removal is necessary to enable maintenance or repair work to be carried out to the dock or to an adjacent part of the dock.

(3) The harbour master may give a direction to a vessel at the docks for the following purposes:—

    (a) any of the purposes referred to in subsection (1) of this section

    (b) requiring the vessel to comply with a general direction made under this section.

(4) In this section reference to a vessel at a dock includes reference to a vessel entering or about to enter a dock and to a vessel leaving or having just left a dock.

## Publication of general directions

**23.**—(1) Notice of the giving of a general direction and of any amendment or revocation of a general direction shall, except in case of emergency, be published by the Authority once in Lloyd's List and Shipping Gazette newspaper or some other newspaper specialising in shipping news, and, if the notice relates to the giving or amendment of a general direction, shall state a place at which copies of the direction may be inspected and bought and the price thereof.

(2) In an emergency, notice of the giving of a general direction or of any amendment or revocation of a general direction may be given in any manner the harbour master considers appropriate.

## Manner of giving special directions

**24.** A special direction may be given in any reasonable manner considered appropriate.

## Master's responsibility to be unaffected

**25.** The giving of a general direction or a special direction shall not diminish or in any other way affect the responsibility of the master of the vessel to which the direction is given in relation to his vessel, persons on board, its cargo or any other person or property.

## Failure to comply with directions

**26.**—(1) The master of a vessel who fails to comply with a general or special direction shall be liable to a fine not exceeding the prescribed sum.

(2) It shall be a defence to the master of a vessel charged with an offence under subsection (1) of this section to prove that he had reasonable ground for supposing that compliance with the direction in question would be likely to imperil his vessel or any person for whom he is responsible or that in the circumstances compliance was impracticable.

## Enforcement of directions

**27.** —(1) Without prejudice to any other remedy available to the Authority, if a special direction is not complied with within a reasonable time, the harbour master may, where practicable, put persons aboard the vessel to carry out the direction or may otherwise cause the vessel to be handled in accordance with the direction.

(2) If there is no one on board a vessel to attend to a special direction, the harbour master may proceed as if the direction had been given and not complied with:

Provided that the powers of this subsection shall not be exercised—

(a) in relation to a vessel other than a lighter, unless after reasonable inquiry has been made the master cannot be found; or

(b) in relation to a lighter, unless it is obstructing the access to or exit from a dock or otherwise interfering with navigation.

(3) Expenses incurred by the Authority in the exercise of the powers conferred by subsection (1) of this section shall be recoverable by the Authority as a simple contract debt.

# APPENDIX G

# BY-LAWS

**709** ## I. SECTION 83 OF HARBOURS, DOCKS AND PIERS CLAUSES ACT 1847

83. Byelaws may be made for all or any of the purposes herein named.—The undertakers may from time to time make such byelaws as they shall think fit for all or any of the following purposes; (that is to say,)

For regulating the use of the harbour, dock, or pier:

For regulating the exercise of the several powers vested in the harbour master:

For regulating the admission of vessels into or near the harbour, dock or pier, and their removal out of and from the same, and for the good order and government of such vessels whilst within the harbour or dock, or at or near the pier:

For regulating the shipping and unshipping, landing, warehousing, stowing, depositing, and removing of all goods within the limits of the harbour, dock, or pier, and the premises of the undertakers:

For regulating (with the consent of the Commissioners of Her Majesty's Customs) the hours during which the gates or entrances or outlets to the harbour, dock, or pier shall be open:

For regulating the duties and conduct of all persons, as well [as] the servants of the undertakers as others, not being officers of Customs or Excise, who shall be employed in the harbour, dock, or pier, and the premises of the undertakers:

For regulating the use of fires and lights within the harbour, dock, or pier, and the premises belonging thereto, and within any vessel being within the harbour or dock, or at or near the pier, or within the prescribed limits (if any):

For preventing damage or injury to any vessel or goods within the harbour or dock, or at or near the pier, or on the premises of the undertakers:

For regulating the use of the cranes, weighing machines, weights and measures belonging to the undertakers, and the duties and conduct of all weighers and meters employed by them:

For regulating the duties and conduct of the porters and carriers employed on the premises of the undertakers and fixing the rates to be paid to them for carrying any goods, articles, or things from or to the same:

And the undertakers may from time to time, as they shall think fit, repeal or alter any such byelaws: Provided always, that such byelaws shall not be repugnant to the laws of that part of the United Kingdom where the same are to have effect, or the provisions of this or the special Act; and such byelaws shall be reduced into writing, and have affixed thereto the

196

common seal of the undertakers, if they be a body corporate, or the signatures of the undertakers, or two of them, if they be not a body corporate, and, if affecting other persons than the officers or servants of the undertakers shall be confirmed and published as herein provided.

## 710    II. SECTION 78 OF MEDWAY PORTS AUTHORITY ACT 1973

### General byelaws

**78.** Subject to the provisions of this Act, the Authority may make byelaws for all or any of the following purposes:—

(a) for regulating the use, operation and superintendence of the port and the docks, berths, wharves, quays, piers, jetties, staiths, warehouses, sheds, landing places, locks, sluices, equipment, works and conveniences (including moorings) in the port;

(b) for regulating the admission to movement and berthing within, and the departure of vessels from, the port, or the removal of vessels, and for the good order and government of vessels whilst within the port;

(c) for regulating the shipping and unshipping, landing, warehousing, stowing, depositing and removing of goods within the limits of the port, and at the premises of the Authority;

(d) for regulating the navigation, berthing and mooring of vessels within the port and their speed and manner of navigation, and the use of tugs within the port;

(e) for preventing damage or injury to any vessel, goods, vehicle, plant, machinery, property or persons within the port, or on the premises of the Authority;

(f) for regulating the conduct of all persons in the port, not being members of a police force or officers or servants of the Crown whilst in the exercise of their duties;

(g) for regulating the placing and maintenance of moorings;

(h) for preventing and removing obstructions or impediments within the port;

(i) for prohibiting or regulating the discharge or deposit of ballast, ashes, refuse, rubbish or other material (including any polluting liquid) in the port;

(j) for regulating the use of ferries within the port;

(k) for regulating the use of yachts, sailing boats, rowing boats, pleasure craft and other small craft and the holding of regattas and other public events within the port;

(l) for regulating the launching of vessels within the port;

(m) for prohibiting persons working or employed in or entering the port, or any part thereof, from smoking therein;

(n) for regulating or preventing the use of fires and lights within the port and the premises belonging thereto, and within any vessel within the port;

(o) for regulating traffic on railways within the port and the use of locomotives thereon;

(p) for regulating the movement, speed and parking of vehicles within the port;

(q) for regulating the exercise of the powers vested in the harbour master.

# 711    III. MODEL GENERAL HARBOUR BYELAWS

The                              Port/Harbour Authority, in exercise of the powers conferred by section/article        of the                                  Act/ Order 19      and of all other powers them enabling, hereby make the following byelaws.


PART I—PRELIMINARY

## Title and commencement

1. These byelaws may be cited as the                Byelaws 19            and shall come into operation on the expiration of 28 days from the date of confirmation thereof by the Secretary of State.

[*Note: the period of 28 days referred to in byelaw 1 may be varied in some cases.*]


## Application

2. These byelaws shall apply to all parts of the port/harbour the limits of jurisdiction of which are set forth in the Schedule hereto and to the harbour premises/dock estate as defined in byelaw 3 hereof.

[*Note: in some cases it may be useful to annexe to the prints of the byelaws, on an informal basis, a map indicating the limits of jurisdiction.*]


## Interpretation

3. In these byelaws, unless the context otherwise requires, the following words or expressions have the meanings hereby respectively assigned to them "the Authority" means the                            Port/Harbour Authority as defined by section/article          of      the                                  Act/order                              ;

"Collision Regulations" means regulations for the prevention of collisions made under section 21 of the Merchant Shipping Act 1979;

"goods" means all articles and merchandise of every description and includes fish, livestock and animals;

"the harbour master" means the person appointed as such pursuant to section/article        of the                          Act/Order 19            and includes his authorised deputies, assistants and any other person authorised by the Authority to act in that capacity;

"the harbour premises/dock estate" means the docks, quays, jetties, stages and all other works, land and buildings for the time being vested in or occupied or administered by the Authority;

"hovercraft" means a vehicle which is designed to be supported when in motion wholly or partly by air expelled from the vehicle to form a cushion of which the boundaries include the ground, water or other surface beneath the vehicle;

[*Note: the definition of "hovercraft" is similar to that set out in section 4 of the Hovercraft Act 1968.*]

"master" when used in relation to any vessel means any person having the command, charge or management of the vessel for the time being;

"owner" when used in relation to goods includes any consignor, consignee, shipper or agent for the sale, receipt, custody, loading or unloading and clearance of those goods and includes any other person in charge of the goods and his agent in relation thereto; and when used in relation to a vessel includes any part owner, broker, charterer, agent or mortgagee in possession of the vessel or other person or persons entitled for the time being to possession of the vessel [and when used in relation to a vehicle includes any part owner or agent or person having charge of the vehicle for the time being].

[*Note: the definition of "owner" is not used in relation to vehicles in this code and will only be necessary, therefore, where individual authorities propose additional byelaws which require the definition to extend to vehicles.*]

"quay" means any quay, wharf, jetty, dolphin, landing stage or other structure used for berthing or mooring vessels, and includes any pier, bridge, roadway or footway immediately adjacent and affording access thereto;

"small vessel" means any vessel of less than 20 metres in length or a sailing vessel and for the purposes of this definition "sailing vessel" means a vessel designed to carry sail, whether as the sole or as a primary or supplementary means of propulsion;

"vehicle" includes any vehicle propelled on rails, any machinery on wheels or caterpillar tracks, trailers, caravans and mobile homes and includes a hovercraft or any other amphibious vehicle;

"vessel" [*Note: it is suggested that the first choice for this definition should be that which is included in a harbour authority's own legislation; the second choice should be that which is included in the Collision Regulations (viz. " 'vessel' includes every description of water craft, including non-displacement craft and seaplanes, used or capable of being used as a means of transportation on water"); the third choice is that which follows and was devised to extend to unusual but navigable objects found in some harbours, such as oil rigs, but the third choice should only be adopted where the authority are dealing, or anticipate that they will deal, with such unusual objects*] means a ship, boat, raft or water craft of any description and includes non-displacement craft, seaplanes and any other thing constructed or adapted for floating on or being submersed in water (whether permanently or temporarily) and a hovercraft or any other amphibious vehicle.

## Application of Collision Regulations

4. Insofar as the rules contained in Schedule 1 to the Merchant Shipping (Distress Signals and Prevention of Collisions) Regulations 1983 do not apply within the harbour by virtue of Rule 1 (a) of the said Schedule 1, the like rules shall so apply as part of these byelaws but subject to the other provisions of these byelaws [and references in these byelaws to the Collision Regulations shall include references to the said rules as applied by this byelaw].

*Note: generally, the Collision Regulations apply of themselves within harbours. Although byelaws applying the Collision Regulations are not uncommon they are usually unnecessary and, unless (like the above model byelaw) drafted by reference to a specified order containing the text of the Collision Regulations, may well be ultra vires. Furthermore, such a byelaw may well result in a breach of the Collision Regulations being treated as a breach of the byelaws rather than as an offence under the Merchant Shipping Acts with the consequence that the maximum penalty will be substantially reduced. It has, however, been held by the courts that the Collision Regulations do not apply of them-*

*selves in landlocked artificial channels. Where, therefore, a harbour, or part of it, consists of such a channel a byelaw on the lines of the above may be appropriate. The words in square brackets at the end should not, of course, be included unless the other byelaws refer to the Collision Regulations.*

## Vessel movements

5. The master of a seagoing vessel shall give prior notice to the harbour master of the vessel's arrival at, departure from or movement within, the harbour.

## Declaration of particulars of vessel

6. The master of a vessel arriving at the harbour shall, if required by the harbour master, furnish to him a declaration in the form to be obtained from him containing a correct statement of the tonnage and draught of the vessel, its last port of call, ownership and destination, and particulars of its cargo.

## Vessels to navigate with care

7. The master shall navigate his vessel with such care and caution and at such speed and in such manner as not to endanger the lives of or cause injury to persons or damage to property and as not to interfere with the navigation, manoeuvring, loading or discharging of vessels or with moorings, river banks or other property.

## Speed of vessels

8. Except with permission of the harbour master and, subject to byelaw 7 and the Collision Regulations, the master of a vessel shall not cause or permit the vessel to proceed at a speed greater than        knots.

## Small vessels not to obstruct fairway

9. The master of a small vessel which is not confined to a fairway shall not make use of the fairway so as to cause obstruction to other vessels which can navigate only within the fairway.

## Vessels not to be made fast to navigation buoys or marks

10. The master of a vessel shall not make fast his vessel to or lie against any buoy, beacon or mark used for navigational purposes.

## Notification of collisions, etc.

11. The master of a vessel which—
    (a) has been involved in a collision with any vessel or property, or has been sunk or grounded or become stranded in a harbour area; or
    (b) by reason of accident, fire, defect or otherwise is in such a condition as to affect its safe navigation or to give rise to danger to other vessels or property; or
    (c) in any manner gives rise to an obstruction to a fairway; shall forthwith report the

occurrence to the harbour master (and as soon as practicable thereafter) provide the harbour master with full details in writing and where the damage to a vessel is such as to affect or be likely to affect its seaworthiness the master shall not move the vessel except to clear the fairway or to moor or anchor in safety, otherwise than with the permission and in accordance with the directions of the harbour master.

## Vessels adrift

12. The master of a vessel which parts from its moorings shall as soon as possible report the same to the harbour master.

PART III—BERTHING AND MOORING

## Provision of proper fenders

13. The master and the owner of a vessel shall ensure that it is provided with a sufficient number of fenders adequate for the size of their vessel and, when berthing and leaving or lying at a quay or against other vessels, the master shall cause the vessel to be fended off from that quay, or those other vessels so as to prevent damage to that quay, those other vessels or other property.

## Vessels to be properly berthed

14. The master of a vessel shall at all times keep his vessel properly and effectively moored when berthed or lying at any quay.

## Access to and egress from vessels

15. The master and the owner of a vessel (other than a small vessel) while berthed alongside a quay shall provide and maintain a sufficient and proper gangway for the access and egress of all persons having lawful business on the vessel and shall during the hours of darkness provide sufficient lighting to illuminate the whole length of the gangway.

## Sufficiency of crew

16. Except with the permission of the harbour master, the master of a vessel shall at all times when his vessel is within the harbour ensure that his vessel is capable of being safely moved and navigated and that there are sufficient crew or other competent persons readily available—
(a) to attend to his vessel's moorings;
(b) to comply with any directions given by the harbour master for the unmooring, mooring and moving of his vessel; and
(c) to deal, so far as reasonably practicable, with any emergency that may arise.

## Vessels to be kept in a movable condition

17.—(1) The master of a seagoing vessel shall not, except where his vessel is lying aground, take any steps to render his vessel incapable of movement without first notifying the harbour master and, subject as aforesaid, shall at all times keep his vessel so loaded and ballasted and in such condition that it is capable of being safely moved.

(2) Where a vessel is at any time not capable of being safely moved by means of its own propulsive machinery, the master or owner shall inform the harbour master forthwith and give to him any further information which the harbour master may reasonably require.

## Use of engines while vessel moored or berthed

18. The master of a vessel which is at a quay or attached to any mooring device shall not permit the engines of his vessel to be worked in such a manner as to cause injury or damage to the bed or banks of the harbour or to any other vessel or property.

## Vessels not to make fast to unauthorised objects

19. No person shall make a vessel fast to any post, quay, ring, fender or any other thing or place not assigned for that purpose.

## Access across decks

20. The master of a vessel alongside a quay or alongside any vessel already berthed within the harbour shall, if required so to do by the harbour master, give free access across the deck of his vessel for persons and goods to and from vessels berthed alongside his vessel.

## Lost anchor, cable or propeller

21.—(1) The master of a vessel which has slipped or parted from or lost any anchor, chain, cable or propeller, shall forthwith give to the harbour master notice thereof and, if possible, of the position of the anchor, chain, cable or propeller and, if the harbour master so directs shall cause it to be recovered as soon as practicable.

(2) The master of a vessel slipping or parting from an anchor or propeller shall leave a buoy to mark the position thereof.

PART IV—GOODS AND ROAD AND RAIL TRAFFIC

## Requirements as to handling and movement of goods in the harbour

22.—(1) The owner of any goods loaded or discharged at the harbour shall ensure that the goods are removed therefrom as soon as practicable and in any case within 48 hours unless the harbour master otherwise agrees.

(2) The owner of any goods shall comply with such directions as the harbour master may from time to time give for regulating the time, place and manner of discharging, loading or otherwise bringing into or removing those goods from the harbour premises/dock estate.

## Precaution against goods, etc., falling into harbour waters or the Authority's premises

23. The master of a vessel and a person undertaking the loading of cargo into, or the discharging of cargo from, a vessel shall use or cause to be used such methods as the harbour

master may direct for the prevention of any cargo, dunnage, ballast or other materials from falling or escaping into the waters of the harbour or onto the premises of the Authority.

## Obstruction or interference at harbour premises/dock estate

24. No person shall—
   (a) except with the permission of the harbour master, deposit or place on any part of the harbour premises/dock estate any goods or park any vehicle so as to obstruct any road, [railway], building, mooring place, plant, machinery or apparatus or the access thereto; or
   (b) without lawful authority, use, work, move or interfere with any plant, machinery, equipment or apparatus at the harbour premises/dock estate.

## Safe driving of vehicles

25. No person shall drive or otherwise operate a vehicle in the harbour premises/dock estate without due care and attention or without reasonable consideration for other persons using the harbour premises/dock estate.

## Speed limit for vehicles

26. No person shall allow a vehicle to proceed anywhere in the harbour premises/dock estate at a speed greater than         miles per hour in the case of road vehicles, and         miles per hour in the case of vehicles on rails.

## Supervision of vehicles

27. A person having charge of a vehicle in the harbour premises/dock estate shall at all times comply with any directions of the harbour master with respect to the loading, discharging, manoeuvring and removal thereof and shall not, without the permission of the harbour master—
   (a) leave the vehicle unattended anywhere within the harbour premises/dock estate; or
   (b) take it into any shed or working area.

## Loads not to leak, spill or drop

28. The owner, driver or other person having charge of a vehicle in the harbour premises/dock estate shall not permit any substance to leak, spill or drop from the vehicle.
   [*Note: vehicles transporting fish in bulk would find it difficult, if not impossible, to comply with this byelaw. The defence of due diligence or reasonable excuse contained in byelaw 49(3) would probably prevent a conviction in the case of such vehicles. A port which trades in fish should consider whether to adopt this byelaw at all or adopt it subject to the following qualification—*
   "(2) This byelaw shall not apply to any spillage from a vehicle in which fish are being transported in bulk where that spillage could not have been reasonably prevented".]

## Loads to be secured

29. The owner, driver or other person having charge of a vehicle in the harbour premises/dock estate shall ensure that any load carried thereon or therein is properly secured and that it complies with all such statutory restrictions on the weight of goods to be so carried as are applicable on public roads.

## Refuelling, etc., of vehicles

30. No person shall within the harbour premises/dock estate charge or recharge any vehicle with, or empty it of, fuel except with the permission of the harbour master.

## Precedence of locomotives, etc.

31. A person driving or otherwise operating a road vehicle within the harbour premises/dock estate shall give way to any locomotive, railway rolling stock or other rail vehicle.

## Driving on weighbridges

32. No person shall drive or otherwise operate a vehicle across any weighbridge within the harbour premises/dock estate except for the purpose of weighing the vehicle.

## Accidents to be reported

33. Any person driving or otherwise operating a vehicle involved in an accident in the harbour premises/dock estate whereby any injury is caused to any person or any damage is caused to any property, shall stop the vehicle and report the accident to the harbour master and shall give his name and address to the harbour master.

### PART V—GENERAL

## Inspection facilities, etc., to be made available to harbour master

34. The master of a vessel shall so far as may be required by the harbour master in the exercise of his duties, afford the harbour master access to any part of the vessel and provide all reasonable facilities for its inspection and examination.

## Navigation under influence of drink or drugs prohibited

35. A person shall not navigate any vessel in the harbour whilst under the influence of drink or drugs to such an extent as to be incapable of taking proper control of the vessel.

## Vessels not to be fumigated without permission

36. The master or owner of a vessel shall not cause or permit it to be fumigated without the prior permission of the harbour master.

### Laying down moorings, buoys and other tackle

37.—(1)  No person shall lay down any mooring, buoy, or similar tackle without a licence or prior consent in writing of the Authority/harbour master nor except in accordance with such conditions as the Authority/harbour master may impose.

(2)  A mooring, buoy or similar tackle shall forthwith be removed by its owner or any other person claiming possession of it if the harbour master so directs.

### Dumping in harbour water prohibited

38.  No person shall deposit or throw into the waters of the harbour any rubbish or other material whatsoever or place it in a position that it can fall, blow or drift into the harbour.

### Drift or trawling nets not to obstruct vessels

39.  No person shall cast or place any drift, trawl or other net in such a position as to be likely to become an obstruction or danger to any property including in particular, but without prejudice to the generality of the foregoing, any vessel or mooring.

### No dragging or grappling without permission

40.  No person shall drag or grapple for any material or article nor remove the same from the bed of any water area of the harbour without the written consent of the harbour master.

### Vessels to have names marked on them

41.  The owner of a vessel which is not registered as a ship under the Merchant Shipping Act 1894 or the Merchant Shipping Act 1983 and marked accordingly shall ensure that the vessel is marked conspicuously with its name or other means of identification unless otherwise exempted by the Authority.

### Abandonment of vessels prohibited

42.—(1)  No person shall abandon a vessel on the banks or shore of the harbour.

(2)  For the purposes of paragraph (1) of this byelaw, a person who leaves a vessel on the banks or shore of the harbour in such circumstances or for such period that he may reasonably be assumed to have abandoned it shall be deemed to have abandoned it there unless the contrary intention is shown.

### Water skiing, aquaplaning, etc.

43. (1)  No person shall engage or take part in water skiing or aquaplaning except with the written permission of the Authority given either specifically or generally and only in such areas as may be designated and in accordance with such reasonable conditions as may be imposed.

(2)  A master whilst using his vessel for the purpose of towing a water skier or a person aquaplaning shall have on board at least one other person capable of taking charge of the vessel and of giving such assistance as may be reasonably required during the towing and in the recovery of the water skier and shall carry—

(a) for each person on board a life jacket manufactured in accordance with the appropriate British Standards Specification or a personal buoyancy aid of the Ship and Boat Builders' National Federation approved type, two hand held distress signals and a fire extinguisher;

(b) for each person water skiing or aquaplaning, a rescue quoit with line or other sufficient hand thrown rescue device.

(3) No person shall engage in kiting or parachute towing in the harbour without the prior written consent of the Authority given either specifically or generally and in accordance with such reasonable conditions as may be imposed by the Authority.

## Assistance to fire and other services

44. The master of a vessel shall give every reasonable facility and assistance to the fire, police, ambulance and other emergency services for dealing with, alleviating or preventing any emergency.

## Fire precautions

45. The master of a vessel shall take all reasonable precautions for the prevention of accidents by fire.

## Obstruction of officers of the Authority

46. No person shall intentionally obstruct any officer or employee of the Authority in the execution of his duties.

## Meetings

47. Except with the consent of the harbour master, no person shall within the harbour premises/dock estate—

(a) take part in any general meeting; or

(b) gather together, or deliver any address to an audience or gather together any persons whereby any work or business at the harbour or the control, management or use of the harbour is, or is likely to be, obstructed, impeded or hindered.

[*Note: this byelaw should be invoked with caution in that the discretion which it confers on a harbour authority could lay the Authority open to criticism on the grounds of discrimination or bias.*]

## Unauthorised trading prohibited

48. No person shall engage by way of trade, in buying or selling any goods or property in the harbour premises/dock estate without the written consent of the Authority.

[*Note: before making the above byelaw an authority should consider the following points of difficulty:—*

*(1) The byelaw could amount to an unreasonable infringement of a person's right to trade and, for this reason, the byelaw has been limited to the harbour premises or dock estate but, in certain circumstances, it could also apply throughout a totally enclosed harbour.*

*(2) In the case of Parker v. Bournemouth Corporation (1902) 86 L.T.449, 18 T.L.R.372, it was held that it was unreasonable for the defendant Corporation to seek to regulate the selling or*

*hawking of any article on their beach or foreshore by a byelaw which provided that no person should sell, etc., any article except in pursuance of an agreement with the Corporation and in such part or parts of the beach and foreshore as the Corporation should by notice from time to time appoint and that the byelaw was bad since it gave the Corporation power to make any agreement they chose without regard to the question of reasonableness or otherwise and because it reserved to the Corporation a right to refuse to give a licence to any particular person.*]

## Penalties

49.—(1) Any person who contravenes or otherwise fails to comply with any of these bye-laws or any condition, requirement or prohibition imposed by the harbour master in the exercise of the powers conferred upon him by these byelaws shall be guilty of an offence and be liable, on conviction before a court of summary jurisdiction, to a fine not exceeding level 4 on the standard scale and, in the case of a continuing offence, a further fine not exceeding £ for each day during which the offence continues after conviction therefor.

(2) Where the commission by and person of an offence under these byelaws is due to the act or default of some other person, that other person shall be guilty of an offence; and that other person may be charged with, and convicted of, the offence by virtue of this byelaw whether or not proceedings for the offence are taken against any other person.

(3) In any proceedings for an offence under these byelaws, it shall be a defence for the person charged to prove—

(a) that he took all reasonable precautions and exercised all due diligence to avoid the commission of such an offence; or

(b) that he had a reasonable excuse for his act or failure to act.

(4) If in any case the defence provided by paragraph (3)(a) of this byelaw involves the allegation that the commission of the offence was due to the act or default of another person, the person charged shall not, without leave of the court, be entitled to rely on that defence unless, within a period ending seven clear days before the hearing, he has served on the prosecutor a notice in writing giving such information identifying or assisting in the identification of that person as was then in his possession.

## Revocation

50. The                         Byelaws made                         are hereby revoked.

SCHEDULE. LIMITS OF JURISDICTION

# DANGEROUS GOODS

## 712 SECTIONS 67 AND 68 OF FORTH PORTS AUTHORITY ORDER 1969

**As to entry of dangerous goods**

67.—(1) The Authority may—
(a) refuse entry into the port premises of any goods which in their opinion would endanger or be liable to endanger persons or property; or
(b) permit the entry of any such goods subject to compliance with such terms and conditions (including the part or parts of the port premises where such entry is permitted) as they think fit.

(2) The Authority shall publish a schedule of such goods—
(a) entry of which is forbidden by them; and
(b) entry of which is permitted by them only upon terms and conditions specified in the schedule.

(3) A person who after publication of the schedule referred to in subsection (2) of this section—
(a) brings or causes or permits to be brought into the port premises any goods the entry of which is forbidden; or
(b) fails in relation to any goods brought into the port premises to comply with any terms or conditions imposed by the Authority under subsection (1) of this section;
shall—
(i) be guilty of an offence and liable to a fine not exceeding the prescribed sum, and on conviction on indictment, to a fine; and
(ii) indemnify the Authority against all claims, demands, proceedings, costs, damages and expenses which may be made against or recovered from or incurred by the Authority in consequence of the commission of the offence;
and the Authority may remove the goods in question and may recover from the owner or offender the costs of such removal and of placing or storing the goods elsewhere.

**Notice before entry of dangerous goods**

68.—(1) Except in case of emergency, the owner or master of a vessel—
(a) which it is intended to bring into the port carrying dangerous goods; or
(b) which is within the port and on which it is intended to place dangerous goods;
shall, not less than twenty-four hours before that vessel enters the port or before the

dangerous goods are placed on board, as the case may be, give notice to the harbour master of the nature and quantity of the dangerous goods in question and, if such notice is not given, the owner or master of the vessel shall be guilty of an offence and liable to a fine not exceeding the prescribed sum.

(2) Where the owner or master of a vessel is charged with an offence under subsection (1) of this section it shall be a defence to prove that he did not know and could not with reasonable diligence have ascertained the nature of the goods in respect of which the proceedings are taken.

(3) This section does not apply to dangerous goods to which byelaws made by the Authority under the Explosives Act, 1875, or the Petroleum (Consolidation) Act, 1928, for the time being apply.

# 713 HISTORY OF PILOTAGE LAW BEFORE THE PILOTAGE ACT 1913

In 1514 Henry VIII granted to the Trinity House of Deptford Strond, now usually known simply as "Trinity House", a charter which gave them the powers necessary to control the operations of shipment, pilots and mariners, not only in the River Thames but throughout the country. This charter was subsequently confirmed by Edward VI, Queen Mary, and Queen Elizabeth I. In 1604 James I gave Trinity House a new and more comprehensive charter but in 1647, being under suspicion of having Royalist tendencies, their charter was dissolved by Parliament. After the Restoration, Trinity House received a new charter from Charles II on the same lines as that of James I. In 1685 came the charter of James II which strictly charged that no person was to act as pilot in the "river Thames or any other creek belonging to or running into the same" unless he had first been appointed and authorized by the "masters, wardens and assistants" of Trinity House.

Beginning in the early 18th century a succession of Acts were passed relating to London Trinity House, although a number of the provisions they contained were of a general nature. Successive general Acts then followed dealing with all pilotage authorities, with the result that by the beginning of the 20th century the confusion that was created by the variance between the general law contained in the public statutes and the special provisions contained in the local Acts became so apparent that in 1911 a Departmental Committee on Pilotage was appointed. The function of this committee was to examine the existing state of the law and to recommend any changes, and the outcome of their inquiry was the passing of the Pilotage Act 1913.

A brief summary of these earlier statutes now follows.

The first Act relating to pilots was the Act 3 Geo. I c. 13 in 1717, the purpose of which was to give to the Dover Trinity House similar conditions to those granted by James II to London Trinity House. It made pilotage compulsory for all ships navigating between Dover, Deal or the Isle of Thanet and any places in the "Rivers of Thames and Medway"; and granted exemptions to the master, mate, or part owner of any vessel who was a resident of either Dover, Deal, or the Isle of Thanet. Unlicensed pilots could only be employed if licensed pilots were unavailable, and were heavily fined if they contravened this provision (£40 for a persistent offender), the fines being used to provide for superannuated pilots and the widows of pilots. A scale of charges was laid down and "no greater or other prices" were to be accepted or demanded.

An Act of 1732 (5 Geo. II c. 20) gave to London Trinity House general confirmation of the powers granted in the charter of James II. Its provisions were generally the same as those in the Act of 1717 except that exemption from compulsory pilotage was extended to vessels engaged in the coal trade.

In 1808 an Act (48 Geo. III c. 104) was passed setting out the basic scheme whereby

London Trinity House became the largest pilotage authority in Great Britain. It reaffirmed the power granted to the London and Dover Trinity Houses in the previous statutes and in addition empowered the London Trinity House to appoint subcommissioners to examine and license pilots at "such ports and places in England as they may think requisite", except in those places where pilotage was already under the control of some statutory authority.

Although this Act applied principally to the London and Dover Trinity Houses it contained a number of provisions which could be interpreted as having general application. For example, section 51 stated that "no pilot shall be taken to sea beyond the limits of his district by the Commanding Officer of any of His Majesty's ships or by the master of any ship in the Merchant Service" without the consent of the pilot except in cases of "unavoidable necessity". Compensation for being taken to sea in such circumstances was to be paid at the rate of 10 shillings and sixpence per day, a figure which remained unchanged until 1979. It would also appear that it was intended that pilotage should be compulsory in all districts because section 55 stated that "the Master of every ship . . . which shall be conducted by any other person than a duly licensed pilot, within any limits for which any pilots have or shall be appointed by *any lawful authority* shall forfeit double the amount of the sum which would have been demandable for the pilotage . . .".

Section 67 of the Act of 1808 stated that it was to remain in force for only four years. Thus, in 1812, a further Act was passed (52 Geo. III c. 39) which repealed, and in the main re-enacted, all the provisions contained in its predecessor. In addition, the right to appoint subcommissioners was extended to the Trinity Houses of Hull and Newcastle. A further important provision was section 30, which stated that the owner or master of a ship would not be answerable for any loss or damage caused by "the incompetence or incapacity of any pilot taken on board . . . under or in pursuance of any provision of this Act".

In 1825 the Act of 1812 was also repealed, and a new Act (6 Geo. IV c. 125), which contained most of the original provisions, replaced it. Exemptions from compulsory pilotage were again extended, this time to British vessels engaged in a variety of trades, such as vessels trading to either Norway, the Kattegat or Baltic, and vessels "wholly laden with stone from Guernsey, Jersey, Alderney, Sark or Man and being the production thereof". In addition, His Majesty in Council could permit certain vessels not having British Registers to be conducted without pilots. Another important inclusion was contained in section 57 which stated that a pilot who had executed a bond would not be liable beyond the amount stated therein (maximum £100) for any damage arising from "neglect or want of skill".

In 1836 a Royal Commission appointed in the previous year reported on "the existing laws, regulations and practices under which pilots were appointed, governed, and paid in the British Channel and the several approaches to the Port of London, and also in the navigation connected with the other principal ports in the United Kingdom".[1] With regard to compulsory pilotage it reported that in nearly all the important ports in the United Kingdom all vessels above a certain tonnage, unless specifically exempted and irrespective of nationality, were obliged to receive on board a licensed pilot "if he shall present himself". The report stated that to make pilotage entirely optional would "only hold out a boon to the foolhardy"[2] and recommended that it should be compulsory everywhere with certain specific exemptions. The recommended exemptions were the coasting trade and ships trading between the United Kingdom and foreign ports within 24 hours steaming. It pointed out

1. Report from the Commissioners appointed to inquire into the Laws and Regulations relating to Pilotage in the U.K. (1836) [56] xxviii).
2. *Ibid.*, p. 17.

that to allow too many exemptions would put "too great a charge on the remainder".[3] With regard to pilotage authorities the report commented on their great variety and pointed out that in some ports the regulations they imposed were "inexpedient and onerous"[4] while in others no sufficient regulations had been adopted at all. The report concluded, therefore, that the abuses and complaints that had resulted demonstrated "the want of a superior body to control the acts of local authorities".[5]

The report also recommended the repeal of all existing Pilotage Acts (including local Acts) and the introduction of a general Act which would be in force throughout the United Kingdom. Trinity House would, in effect, become the central pilotage authority with the power to revise and sanction by-laws made by local pilotage authorities and to make new by-laws and fix pilotage rates.

The report appears to have been largely ignored, however, and by an Act passed in 1840 (3 & 4 Vict. c. 48) exemptions were extended to "the subjects of foreign countries having Treaties of Reciprocity with the United Kingdom". In 1853, the Pilotage Law Amendment Act brought about the amalgamation of the London and Cinque Ports pilots under the jurisdiction of the London Trinity House. It also contained a number of general provisions. It stated, for the first time, the powers and duties of pilotage authorities other than Trinity House, empowering them "with the consent of Her Majesty" to determine pilots' qualifications, to make regulations for the government of pilots and of certificated masters and mates, and to fix pilotage rates. They were also empowered to make and extend exemptions from compulsory pilotage and to arrange the limits of pilotage districts. They were required to make full returns to the Board of Trade of various particulars connected with pilotage, and if they failed to do so they were liable to be deprived of their authority, and the power to appoint pilots would be invested in Trinity House. The Board of Trade were empowered to examine and grant pilotage certificates to masters and mates in the event of an authority's refusal to do so.

In 1854 the Merchant Shipping Repeal Act repealed all previous provisions in public Acts relating to pilotage. It came into force on the same day as the Merchant Shipping Act 1854, Part V of which was devoted to pilotage. It re-enacted most of the general provisions contained in the earlier statutes, and kept alive all provisions contained in local Acts which were not inconsistent with it. Subject to alteration by by-law, compulsory pilotage was to continue in all districts where it was currently in force and similarly all exemptions therefrom were to continue.

Home Trade passenger ships were to employ qualified pilots unless they had on board masters or mates holding pilotage certificates. Trinity House retained the special position it enjoyed under previous statutes but was not permitted to extend its jurisdiction without the consent of Her Majesty in Council. Pilotage continued to be compulsory in all London and Trinity House outport districts, and similar exemptions applied to those embodied in the earlier statutes except that they were no longer granted on the basis of reciprocity.

After the passing of the Merchant Shipping Act 1854 a strong reaction appears to have set in against the principle of compulsory pilotage. In 1860 a select committee of the House of Commons, appointed to inquire into the general state of the shipping industry, recommended that pilotage should be non-compulsory throughout most parts of the British Empire. They added that they had "the most convincing evidence that where the system of

3. *Ibid.*, p. 17.
4. *Ibid.*, p. 7.
5. *Ibid.*, p. 7.

voluntary pilotage prevails the supply of pilots is more abundant, their efficiency is no way inferior, and the rates generally lower than at any ports where compulsory pilotage is still in force".[6]

In 1862, no doubt prompted by the report of the select committee, Parliament's antipathy towards compulsory pilotage began to make itself felt. Under the Merchant Shipping Act Amendment Act the Board of Trade were empowered, in a non-compulsory district in which there was no restriction on the number of licensed pilots, to give a pilotage authority the power to raise rates and additional facilities for their recovery, and also to give them the power to prevent unqualified persons from obtaining licences and to assist qualified persons to obtain licences. They were also empowered to create new pilotage districts.

Between 1870 and 1888 various select committees examined the problems of pilotage and although they differed in their attitudes towards compulsory pilotage they were all of the opinion that the shipowners' defence of compulsory pilotage in respect of a claim for loss or damage caused by a vessel while under pilotage should be abolished.

In 1889 the power of the Board of Trade to make provisional orders with respect to pilotage matters was again extended. By the Merchant Shipping (Pilotage) Act they were empowered to extend pilotage districts but the Act specified that in any new district pilotage was to be non-compulsory and there was to be no restriction on the right of duly qualified persons to obtain licences. Also, subject to the condition that pilots were directly represented thereon, pilotage authorities were empowered to suspend or dismiss pilots, and any pilot so dealt with had the right to appeal to a County Court or stipendiary magistrate.

Part X of the Merchant Shipping Act 1894 repealed and re-enacted practically all the provisions appertaining to pilots in the Merchant Shipping Act 1854; The Merchant Shipping Act Amendment Act 1862; and the Merchant Shipping (Pilotage) Act 1889. Like the Merchant Shipping Act 1854, although it purported to be a consolidating Act, it did not embody or supersede any of the various local Acts relating to particular ports.

In July 1909 a Departmental Committee of the Board of Trade was appointed "to inquire as to the present state of law and its administration with respect to pilotage in the United Kingdom, and as to what changes, if any, are desirable".[7] The committee's report was published in 1911. It described the then existing state of the pilotage law as "chaotic", a condition which, it said, was due to the fact that the statute law relating to pilotage was contained partly in general Acts and partly in local Acts, and to the absence of any definite principle governing pilotage legislation in enactments of either description.

The report recommended that, in order to achieve the necessary reforms, all the provisions in local Acts, charters, or customs relating to pilotage should be repealed, and in their place should be substituted:

    (a) A general Act of Parliament laying down the principles governing pilotage.

    (b) Orders of a Central Authority defining the constitution and limits of each pilotage authority.

    (c) By-laws of local pilotage authorities applying to the particular districts under their control.

With regard to the general law, one of the most important changes recommended was that pilotage should be compulsory in all districts except in the case of:—vessels whose masters or mates held pilotage certificates; Naval vessels; vessels under 100 tons gross register;

6. As quoted in *Report of Departmental Committee on Pilotage*, Cd. [5571], London, 1911 (Board of Trade), p. 9.

7. *Report of Department Committee, &c.*, *op. cit.*, p. 1.

vessels passing through a pilotage district. The committee was not unanimous in giving this recommendation, however, and the report contained a minority proposal that compulsory pilotage should remain only in those ports where it already existed.

The other important change recommended was that the immunity from liability of the shipowner or master for loss or damage occasioned by the fault of a compulsory pilot should be abolished, and that this should be coupled with an alteration in the legal relationship between the master and the pilot.

The legal relationship between master and pilot was the subject of considerable discussion by the committee and the opinion of those who gave evidence was clearly divided. Lord Gorell, a former President of the Probate, Divorce, and Admiralty Division of the High Court, was of the opinion that "no-one unaccustomed to a particular ship can handle her as her master and officers can",[8] while Sir Kenneth Anderson, Chairman of the Orient Steam Navigation Company, said that "it is obviously better that the actual giving of orders should rest with the man who has the knowledge than with the man who seeks advice".[9] One shipmasters' organization said that "in a district where pilotage is compulsory, the pilot should have sole and complete charge of the ship",[10] while another said that "under no circumstances should a master give up charge of his ship or the control of his crew".[11] Pilots, understandably, were almost unanimous in the view that the pilot should have complete control. A typical view was expressed by the Manchester pilots who said that the pilot's authority "should be absolute in the control of the ship while within his jurisdiction".[12] Having weighed all the evidence the committee recommended that there should be an express provision in the new pilotage legislation that the pilot should be given a subordinate role.

With regard to pilotage orders and by-laws the report recommended that pilotage commissioners should be appointed for a period of five years to "bring about such changes in the law of pilotage and its administration as may best meet the special requirements of any pilotage district and at the same time, secure, as far as possible, greater uniformity in the general law of pilotage".[13] The report also stated that the Board of Trade was and should remain the central pilotage authority for the United Kingdom, and that the commissioners should be the medium through whom all pilotage questions of an administrative nature should be brought before the central authority for their ultimate decision. Finally, there was a memorandum by the committee's chairman in which he stressed the importance of the continuance of the Pilotage Commissioners or some similar body as an essential part of the organization of the Central Pilotage Authority. He summarized his position as follows:

It is impossible for a department of a central office, where the superintendence of pilotage would only be one out of many subjects under its charge, to possess the technical experience or to give the detailed attention required for the direct control of such questions as are constantly arising in the administration of the law of pilotage.[14]

The outcome of the Departmental Committee's report was the Pilotage Act 1913, which was described in its preamble as "an Act to consolidate and amend the Law relating to Pilotage". It was not a completely new Act, therefore, and many of the general provisions

8. *Report of Departmental Committee, &c., op. cit.*, Minutes of Evidence, p. 231, question 7445.
9. *Ibid.*, p. 321, question 10077.
10. *Ibid.*, Appendix A, p. 7, *per* Hull British Shipmasters' Association.
11. *Ibid.*, Appendix A, p. 9, *per* Mercantile Marine Association.
12. *Ibid.*, Appendix C, p. 68.
13. *Report of Departmental Committee, &c., op. cit.*, p. 84.
14. *Ibid.*, p. 113.

which had appeared in the earlier statutes were again re-enacted. While it gave effect to most of the report's recommendations there were several important variations. For example, despite the committee's emphatic recommendation that the Board of Trade should be the Central Pilotage Authority the Act did not contain any express provision to that effect; indeed the statutory definition of a pilotage authority as stated in the Pilotage Authorities (Limitation of Liability) Act 1936 would appear to have excluded the Board of Trade. Again, although the chairman recommended that the Pilotage Commissioners should become a permanent body the Act provided that they should not continue in office beyond 1922. The intervention of the 1914–1918 war meant that in all probability the greater part of their work was carried out in their last four years of office, as nearly all Pilotage Orders setting up local pilotage authorities were not confirmed by Parliament until 1920 or later. The committee's recommendations on compulsory pilotage were not accepted either, with Parliament preferring the minority proposal that the existing system, with pilotage compulsory in some ports and not in others, should be retained. The Act did give effect to the recommendation abolishing the shipowner's and master's defence of compulsory pilotage but did not include any specific provision altering or defining the legal relationship between master and pilot, a provision which the committee had regarded as an essential adjunct to such abolition.

# INDEX

*All references are to paragraph number*